THE COMPLETE GUIDE TO WOMEN'S COLLEGE ATHLETICS

THE COMPLETE GUIDE TO WOMEN'S COLLEGE ATHLETICS

Includes over 10,000 women's athletic scholarships and recruiting rules and regulations

Carolyn Stanek

Contemporary Books, Inc.
Chicago

Library of Congress Cataloging in Publication Data

Stanek, Carolyn.
  The complete guide to women's college athletics.

  Bibliography: p.
  Includes index.
  1. Sports for women—United States.   2. College
sports—United States.   I. Title.
GV709.S73   1981   796'.0973   80-70635
ISBN 0-8092-5986-9
ISBN 0-8092-5985-0 (pbk.)

Published by Contemporary Books, Inc.
180 North Michigan Avenue, Chicago, Illinois 60601
Manufactured in the United States of America
Library of Congress Catalog Card Number: 80-70635
International Standard Book Number: 0-8092-5986-9 (cloth)
                                   0-8092-5985-0 (paper)

Published simultaneously in Canada by
Beaverbooks, Ltd.
150 Lesmill Road
Don Mills, Ontario M3B 2T5
Canada

CONTENTS

ACKNOWLEDGMENTS

Many thanks to the following individuals, whose inspiration and perspiration made this project possible:

Holly Turner and Eva Auchincloss of the Women's Sports Foundation for their advice and networking;

Lori Fradin and John Griffith of the *Athletic Journal* for their assistance with resources and photographs;

the librarians, coaches, athletes, and other friends at Arlington High School for their assistance and support;

dozens of high school and college players, coaches, and athletic directors from all over the United States for their ideas;

Nessa Calabrese for her courage and interest;

the Lakeshore Women's Rugby Club for their friendship and for keeping me sane;

Veronica Murphy and her Forest View High School yearbook staff who, along with Anthony Photographers, supplied many photos;

my sister Susan who helped type the manuscript and my sister Nancy who offered illustrations;

my friend Sharon Friend of Evanston who mercilessly edited much of the manuscript;

my folks Emil and Lil of La Grange Park for their love.

THE COMPLETE GUIDE TO WOMEN'S COLLEGE ATHLETICS

CHAPTER 1
WHY YOU SHOULD
BOTHER TO READ THIS

It doesn't matter if you're a high school sophomore or senior or even a college freshman, if you've been all-conference for four years or if you've just begun conditioning.

If there's any chance you might want to participate in college or junior college athletics—this book is for you. You'll never know just what you can achieve until you try. And with opportunities for women in sports increasing by record-breaking leaps and bounds, now is the time to "go for it," as we often say.

Because of a variety of factors, things have changed. This book could not have been written a decade ago, or even five years ago, for that matter. The idea would have been considered a dream, something entirely impossible, even radical. Yet who knows, athletics could pay your way through school, perhaps at an institution you never could have afforded otherwise. And we all know how high college costs have climbed within the past few years, rising even faster than the inflation rate.

1

Since 1970, college tuition alone has doubled at most schools; at many others it has soared even higher. State schools that charged only $200 or $300 per year for tuition in 1970 have upped their rates to $800 and more. Private universities with tuitions of $2,000 to $3,000 ten years ago now are demanding $4,000 to $5,000.

Perhaps, in view of colleges' costs and academic demands, you have considered giving up athletics to take on a part-time job while in school. Well, there is another way to reduce the financial burden on your folks and yourself: obtaining an athletic scholarship. You might receive more money for your education by pursuing this course, staying in shape and having more fun at the same time.

You see, it's happening all over the country in public and private institutions alike. Schools that had no funds for women competing in intercollegiate sports eight or ten years ago are now discovering hundreds of thousands of dollars in the athletic coffers for a number of women's sports.

At the University of Illinois, for instance, not a single dollar was budgeted for women's intercollegiate sports in 1973–74. Then, in 1974–75, the women's program began with seven sports and $35,000—not much compared to the nearly $800,000 spent for men's sports that year. In 1980–81 the same university spent more than $900,000 on women's sports.

In 1971 only 200 athletic scholarships were given to women in the United States. But in 1980 the Women's Sports Foundation reported that more than $7 million was available to female athletes at more than 700 schools. And scholarships are now offered for an amazing variety of sports. Funds are available for such sports as squash, bowling, skiing, bronco-busting, and lacrosse.

The main purpose of this book is to make you, your coach, your athletic director, and your parents aware of the opportunities now open to college athletes. Hopefully, you will be encouraged to continue or begin participating in a college sports program. Who knows, you might even become involved in starting a women's sports program. But first you should learn about the demands, the pressure, the price, and, perhaps most important, the satisfaction and rewards to be gained from being a college athlete.

You might want to know how true the slogan "You've come a long way, baby" is for women athletes. While progress has certainly been made, women still have a long way to go before their athletic programs will attain the magnitude and notoriety of the men's programs.

Reluctance to accept women in sports dates as far back as 776 B.C., when women in ancient Greece were not allowed to compete in the first Olympic Games. Nor were they allowed to be spectators because the men performed in the nude. To this day, women have been limited to running only the 1,500-meter race, although in the 1984 Olympics a 3,000-meter race will be added. Crew and basketball were not open to women in the Olympics until 1976. Finally, no woman has even been chosen as a member of the International Olympic Committee.

Chapter 2 documents some of the advances women have made in sports. It also emphasizes how attitudes toward women athletes have been changing. What was once considered unladylike, even disgusting, is now considered perfectly normal, acceptable, and even desirable. For example, many women wouldn't have dreamed about sweating it out in the weight room a few years ago. Today, however, most women realize that weight training is absolutely necessary for numerous sports.

More background on the advances in women's athletics from the legal standpoint is outlined in chapter 3, which discusses the federal and state laws and court cases that have produced positive results for women in sports.

Several chapters in this book are devoted to giving you an idea of the best and the worst things that can happen to a college athlete. For although many changes have been made and the overall picture for women looks good, there are still some inequities. For those situations that warrant such action, chapter 3 also tells you how to report discrimination.

Another concern of yours probably is, "So when will I

have time to study? After all, isn't that why I'm going to college?" This is an important concern and chapter 4 will present both sides of the topic. It *is* possible to be a top-notch athlete and student at the same time. You don't need to sacrifice one for the other. Sports can be important, yet secondary to your career goals. Also consider the fact that sports, as many coaches say, is an education in itself.

What happens once you do decide to make the commitment to college athletics? First, you have to get there. And then you have to try out. Even if you've been recruited and awarded a scholarship at a certain campus, you still must compete for a spot on the team. Chapters 5 and 6 are directed to this topic: chapter 5 outlines what to do if you are recruited; chapter 6 details what to do if you're not recruited.

You may or may not be aware that the Association for Intercollegiate Athletics for Women (AIAW) has strict rules governing recruiting practices. For instance, a coach may not contact a high school athlete until she is a senior. Fortunately, the women's recruiting game has not yet reached the scandalous proportions that men's recruiting has. The news media are constantly exposing scandals among the National Collegiate Athletic Association (NCAA) member schools—with certain men being offered luxury accommodations in dorms and apartments, cars, even good grades and forged transcripts in return for donating their bodies to the football or basketball team. It's not the same with women's recruiting, but you'd better check out all recruiting details to best protect yourself.

Whether or not you are recruited, you must study many aspects of any athletic program before deciding to go for it. The best way to do this is to visit the college. There you can check the academic department you are interested in and at the same time meet the coach and team you think you might want to play with. Major considerations include availability and quality of trainers, availability and proximity to practice and playing areas, and amount of travel required. Chapter 7 provides a detailed checklist for your college visits.

Chapter 8 helps you decide what kind of coach you would prefer, assuming you have a choice. Do you want a coach who is obsessed with winning? Do you want a coach who plays out the entire team or only the best? Someone who takes a personal interest in everyone or someone who remains outside of personal affairs? Someone who wants sports to come before everything else in your life, including studies, job, family, and friends? You need to think about the types of coaches you could work under. Most professors and instructors have to be tolerated for only a quarter or a semester. A coach has to be dealt with for as many years as you spend on a team. Consider the possibilities.

Also consider the size of the school. There are advantages to the large campus and the small one, too, academically and athletically. You also might find a good reason for choosing to play at a junior college.

No matter how far in the future college is for you, you might think about attending one of the hundreds of camps and workshops that cover almost every sport and can be found in nearly all parts of the country. You might also meet some college coaches at these camps. They are often there to find out about you, and you would do well to find out from them what college athletic programs are like. Chapter 9 deals with this aspect.

If you're good—really good—you might wonder about turning pro. Many pros have never finished college. Tennis star Andrea Jaeger, 14 in 1980 when she turned pro, constantly has to arrange for makeup work from her high school. There are risks involved, of course, when you leave school to make sports your career. Many athletes leave school and never return.

Throughout the book, state-to-state differences are emphasized. Scholarships are easier to obtain in some areas and in some sports while they are virtually nonexistent in others. Some schools do not award athletic scholarships to either men or women. Some sports are not available at all campuses. Some campuses are still ten years behind in offering women's programs a fair share of the funds. The Women's Sports Foundation guide to scholarships is listed in the Appendix.

And don't overlook the importance of the footnotes and the bibliography at the end of this book. If your interest in the history and progress of women's sports has been stimulated in reading this, then you'll surely enjoy reading more.

This guide is primarily intended to motivate you, to encourage you to start believing that Johnny-the-star-quarterback-next-door is not the only one who's going to attend college on an athletic scholarship. Perhaps Jill and Jane will also be cashing in on the funds set aside for college athletes. And perhaps you, too, will benefit.

This is the kind of book you will want to pass along or recommend to your teammates, to your coach, to your athletic director, and, of course, to your parents. After all, they might want to know more about the women's sports scene, too.

CHAPTER 2
JUST HOW FAR HAVE WE COME?

Men laugh. Boys chuckle and tease. Let them. In twenty years, no, even ten, they'll want to eat their gym shoes. The truth is that female athletes are improving their times, distances, and scores at a far swifter rate than male athletes ever have. And it's all happening as a result of better training, better coaching, and greater participation. In the past, far fewer women were involved in athletics and most of them were not concerned with the competitive aspects of sports. Now, as the number of female athletes rapidly approaches the number of male athletes, the competition is finally greater.

A decade ago, 7 percent of high school athletes were female. Today more than 30 percent are women. On most college campuses, there is one female athlete for every two male athletes. A decade ago sports scholarships for college women were virtually nonexistent. There were a total of 200. Today more than 700 colleges offer more than $7 million in aid.

The Department of Health, Education, and Welfare reports a 600-percent increase in the number of women in sports, from 204,000 in 1971 to 2.1 million in 1978.

Newsweek found that 25,000 women were regular joggers or runners in 1972; now more than half a million women run or jog. And age doesn't seem to make any difference either. Running boasts the likes of Miki Gorman, now in her mid-forties, who held the world's record in the marathon at age thirty-eight. Another example is forty-year-old Dr. Joan Ullyot, who not only runs marathons, but also writes books and magazine columns for women runners.

There are countless stories of the thirty-six-year-old who discovered softball, the twenty-eight-year-old who discovered weight lifting, the thirty-seven-year-old who is still a tennis pro (Billie Jean King). Women of all ages, all sizes, all abilities are finding that sports and physical activities make them feel healthier, more alive, more confident.

Yes, women's participation in sports is increasing because encouragement as well as benefits have been on the rise. Your mother, your aunt, even your older sister probably didn't have it as good as you do today. Janie Fincher, guard for the Chicago Hustle, said that if she were a teenager today she would be practicing five or six hours a day "because I would know that someday it would pay off." Even women basketball players a couple of years younger than Fincher have been able to demonstrate the positive effects that basketball programs have had on competition. With the likes of Old Dominion's Nancy Lieberman and Inge Nissen graduating in 1980, some veterans of the pro ball circuit, which was born in 1978, found themselves whisked off the courts and out of professional sports. The younger they come, the better they seem to be.

While some states have always supported certain women's sports, in most states, the struggle has been long and wearisome. Everyone knows that women's basketball has been around Iowa just about as long as the corn. And other states, such as California, Texas, and Arizona, also have had reputations for building and maintaining girls' and women's sports.

Volleyball has been big in California, field hockey on the Eastern seaboard. And where good tennis clubs existed, there have been fine tennis players, men and women alike. But not until the last ten years, particularly the last five years, have women's sports received so much attention.

Never before have so many sports been offered to women of all ages in so many places. Never before have so much money, time, interest, and enthusiasm been dedicated to this cause. Never before have women felt better about themselves for doing more with their bodies.

Yet there are still a couple of problems. While things have improved vastly, there's still a distance to go. The Women's Sports Foundation (WSF) is one organization that believes in continued support for women's athletic programs. Formed in 1974 by Billie Jean King and other concerned athletes, the WSF sends its members the monthly *Women's Sports* magazine and provides resources and support for women athletes. According to the WSF the Equal Opportunity Act is not being enforced in sports. Although Title IX has resulted in better and more scholastic and collegiate sports, local programs have not provided adequate facilities and activities for girls and women. The WSF also says girls have too few role models in sports, since women comprise less than 10 percent of the top positions in sports organizations. And while sports are growing in popularity among youths and young adults, most older women in the United States are totally sedentary.

Perhaps we won't see a real change until ten or twenty years from now. By then it might be as common for a ten-year-old girl to ask for a baseball bat for her birthday as it now is for a boy. At that point, fans will have to specify the women's team or the men's team when discussing which college team is rated number one in basketball. Perhaps the struggle for women and girls in sports will finally be over, and they will no longer need to justify their existence. It is hoped, of course, that women will never have to justify their programs by proving they can compete as well as men. For although women are improving overall, they have a long way

fore they can overtake men in most sports. And besides,
ally not the object.

Women vs. Men

While some of the differences between men's and women's
performances are physiological, many are the result of inexperience and ineffective training. The following findings indicate why men usually perform better than women in some
sports:

- Women have a wider pelvic structure and a lower center
  of gravity which tend to slow them down.
- Women take shorter strides.
- Women's bodies contain more fat.[1]

Yet studies have shown that there is no difference between
men's and women's reaction times. However, boys can throw a
ball farther than girls can. This is partly because most girls
just haven't practiced that particular motion.

A top woman athlete has legs just as strong as those of
a man her size in the same condition, but the man's arms
would be twice as strong. Women have trouble throwing a
ball as far as a man not only because their arms are
relatively shorter and their shoulders not as broad. The
result is less leverage and power.[2]

On the other hand, women are said to have certain
advantages. For instance, women's ovaries are less likely to be
injured than men's scrotums; and women are more loose-
jointed, more flexible than men and therefore less likely to
hurt or dislocate shoulders.

Women's menstrual cycles do not inhibit or restrict their
performances. Olympic records have been set by women
during menstruation.[3] Pregnant women and women who have
just had babies have demonstrated the ability to achieve peak

athletic performances. Yet while some sports are not recommended during pregnancy, the most common—jogging, tennis, and cycling—are permissible until the time of birth. Exercise and conditioning are encouraged rather than discouraged. In fact, studies show that conditioned women give birth faster, more easily, with fewer complications. Pregnant women who have kept in shape also have bettered their performances upon returning to sports.[4]

In some sports, men and women can compete on an equal basis and women *can* surpass men. Race car driver Janet Guthrie, the first woman to enter the Indy 500, placed ninth out of thirty-three in 1977. She said that strength was not important in racing: "You drive the car; you don't carry it. Ninety percent of racing is in the mind, not in brute strength." A reasonable amount of endurance is also involved, Guthrie says, but women are long on endurance.

In long-distance swimming, women have outdone men, holding the most records. Diana Nyad bettered any male performance by two hours when she swam around Manhattan Island. Women's swim records from Australia, East Germany, and Italy have topped the men's records in New Zealand, the United States, Canada, and some European nations.[5]

Distance running may be the next area in which women overtake men. Dr. Joan Ullyot and others suggest that a woman's body, with its greater fat storage, may be more suitable than the male body for marathon runs.

Cycling may be another sport in which men and women can compete equally, for leg strength proportional to one's weight is said to be about the same for both sexes.[6]

Women have bested men in parachuting, which did not become a world championship event until 1951 and did not include women's events until 1956. Great Britain's Jacqueline Smith holds the world record for accuracy, scoring ten consecutive dead-center strikes at Zagreb, Yugoslavia, in 1978.

As far as youth goes, the youngest champion with a world title in rodeo events is Metha Brorsen from Oklahoma, an eleven-year-old when she won the barrel racing competition in 1975.

And if women's endurance is in question, the record for the longest roller skating journey is Jackie Jacob's California-to-Georgia skate, taking her five weeks to do the 2,389 miles at age twenty-one.

Other feats of the so-called weaker sex include car lifting. No, it's not a new sport, but circumstances requiring the rescue of persons pinned beneath automobiles have spurred at least a couple of women to action. In one case, a Florida woman lifted a 3,600-pound car off her son after the car had toppled from a jack. In another case, a 5-foot-3-inch woman weighing 118 pounds lifted a 4,500-pound Cadillac off a child who had been run over and dragged for twenty feet. The police reaction: "Things like this have happened before, but I can't recall it being done by anyone so small."

Although these examples have not been provided to suggest that women will ultimately overtake men in sports, at least one great sports personality did believe that women will someday outdo men. The late Jesse Owens, Olympic track star in the 1930s, commented:

> Women have been oppressed and suppressed in athletics longer than any other group. Their motivation has been burgeoning geometrically, and this is the decade when it will explode, when we will see the "weaker" sex dominate sports. Because sports, except for weight lifting and some positions in football, seldom favor the strongest. Bulk isn't where it's at. It's what you've got *inside* that counts.[7]

Women, Owens said, have always been able to survive better than men. With this superior ability to survive, plus a lot of motivation, Owens believes women will actually outdo men in many sports before the 1980s are over.

How Women Were Held Back in Sports

When you examine the psychological and cultural barriers of the past, it is no wonder that it has taken so long for women to become involved in sports. As mentioned earlier, women were not allowed to participate in the first Olympics, staged nearly 3,000 years ago. In fact, women weren't even welcome to watch, because male participants wore no uniforms—they wore nothing at all. Peeping Thomasinas, if discovered, were punished by death, being flung from a mountain peak. But instead of running home to do the dishes, these women of ancient Greece decided to run their own loosely organized competitions. Eventually, after 127 Olympics, women were invited to participate in the games.[8] The Olympics died in 392 B.C. and were not revived until 1896; women were included, but not in nearly as many events as men were. In fact, women are still trying to establish some distance events in track along with additional cycling competition. The chart below indicates how slowly women have been admitted to modern Olympic competition.[9]

Summer Games		Winter Games	
Year	*No. of Women Competitors*	*Year*	*No. of Women Competitors*
1896	0	1908	7
1900	11	1920	12
1904	8	1924	13
1906	7	1928	27
1908	36	1932	32
1912	57	1936	80
1920	64	1948	77
1924	136	1952	109
1928	290	1956	132
1932	127	1960	144
1936	328	1964	200
1948	385	1968	228
1952	518	1972	217
1956	384	1976	276
1960	610		
1964	683		
1968	781		
1972	1,070		
1976	1,274		

Although ancient artwork shows women did engage in sports ranging from ball games to swimming and wrestling, many religious and social customs forbade women from participating in most physical activities other than dancing. Yet women were not always alone in being barred from athletic competition. Religious asceticism prevented many men from participating in sports during the Middle Ages. In a later era, when Puritanism reigned and anything resembling fun was considered sinful, athletics was shunned for prayer.

For the most part, sports was considered the realm of men, just as hunting and building, for example, were thought of as male tasks, and feeding and cooking were believed to be the responsibilities of the women. Men were looked upon as the stronger sex, yet women, paradoxically, were required to serve as beasts of burden in some societies. Women have substituted for donkeys when those animals were in short supply. Women have carried crops, water vases, and barrels and have towed carts of goods, often when the men would not.[10]

Further evidence that women were required to use their strength is indicated by the Sarmatian custom that women could not wed until after they had taken the life of an enemy in battle.[11]

What held women back from participation in sports, not to mention other significant aspects of society from which they were excluded, were the prevalent attitudes toward women— attitudes of philosophers, religious men, authors, politicians, psychologists. Women were considered inferior and were restricted to their homes; they were slaves to some extent and won the right to vote years after black men did.

Men used to question the femininity of women who wished to participate in sports. Some still do. But back in the nineteenth century the supposed emotional and physical fragility of women was emphasized—that is, until croquet became popular.[12] Then sport became a way for men and women to socialize with each other. After croquet became socially acceptable for women, other sports gradually gained popularity. Archery was one, because it required no great endurance. Lawn tennis was another, largely because it was a woman who brought the sport to Great Britain after having seen it played in Bermuda. Then came participation in such leisure-time sport activities as horseback riding, swimming, bowling, boating, and roller skating.

But the real boost for women in sports was the popularity of bicycling, although women first rode tricycles because the bicycle was at first considered too dangerous. The bicycle was seen as the great liberator of women since its popularity led to a breakdown of the restrictive dress code for Victorian women. Finally, women were able to set aside their long dresses and corsets to wear bloomers, split skirts, or knickers. In fact, the influence of the bicycle was so great that one women wrote in a magazine in 1895, "To men, rich, and poor, the bicycle is an unmixed blessing; but to women it is deliverance, revolution, (and) salvation." Because of their Victorian dress habits, it is said that when schools started to offer women physical education classes in the 1890s, the women were embarrassed to wear the bloomers, which they considered revealing.

Finally, at the turn of the century, scholastic competition for women began. It grew in the high schools and colleges of America, not exactly by leaps and bounds, but slowly and steadily. Women's interscholastic competition took far longer to start than did men's. But development of sports programs varied significantly from state to state and from school to school.

High School Girls' Sports: 1900–1960

Once girls convinced themselves it was all right to wear suitable sports clothing and to participate in a previously all-male activity, they became involved in sports. Of course, the encouragement and financial support available to boys was inaccessible to girls. But compared to the 1800s, the twentieth century became a period of growth and development for both girls' and boys' high school sports. Obviously, boys' sports developed much more swiftly, because of the great enthusiasm and interest shown by both players and spectators. Although baseball was becoming as American as apple pie with the popularity of the major leagues, it failed to attract throngs at most high schools. This was partially because many Northern schools closed for the summer in May or June, and the weather permitted few weeks of competition in the spring.

The earliest annals of high school sport history show that sports for girls ranged from virtually nonexistent to thriving growth from school to school.

At the time of the Depression, when it is a wonder that budgets allowed for any sports at all, some states reported gains for their girls' programs. Other states still had no competitive programs for girls. Small schools and schools lacking facilities sometimes could depend on a local college or university to sponsor athletic contests for them, which was the case in Arizona.

In the spring of 1930, *Athletic Journal's* survey of state high school athletic associations indicated the following:

- In Arkansas, 6,000 boys and 3,000 girls were on basketball rosters. No other sports were mentioned for Arkansas girls. Yet many states did not have such a large proportion of girls in basketball even ten years ago.
- In 1930 the Illinois state association decided to earmark the first funds (about $5,000 a year) to girls' athletics.
- The fall of 1930 brought the first girls' (and boys') intramural programs to Kansas high schools.
- Kentucky had a girls' basketball program that was solid enough that year to offer both A and B level competition and a state tournament in which the A champion met the B champ.
- Nearly 2,000 girls competed in Maryland's seventh annual "Field Ball Tournament."
- In 1930 Minnesota girls had a state swim meet—an event not initiated in many other states until the 1970s.
- In Nevada, "A play day for girls held at Reno and Las

Vegas, where practically all of the girls of the participating schools take part in a varied sports program, is coming to be a definite part of the physical education program. Transportation is the most insurmountable difficulty."

It was not until the '70s that girls' sports began to receive any significant financing or recognition, plus the opportunity to compete interscholastically to any great extent.

High School Girls' Sports in the '60s: From Pinnies and Playdays to Interscholastic Sports

Girls' athletic programs of the 1960s varied from state to state and from sport to sport, yet this general statement from a British book for girls accurately described the situation both in England and in the United States:

> In most schools it is now possible for girls to "have a go" at athletics, but too often it is still a case of a short period for practice before a "sports day" or special coaching for those girls with obvious physical skill. In either case many girls are left out.[13]

Social and financial pressure from state to state largely dictated that girls' scholastic sports programs, if offered at all, were little more than an extension of physical education classes. Organizations such as the Girls Athletic Association, which thrived through the early '70s, made it possible for large numbers of girls to participate in after-school intramurals in such sports as tennis, softball, volleyball, and basketball. Some schools had even more extensive programs. But the coaching was not available, the equipment was often barely adequate, and participation was usually limited to a couple of days a week. Very few states offered interscholastic competition or state tournaments.

Frequently, the girls obtained only pinnies rather than uniforms and sports days or play days instead of interscholastic competition. Typically, girls from several schools would get together for play days and divide into teams (usually not in school vs. school competition) for volleyball, basketball and other team sports. Others would participate in swimming, relay races, and dancing. Yet competition was not stressed:

> Victory would obviously mean less in a basketball game in which none of the participants had previously played together than if a team from one school had practiced as a unit for a period of weeks. Competition was deemphasized in the play day; socialization was maximized. Frequent breaks with "cookies and juice" prevented overexertion while increasing social interaction.[14]

Play days and GAA took care of the women and girls for a long time, although a few states took the trouble to sponsor more competitive programs, usually in basketball, volleyball, and softball. Some GAA programs offered as many as ten or eleven sports per year. Yet many GAA programs were limited, even in the states that catered most to female athletes. For instance, Billie Jean King recalls her junior high's inadequacies:

> . . . I like volleyball well enough and the GAA put a lot of pressure on me to play because I was one of the best athletes in school. But by then I was already taking tennis lessons every day of the week and I played the year round. That's really what I wanted to do. So I asked the head of the GAA if my tennis could count toward my GAA letter. No way. Tennis wasn't a GAA sport. That was discrimination, all right, but I felt it was discrimination against tennis, not against me. . . . Little boys could play tennis in junior high, but not little girls, not even in Southern California.[15]

It wasn't until the early 1970s that GAA, play days, and pinnies faded from the scene. Political and social attitudes signaled advances and greater opportunities for women in our society. Title IX of the Education Act of 1972 is credited with revolutionizing women's sports. For high school girls, Title IX meant the expansion of interscholastic competition for some schools and the beginning of it for most. Coaches were hired to sponsor basketball, volleyball, swimming, and other surefire popular sports. Girls who showed interest in other sports requested teams and at times were able to form them. For many sports, there would be a trial year in which a school could designate the sport a club sport and determine the level of interest. Then, if enough interest was shown, the club sport would enter further interscholastic competition. Some girls fought (at times with lawsuits) to be allowed on boys' teams in sports that interested no other girls. In some cases, they won; in others, they gave up. In a Los Altos, California, case filed in August 1980, a girl charged her high school with sex discrimination when she and other girls were not allowed to try out for the varsity football team.

In many high schools today, the number of girls' sports exceeds or equals the number of boys' sports. But on the average, boy athletes outnumber the girls by two to one. At times girls' sports have been established at the expense of boys' junior varsity sports. With the greater involvement of girls, however, Booster Clubs report having to work harder and school athletic budgets have been planned more judiciously.

Although some female physical education instructors preferred to stick with play days and cultivation of the social aspects of sport, at least one study shows that competition also contributes to social development. In 1978 a Utah Board of Education study showed "students who participate heavily in extracurricular activities score about the same as or slightly worse than other students in the traditional academic achievement areas. They tend, however, to be more self-assured in social situations, are better at peer relationships and more effective in leadership situations. They also tend to enjoy school more than their peers."

Women's Collegiate Sports—Just for Fun for Some

As in high school sports, college women were rarely allowed more than pinnies and play days until the 1950s. Only eleven of fifty colleges in a 1923 survey indicated they had intercollegiate competition for women. Opposition to women's competitive athletics stemmed from the misguided notion that sports would harm a woman's reproductive system and the belief that women's athletics would become too much like men's, with highly competitive, commercialized competition. In 1931 a similar survey showed twelve out of one hundred colleges permitting intercollegiate athletics, with eighty allowing play days.[16] One male physical education leader further discouraged women in 1930 when he said:

> Games like basketball and baseball are combative sports. They develop ugly muscles—muscles ugly in girls—as well as scowling faces and the competitive spirit.[17]

Women who tried to bring about more competitive programs were often ostracized. When the Ohio State University women organized the first Women's National Collegiate Golf Tournament in 1941, the anticompetitive spirit was so strong that many coaches and their teams stopped speaking to the OSU women. For years no OSU women were elected to national athletic association offices.[18]

Slow progress continued to be made over the following years. After World War II, about one-third of the colleges in the East were involved in intercollegiate athletics for women. But it was not until the 1960s and the advent of the women's movement that women's college athletics grew to significant proportions. In the 1940s, OSU women who had proposed a national women's athletic organization similar to the men's long-standing NCAA were disregarded and criticized. By 1967, however, women were ripe for forming the Commission on Intercollegiate Athletics for Women (CIAW). And in 1971–72 the Association for Intercollegiate Athletics for Women

(AIAW) was born, attracting 280 two- and four-year colleges as members. Now nearly 1,000 schools belong to the AIAW. Whereas the AIAW had only nineteen sports with seven national championships in 1973, the 1980–81 program was expanded to thirty-seven national championships in seventeen sports, with additional open championships in several and three-level competition in a few more.

The AIAW governs women's collegiate sports by sponsoring championships and regulating recruiting, scholarships, and eligibility. The AIAW also stresses a code of ethics. For the last several years, however, one of the AIAW's greatest concerns has been fighting the NCAA, which is trying to take it over. The AIAW believes there would be diminished opportunities for women athletes under the auspices of the NCAA.

However, the AIAW has been somewhat conservative in its policies, since it has limited scholarships and recruiting practices. Some women's athletic directors and instructors have actually helped block or sabotage efforts to equalize opportunities for women. It even took a court case to bring the AIAW to allow athletic scholarships for women. After Title IX was passed, a Federal court persuaded the women's governing organization to permit athletic grants. Many AIAW members opposed such action, fearing women's sports would begin to have the same problems the men's sports have had.

Yet the conservative element has been resisted and competitive programs have been developed. Ann Johnston, softball coach at Eastern Michigan University, said, "I've been called a troublemaker and a rebel, just because I've wanted more than I've had. Too many women are satisfied with what they have and are not willing to develop their programs. And a lot of women athletic directors are hired because they are puppets and will do exactly what their male superiors want them to do."

Jill Hutchison, basketball coach at Illinois State University, thinks coaches ought to try to get what they're entitled to: "We can no longer afford to go second class. My kids are giving up too much; they make too much of a commitment.

Psychologically I believe it affects my teams. We should do everything we can to allow them to perform their best. We've got to go first class."

Strides in Women's Professional Sports

Women in sports have always had a few noteworthy standouts, but for the most part they were ignored. Their best accomplishments were still far from the men's best. Sure, a woman tennis player could beat a male player—an ex-pro who was twenty some years her senior. Nonetheless, women's accomplishments have been recognized because of those who excel.

It seems that women athletes often made the greatest strides when one woman in a particular sport stuck her neck out for the rest or when one performed exceptionally well, or both.

For a long time it was difficult to find an individual who was willing to encourage female athletes. But even back in the good old days there were some who could detect a great athlete, and it didn't matter much whether the athlete were male or female. Betty Robinson, the first woman on a U.S. Olympic Team to bring home a gold medal (winning the 100-meter dash in 1928), said her high school teacher once saw her running to catch a train and, amazed at her speed, timed her and then offered to coach her. After five months of competition and only four races, the sixteen-year-old Robinson took home the gold. However, Robinson later demonstrated that she could overcome inexperience along with a greater handicap—an injury received in a plane tragedy that nearly took her life. Emerging from the accident with one leg shorter than the other, Robinson persisted in her training. Following a four-year rest, she returned to the 1936 Olympics to help the relay team take the gold.[19]

Not too many years later, Wilma Rudolph first began running as a twelve-year-old in Tennessee. Motivated by the fact that she was the fastest female runner at her grade school, she kept going and found that she was the fastest in her state. She kept running right up until she won two Olympic medals in 1960.

Mildred ("Babe") Didrickson Zaharias (1914–1956) will be remembered not only for her golf but also for her achievements in track and field, swimming, figure skating, and basketball. She may be not only the greatest woman athlete of all time but also the greatest athlete ever. The world renowned Olympic athlete cofounded the Women's Pro Golf Association and won big on the golf circuit for years, taking the 1954 U.S. Women's Open two years before she died of cancer.

Although women golfers were pioneers in the pro sector, interest in them waned with the disappearance of the popular "Babe" and was not really revived until the likes of Nancy Lopez, Donna Caponi-Young, and other contemporary superstars appeared on the tracks. Lopez showed that golf could mean six-figure salaries for women when she won nearly $200,000 in 1978, her second season with the LPGA. Kathy Whitworth made $822,214 through the end of 1978, the largest sum earned cumulatively by a woman golfer.

Yet while golf used to be *the* money-making sport for women, a golfer's earnings hardly compare to the $900,000 Martina Navratilova made in 1979. Tennis prizes once lagged, but now have surpassed the prize money offered in golf. And if money is the object, consider Sonja Henie, who skated her way to $47.5 million starring in more than ten movies before she died in 1969.

Of course, no one can deny the importance of Billie Jean King in promoting women's sports. However, her efforts in establishing women's tours—broadening their schedules and obtaining higher cash awards—were not really recognized until 1973. That's when she walloped self-proclaimed "male chauvinist pig" Bobby Riggs, more than twenty-five years her senior, in straight sets—a battle of the sexes watched by millions on nationwide prime-time TV.

At age thirty-seven in 1980, Billie Jean was still ranked number five on the women's pro circuit among the likes of seventeen-year-old Tracy Austin and fifteen-year-old Andrea Jaeger. It's not only women's tennis that has become respectable, popular, and lucrative because of King, but also women's athletics in general.

Remaining a top competitor all along, King has been an organizer of a women's pro tennis league that eventually folded, founder of the Women's Sports Foundation, publisher of *Women's Sports* magazine, and a business partner in tennis clubs, camps, clothes, and tournaments.

The world was astonished a decade ago when King became the first woman in tennis to win $100,000 in a year. Her efforts paved the way for women like Martina Navratilova and Tracy Austin to earn close to $1 million in a single year. The first time *Sports Illustrated* ever named a woman athlete of the year was in 1972—Billie Jean. The Associated Press gave her the same distinction in 1967 and 1973.

Many other women have promoted their professional sports not so much with their performances or politics but with their personalities. For instance, one figure who has helped women's pro basketball attain its reputation since its inception in 1978 is Chicago Hustle's Janie Fincher. Although she is a feisty guard and better than a fair shooter, her real claim to fame is being able to draw the crowds. When she was traded to another team, the fans beefed so much that the management got her back during the next month. One *Chicago Tribune* sportswriter said Fincher's return to the Hustle was good news for "fans who enjoy watching a skilled ballhandler and defender . . . or for anybody who enjoys watching an attractive blond."[20] The Hustle, it might be mentioned, has been one of the few Women's Basketball League franchises able to keep their financial heads above water since the league began in 1978.

In total, women athletes have gained a lot more recognition, a lot more media coverage, a lot more funding, and fewer and fewer sneers and jeers. Nonetheless, they are still doubted and resented. And these attitudes do not always belong to only the male athletic directors who hesitate to share their athletic coffers with the women. For example, columnist Sally Helgesen claimed that women athletes have no class, that watching women is not as exciting as watching men because women play a "markedly inferior" game:

> Women's pro basketball teams are like teams in the minor leagues; they may be respectable and provide fun for the participants, but they're still the minors. . . . they can't offer the connoisseur of Kareem anything to challenge the imagination.[21]

Perhaps Billie Jean King can best argue the other side. Referring to her pursuit of more tournaments and prize money for women tennis pros, she said, more than five years ago:

> At first, my argument wasn't for equal prize money. We couldn't argue that we were as good as the men, or as strong, because we weren't. In the major tournaments the men did play the best-of-five sets while we played the best-of-three. All what the other women and I agitated for initially was for a better ratio, maybe five to three or even just two to one.

> But even that was unfair to us, because it meant that as entertainers we were still getting short-changed. I began to realize that women should get paid not only for their skill and talent, but because people wanted to watch them play. The best men players were better than the best women, and I'd never said they weren't (although I do wonder what would happen if we played against men on equal terms right from birth; it might be interesting). . . . If our show was as entertaining as the men's, then we should have been getting equal pay. It was really that simple.[22]

CHAPTER 3
TITLE IX AND ITS IMPLICATIONS

Imagine being a swimmer and having nowhere to train or display your talents except at a park district pool. Your high school offers swimming once a year in PE. There's a synchronized swim club you can try out for, if you're interested. What do you do? Try to get on the only swim team you can at school—the boys' team. No girls allowed on it? You sue. At least that's what Sandy Bucha did in 1972 in Illinois. She lost her case, but her suit led to girls' interscholastic swim competition in that state.

Imagine being on a basketball team that is pretty competitive and well supported by local fans. That's nice. Basketball is popular in your state. You're lucky. You get to play; only you're a guard and, in playing by the six-person half-court girls' rules, you never have a chance to develop your shooting game. Shoot! How are you even supposed to be considered for a college athletic scholarship if the recruiters are looking only at the forwards? Good luck. Go to court. Do not pass "go" yet. Spend lots of money suing the state high school association. That's what Victoria Ann Cape did in 1976 in Tennessee, leading to boys' rules for girls' basketball. Many other states have followed suit—and their guards no longer go unnoticed.

Imagine you're a volleyball and track standout at a big, actually a Big Ten, state university. The male athletes receive lots of scholarships covering tuition, fees, room and board, book loans, and employment opportunities. The women's aid, on the other hand, is limited to tuition waivers and fees. The men travel in style—usually four to a university car. Or in university planes, chartered buses, or commercial planes. The women cram eight or nine in a van for trips, sleeping four to a room, two per bed at hotels, while the guys go two to a room. In general, more athletic shoes, racquets, practice uniforms, better and more competitive schedules (playing against schools with tougher teams more than fifty miles away), and more adequate facilities are available to men than to women. After all, six-and-a-half times as much money is budgeted for men's sports as for women's sports. Want to cry? That won't help. Already tried filing complaints and reports and they didn't help? Maybe you even contacted the U.S. Department of Education and they never answered your letters, which contained documented proof of discrimination. What do you do?

In one milestone case, Vanessa Calabrese contacted lawyer Edward Rawles, who suggested that a couple of younger students join her in pressing charges against the college for the discrimination described above. Nancy Knop, a member of the track and cross-country teams, joined the effort as did another athlete, who soon after dropped out of the case to transfer to another school with better athletic opportunities for women. In a dramatic out-of-court settlement reached on the eve of the trial in 1977, their efforts resulted in equalized opportunities for women athletes at the University of Illinois at Champaign-Urbana. It was a start. It had been long overdue.

The cases described above are just three of the dozens of suits and confrontations of the 1970s that led to:

- Expanded competition for female athletes
- Elimination of rules and practices that discriminated against female athletes
- Increased funding and scholarships for women athletes

Yes, women athletes were never taken seriously enough until they got the law on their side. And even though women's rights are protected under Federal and many state laws, women have had to struggle, either threatening or pressing lawsuits to get their chance at bat. Although many state laws have mandated equal opportunities for women athletes, the Federal law known as Title IX is credited with expanding intercollegiate and interscholastic sports for women.

Perhaps a few answers to common questions concerning Title IX would be helpful.

What is Title IX?

Title IX is simply a stipulation in the Education Amendments of 1972 that states: "No person in the United States shall, on the basis of sex, be excluded from participation in, be denied the benefits of, or be subjected to discrimination under any education program or activity receiving Federal financial assistance." That means any educational institution receiving Federal funds must not discriminate on the basis of a person's sex. Although Title IX and its implications for athletics will be discussed in this chapter, it should be noted that Title IX covers equal opportunity in all departments and aspects of educational institutions.

When did Title IX begin to bring about some changes in athletic programs?

Although Title IX did not become effective until July 21, 1975, schools became aware of the expectations it would bring and the changes that would have to be made in the period

1972–75. Many gradually began to develop their women's sports programs before 1975, while others resisted changes and then furiously, in one fell swoop, started to hire women's coaches and offer women's sports. It was not uncommon for a university to have no women's sports or coaches in 1974 and then six sports and a couple of coaches in 1975. Thus women's collegiate sports finally began to receive the same treatment and funding that men's collegiate sports had received for ages. It is interesting to note this progress in financial terms: The University of California budgeted $108,000 for women in 1973–74 and $500,000 in 1978–79. Similarly, at North Carolina State the funding increased from a paltry $20,000 to more than $300,000 in four years. Many large universities are now spending more than a million dollars on women's athletics.

Who handles Title IX complaints and how is the law enforced?

Helen Walsh, an attorney who handles Title IX complaints in Washington, D.C., said more than 124 complaints about eighty institutions have been received over the years and that it was not until late 1980 and early 1981 that these complaints were investigated. "We received many requests from institutions to clarify Title IX and we had numerous complaints, but we had to keep everything on hold. We couldn't act on anything until an official policy was established. And that wasn't until December 1979. Now we're going over all the complaints, and many institutions have already changed their programs and increased the opportunities for women significantly."

Did Walsh know of the grievances filed by Vanessa Calabrese, as mentioned earlier in this chapter? "We have complaints about the U of I dating back to 1974. But we did visit the campus in '78 and saw a lot of changes."

Nonetheless, Title IX was around for eight years before the Federal government began to answer complaints. In essence, Title IX has been self-enforced. In other words, schools have been on their honor to abide by its provisions. In most cases, institutions have changed their programs significantly enough to argue that they have complied with Title IX. When threatened by a lawsuit, high schools and colleges generally have taken the path of negotiation and have conceded to the women's programs.

One Midwestern coach suggested that some schools comply or at least attempt to comply with Title IX guidelines in order to remain in the good graces of benefactors and alumni and to attract potential students. "What parents," she asked, "would want to send their daughter to a school that discriminates against women?"

At first Title IX was under the auspices of the Department of Health, Education, and Welfare (HEW). Since HEW has now become the Department of Health and Human Services, Title IX has been the responsibility of the Department of Education, established in May 1980.

What kinds of changes have been made as a result of Title IX?

The list is quite long. Basically, Title IX brought more funds to women's sports. It required schools to make their PE classes coed, which caused a lot of resistance at the high school level. In fact, one Chicago suburban high school still had sex-segregated PE classes in 1980.

Title IX also forced schools to provide women's coaches with better salaries (closer to and occasionally equal to the amounts men's coaches are earning). It allowed women's sports to provide athletes with heavier competitive schedules, better travel allowances, more equipment, and more assistant coaching. Title IX also required schools to provide a sport where a need was shown.

Probably the most important implication of Title IX is the Department of Education policy ruling of December 1979 stating that a proportional amount of scholarship funds be available for women athletes based on the number of women in athletic programs. Simply, if 35 percent of a university's athletes are women, then 35 percent of its athletic scholarship funds must go to women. This policy does not imply that 35 percent of the total athletic budget should be set aside for women in this example, however. It's not a matter of equal funding, but a matter of providing *equivalent* opportunities, insuring that each sport has equipment and supplies, adequate facilities, coaching, training services, secretarial services, publicity, recruiting, scheduling, transportation, tutoring services, and housing and dining on road trips.

On the high school level, Title IX seems to have spurred more female students to participate. Even though the number of high school-aged persons is dropping nationwide, the number of girls in high school sports has jumped from 300,000 in 1971 to 800,000 in 1973, 1.3 million in 1974 to more than 2 million in 1980.

Of course, Title IX covers a lot more, but only areas relevant to the student-athlete are summarized above.

Is Title IX the only law providing for equal opportunity for women in sports?

No. Lawsuits demanding equality of opportunity for women athletes have not been based on Title IX, largely because no official policy had even been developed until December 1979. Some attorneys have successfully based their cases on state equal rights legislation. In the aforementioned University of Illinois case, attorney Edward Rawles prepared a suit based on the Illinois Equal Rights Amendment instead of dealing with the case in Federal court under Title IX.

What guidelines has HEW given for complying with Title IX?

Fortunately, many publications on implementing Title IX have been distributed to institutions, informing them of their responsibilities to the law and outlining procedure for submitting and dealing with Title IX grievances. Now that HEW no longer has jurisdiction over Title IX, the Department of Education has been responsible for disseminating information.

How can I find out more about Title IX?

Find out who your school's Title IX representative is. This individual should have several publications, including *Title IX Grievance Procedures: An Introductory Manual* and *Implementing Title IX and Attaining Sex Equity in Education*, both issued by HEW and available from the U.S. Government Printing Office, Washington, D.C. 20201.

Any one of ten regional Offices of Civil Rights might also be helpful in obtaining more information about Title IX.

Regional Offices for Civil Rights

Region I—CT, ME, MA, NH, RI, VT
Mr. Robert Randolph
Acting Regional Director
Office for Civil Rights, Region I
Dept. of Education
140 Federal Street, 14th Floor
Boston, MA 02110   (617) 223-4248

Region II—NH, NY, PR, VI
Mr. Charles J. Tejada
Regional Director
Office for Civil Rights, Region II
Dept. of Education
26 Federal Plaza, 33rd Floor
New York, NY 10007   (212) 264-5180

Region III—DE, DC, MD, VA, PA, WV
Mr. Dewey E. Dodds
Regional Director
Office for Civil Rights, Region III
Dept. of Education

Gateway Building, 3535 Market Street
Post Office Box 13716
Philadelphia, PA 19101   (215) 596-6787

Region IV—AL, FL, GA, KY, MS, NC, SC, TN
Mr. William H. Thomas
Regional Director
Office for Civil Rights, Region IV
Dept. of Education
101 Marietta Street, 27th Floor
Atlanta, GA 30323   (404) 221-2954

Region V—IL, IN, MI, MN, OH, WI
Mr. Kennet A. Mines
Regional Director
Office for Civil Rights, Region V
Dept. of Education
300 South Wacker Drive
Chicago, IL 60606   (312) 353-2520

Region VI—AR, LA, NM, OK, TX
Mr. Taylor August
Regional Director
Office for Civil Rights,
   Region VI
Dept. of Education
1200 Main Tower Building,
   Room 1930
Dallas, TX 75202   (214) 767-3951

Region VII—IA, KS, MO, NE
Mr. Jesse L. High
Regional Director
Office for Civil Rights,
   Region VII
Dept. of Education
Twelve Grand Building
1150 Grand Avenue, 7th Floor
Kansas City, MO 64106   (816) 374-2223

Region VIII—CO, MT, ND, SD, UT, WY
Dr. Gilbert Roman
Regional Director
Office for Civil Rights,

Region VIII
Dept. of Education
Federal Office Building
1961 Stout Street, Room 1185
Denver, CO 80294   (303) 837-5695

Region IX—AZ, CA, NV, HI, GU, TT, AS
Mr. Robert Brown
Acting Regional Director
Office for Civil Rights,
   Region IX
Dept. of Education
1275 Market Street, 14th Floor
San Francisco, CA 94103-
   (415) 556-8586

Region X—AK, ID, OR, WA
Mr. Gary Jackson
Acting Regional Director
Office for Civil Rights,
   Region X
Dept. of Education
1321 Second Avenue, MS/723
Seattle, WA 98101   (206) 442-2990

For immediate attention, call SPRINT, a toll-free hotline designed to handle your Title IX complaints or questions: 800-424-5162.

Women Who Win: Exercising Your Rights in Sports, by Bonnie L. Parkhouse and Jackie Lapin, is a most informative study of women's rights, particularly under Title IX, and is available at most bookstores in paperback for $4.95. This recent book contains information concerning Title IX, sports equality lawsuits, and much more. Perhaps the most salient feature of this book is its practicality. It gives you all the background you need, plus step-by-step directions for lodging a Title IX complaint. For instance, it gives the American Civil Liberties Union directives for what a complaint of discrimination should contain:

1. The names of the individual complainants.

2. The law that was violated. Cite every law that may be applicable such as the Fourteenth Amendment, Title IX, Title VII, Executive Order 11246, the Equal Pay Act, state ERA (if there is one), state public accommodations law (if there is one), state fair employment practices law, other state laws, the written rules or policies of the school itself (check its affirmative action plan if it has one), etc.

3. The precise nature of the discrimination they suffered. Tell the whole story, to the extent you are sure of the facts, including dates, times, people, and places. For example, don't say only that "Mary Smith was not permitted to try out for the varsity track team." You should include facts as to how she applied, who turned her down, dates, reasons given, her background and experience, the fact that there is no women's team or that it is inferior, the details of how it is inferior (less equipment, fewer opportunities for competition, inferior coaching, different level of funding), how she is disadvantaged by not being given the opportunity to try out (i.e., exposure, publicity, opportunity to increase skills, scholarship or pro opportunities).

4. Broader aspects of discrimination, such as lack of affirmative recruiting and funding inequities. If these are relevant to your charge, show how the class of women is disadvantaged by the rule, policy, or system in question.

If the school has an affirmative action plan that is not being enforced, describe how it is not being enforced. For employment issues, you may also want to show that the existing plan is legally inadequate.

5. Data and statistics on women in general as it relates to your charge. For example, relevant physiological data about women athletes, or data relating to the increased participation of women in athletics, or the increased availability of scholarships for women athletes.

6. The remedy you propose, whether it's simple (permit women on the men's team) or complex (change the structure of the physical education or athletics department). If you propose affirmative action, submit an outline of what it should contain. If you are dealing with a non-employment related issue, much of the material from the employment area is still relevant, for example, recruiting requirements.[1]

The following is a sample letter that you might use in filing a Title IX complaint.

_____, Director
Office for Civil Rights, Region ____
U.S. Department of Education
Address for your region

Dear _____ :
    I am/We are filing a complaint of sex discrimination under Title IX of the Education Amendments of 1972 against *name and address of school district, college or other institution receiving federal education aid.*
    The next paragraph should explain what person or group of people you believe is being discriminated against.

You need only identify them generally—"the girls in sixth grade gym classes," for example—unless it's just one or two people who have been victims of specific acts of discrimination. In that case it would be helpful to give the Department of Education their names and addresses, though it is not required.

Follow this with as complete a description of the sex discrimination as you can. Make sure to tell what happened, when it happened and if the discrimination is still going on. Attach any evidence you may have which supports the complaint, such as letters, student handbooks, and so on. Name any people you think were responsible for the discrimination and their position in the school.

The following people have agreed to provide further information to your staff. *Here, list the people willing to talk to the Department of Education. Explain how they can provide valuable information relating to your complaint, and tell the Department of Education where they can be reached. If their names must be kept confidential, note this as well.*

I/We ask that you investigate this complaint immediately and notify me/us when the investigation will begin. Please keep me/us advised of the status of the investigation. And please send me/us a copy of your findings as soon as they are sent to *name of school district or college.* In addition, please send me/us copies of all correspondence with *name of institution.*

Sincerely,

Name

Address

Daytime phone number, unless you prefer not to receive calls about the complaint at work.

If you are sending copies of your complaint to other persons, list them below. For example:

cc: *School Board*
 Senators
 Members of Congress
 Governor
 State Legislators
 National Organizations
 Newspapers
 PEER

For more information, you may want to consult the following:

Additional Resources/References for Information on Title IX

Cracking the Glass Slipper: PEER's Guide to Ending Sex Bias in Your Schools ($5.00)
 Includes the "Title IX Primer" which explains Title IX, describes how to measure your school's compliance, what to look for and what questions to ask. Also suggests ways to work for constructive change.

 Order from: Project on Equal Education Rights
 1112 13th St., N.W.
 Washington, DC 20005

Title IX and Sex-Integrated Programs That Work ($3.95)
 Gives examples of what is being done in junior and senior high schools to implement Title IX by integrating physical education programs. Stock no. 240-26150

Complying with Title IX of the Education Amendments of 1972 in Physical Education and High School Sports Programs ($2.25)

Designed to assist schools and colleges in complying with Title IX regulations. Provides information on what must be done to be in compliance and includes self-evaluation checklists. Stock no. 240-25930

Order the above from: AAHPERD Publications
P.O. Box 174
44 Industrial Park Circle
Waldorf, MD 20601

Title IX and Physical Education: A Compliance Overview ($1.40)
Provides a basic understanding of Title IX compliance requirements and possibilities. Published by the Department of Health, Education and Welfare in 1976. Stock no. 017-080-01712-1

Title IX Grievance Procedures: An Introductory Manual ($2.50)
Suggests a structure within which educational agencies and institutions can systematically review and evaluate their Title IX grievance procedures and modify these procedures or develop new ones according to their needs. Stock no. S/N 017-080-01711-3

The Complete Title IX Regulations ($.75)
Appeared in the Federal Register on June 4, 1975. Vol. 40, No. 108. Defines the Title IX provisions which insure nondiscrimination on the basis of sex in educational programs and activities receiving or benefiting from Federal financial assistance.

Title IX and Intercollegiate Athletics: The Department of Health, Education and Welfare's Policy Interpretation ($.75)
Appeared in the Federal Register on December 11, 1979. Vol. 44, No. 239. Explains Title IX so as to provide a

framework within which complaints can be resolved, and provides colleges and universities with additional guidance on the requirements for compliance with Title IX.

Order the above from: Superintendent of Documents
U.S. Government Printing Office
North Capitol Between G and H
Sts., N.W.
Washington, DC 20402

Are Most Women Satisfied with Title IX's Results?

Most high school and college PE instructors and coaches involved in women's programs will undoubtedly say Title IX has made things much better for female athletes. However, with all the apparent advantages and increased opportunities for women that have followed Title IX, some still have reservations about the effects of Title IX. Katherine Ley, former head of women's PE at the State University of New York at Cortland, said Title IX is the "greatest step forward for females since they were granted the right to vote." Yet she also sees a negative side: "The most unhappy aspect of Title IX, from women's point of view, is the impression one gets that what men are doing is the standard of excellence against which to judge women's programs."

Ley said she does not necessarily want something more for women, but something different for women; she also believes that would be next to impossible "in a male-dominated world."

It is interesting to further consider what Ley says:

It is reasonable for women to want to eliminate those practices acknowledged by men as being detrimental to athletic programs. It would be wise to take advantage of the willingness of the men to help by identifying their most urgent problems. If women are not allowed to change, there is no doubt that women's programs will simply mirror the programs of men—something that seems to be happening all too frequently across the country. We need new designs that circumvent the mistakes they acknowledge in their programs.[2]

In *Women Who Win,* Parkhouse and Lapin said women should try to be like men in one area—thinking for themselves so they can obtain equality:

> But women must begin to think on their own. For too long they have illustrated they cannot function unless they are told what to do. Women need to question what they are told and to question tradition. Athletic tradition has women sewing up old uniforms while men throw them away and buy new ones. . . . Administrators often express a feeling that there is plenty of time to comply with Title IX, thus, women are passively accepting delays instead of pursuing it with a sense of urgency. They must realize they are being lulled into complacency and put an immediate halt to such delay tactics.[3]

CHAPTER 4
ACADEMICS VS. ATHLETICS

It's your decision. You've had to make it before and now you have to make it again. How serious are you about studying? How serious are you about wanting to compete as a college athlete? Will you want to place the same, greater, or less emphasis on sports in college as you did in high school? Are you aware of all the demands on your time that your particular area of study will make? You know it's a lot less time-consuming to be in some curricula than in others. And you might have to work part-time to help pay for your schooling. Finally, if you intend to have any kind of social life, you need to consider what kind of dent that may make in your schedule. Take the time to evaluate your priorities: studying, competing, working, playing. To make these decisions, you must be honest with yourself about your intelligence and athletic ability.

Most of this chapter is based on the assumption that you will make academics your first priority. In most cases, you will have no choice but to relegate sports to second place. Let's face it, while young men have a very small chance of making it to the NFL or NBA (only 2 percent of male college athletes do), women have an even tinier chance—only a fraction of 1 percent of them go pro because the opportunities are still so limited. Since you probably couldn't make a decent living if sports were your only accomplishment in college, you may as well pick a curriculum and get serious!

Another assumption is also made in this chapter: that athletics is a vital part of your life, a catalyst to your intellectual and emotional growth. A final assumption is that you intend to have a career that will be important, if not economically essential, to your future.

Since you want to accomplish the most in both academics and athletics, here are the questions you will have to answer:

- What will you be studying?
- How difficult (challenging and demanding) will the academic program be?
- How much time will athletics take up?

What Will You Be Studying?

Maybe you're undecided about an area of study. If that's true, your college counselor and your common sense will tell you that you will need to choose an institution that offers a variety of choices. You won't want to go to a technological school if you think you'll end up in the liberal arts (social sciences, literature, languages). You won't want to go to a campus without a premedical program if you think there's a possibility you might want to go into medicine. If you want to have the greatest latitude in choosing a curriculum, you really ought to consider an institution that offers a wide range of choices. Frequently a large private or state university is your best option. But if you don't like the size of a large university, consider a smaller school that has the general area in which you're interested—a liberal arts college or a technical school, for example. Or you might be advised to go to a community college if you are that uncertain and want to save some money. There are many books that tell you how to pick a college for your career goals. Consult them and pick your counselor.

Colleges aren't always chosen on the basis of curricula or athletics alone. Although most will say your curriculum is most important in choosing a school, other factors are involved, such as geographical location, your emotional feelings about the campus (too social? too stuck up? the wrong image?), the size, the price tag, whether or not your friends will be going there, the school's reputation, whether or not your relatives or friends have been there. It is possible to make a so-called wrong choice as far as your program goes and still come out OK—educated, employed, and, above all, satisfied with the intellectual and emotional growth you attained in the years you spent there.

Not knowing what your major will be is not an insurmountable obstacle. Many schools, except for very specialized institutions, require one or two years of general study in the humanities, science and/or math, perhaps a foreign language, and the social sciences. Journalism majors at the best journalism schools, for instance, do not take a full load of journalism courses until they are juniors. And engineering majors at large universities and technical schools will find themselves taking general courses along with drawing and heavy science and math courses their first two years. But the point is this: there's room for change in college. However, if you change too often, you'll find yourself attending college for more than four years. This is not necessarily bad, but you're eligible for sports for only four years.

Sometimes it's good to explore your interests further before choosing a school:

- Try part-time or volunteer work in one of the areas you've been thinking about. Perhaps by working in a hospital or nursing home, you'll learn that's not where you'd like to end up.

- Take advantage of your high school counseling services. College catalogs, career booklets and workshops, vocational tests, and computer programs all may aid you in reaching a decision.
- Take advantage of college counseling services. If you think you want to be a research scientist, visit a college's laboratories, talk to the students and professors there, and see what the field is like.
- Examine your hobbies. Perhaps what you do in your spare time will help you decide on a major.

Here are some more points to consider in choosing a college in light of purely academic factors:

- How demanding is the curriculum at a particular school?
- How difficult will that school's curriculum be for you to handle?
- How academically challenging is the school overall?
- Does the school offer a graduate program in your field?

What Are the School's Admission Standards?

Colleges, universities, and junior colleges all set different admission standards. Some will accept all or most in-state or local students; some will accept only the best. Some large universities are divided into several colleges. For instance, one university has a college of engineering, a college of agriculture, a college of liberal arts and sciences, and several others. Since many students apply to the college of arts and sciences, that particular college will have to close its admissions by November. However, there might still be openings in engineering and agriculture. Thus, some students will reapply for admission to one of those colleges and be accepted. A semester or two later, those students can transfer to another college. Of course, you must find out whether or not transferring is possible. Also, are you willing to study a different area until you can transfer into the department you want? (What is a city kid doing in the college of agriculture?)

A college catalog will tell you what grades and test scores you will need to be accepted at a certain school. It's good to check out this information in a catalog, which you may send for by writing to the institution (some charge $1–$2) or by looking at the catalogs in your high school's counseling office or in a library. Some high schools and junior colleges have computer programs that will tell you everything you need to know about a college—entrance requirements, costs, field of study, size, and, of course, sports offered.

Another way to find out how difficult the school is to be admitted to and how good it is in your particular field is to do a bit of research. Consult the *Readers' Guide to Periodical Literature* and newspaper indices. You will find numerous articles in educational magazines and in large metropolitan daily newspapers about schools, their curriculums and how they are rated by experts. For instance, in 1979 the *Chronicle of Higher Education* published the results of a survey two sociologists took in 1977. The survey listed the top schools in more than a dozen areas, including law, education, political science, mathematics, and music. The top schools (anywhere from eight to fourteen were listed, depending on the curricula) in each of these areas were also listed, along with the percentage of faculty votes they received. In this survey of 4,000 faculty members, the best overall schools were Stanford, Harvard, the University of California at Berkeley, the University of Michigan, Yale, the University of Chicago, and the University of Illinois.[1] At these universities, there is a very good chance that you'll find an excellent department in whatever major you choose. However, if your major is something like dance, cinematography, women's studies, or oceanography, you will have to look further. Some of those schools named best by the survey don't even offer these majors. Very often, uncommon majors are available at a limited number of schools and even fewer have very good departments in those majors.

If the school has very high admission standards, perhaps you will need more than grades and test scores to be accepted. You might also need letters of recommendation from teachers and other adults, your own personal statement, and a long list of personal achievements and extracurricular activities. Your participation in sports will often help show you can contribute to campus life in still other ways.

If the school is hard to get into but the coach assures you that you will be tutored and "helped in any way possible" to get through school (see chapter 5 on recruiting), you should have second thoughts. It's no secret that even schools with the toughest admission requirements have made it possible for male athletic stars to be admitted, only to have those athletes struggle through and sometimes never graduate. Television specials have pointed out the sad fate of the top-notch athlete who plays and wins the game but loses his education. *Sports Illustrated* featured this subject as its cover story in May 1980, calling it "The Shame of American Education: The Student-Athlete Hoax." In the accompanying article, "The Writing on the Wall," John Underwood documented all the ways these highly recruited stars get through four seasons of play and then end up without a diploma: they take easy courses; they switch majors frequently so that they are always taking the lowest level courses in a department; they have their credits forged; they have tests taken for them; they get credit for extension courses they never attended. The list of violations is long. It was estimated that often only 60 to 80 percent of a school's football team would graduate—not counting the twenty to thirty students who drop out before their senior year.

Underwood did not mention any such violations among female athletes and coaches. That is not to say it doesn't happen. But most women's coaches will say that women have just not been involved in organized intercollegiate athletics long enough for this sort of thing to become common. And if women's sports do not become big gate receipt sports like men's football and basketball, perhaps recruiting violations and eligibility scandals will not become as common.[2] Maybe such problems and scandals will never affect women's programs the way they continue to plague men's programs.

Many women athletes and their coaches contend that women have an entirely different attitude toward competition than men do, that academics almost always takes precedence over athletics. Others say this situation is starting to change.

A California university PE professor said, "I've seen the girls' grades go down just like the boys' have. The women's programs emulate the men's and then they try to become training grounds for the professionals—and they shouldn't because there's not that much of an opportunity for women. There's too much emphasis on winning, not enough on the all-around development of an individual."

Another said, "I don't think it'll ever be what it's like with the men. My girls study, even on road trips. And when a game or practice gets in the way, I make sure they know to place their studies first. And they have."

How Difficult Will the School Be for You to Handle?

Let's say math is your best subject and you breezed through high school taking an abundance of math and science and loving every minute of it. But perhaps you change your mind about majoring in math and decide it no longer interests you, that ever since you started working on your neighbor's political campaign you've become very involved in politics. So now you want to consider going to law school but never have performed very well in history or English. What it all amounts to is that you'll be majoring in a field that might prove to be too tough for you. You might prefer it but have a hard time with it. Perhaps the fact that it isn't easy for you makes you want to pursue it even more; perhaps you like challenges—most athletes do!

In any case, figure out how much you will have to study to gain what you need from college. Some students have a natural ability to excel in any area with very little effort—with the fewest hours spent in the labs, in the library, at the tutoring and review sessions. But most of us aren't so lucky—

or so brilliant. The old rule they used to give us in college was "Double the number of hours you spend in class and that will be the number of hours you'll need to study outside of class." For most of you who will be taking twelve to eighteen hours of course work that means twenty-four to thirty-six hours of studying per week. Yes, twenty-four to thirty-six hours is quite a switch from the five to ten hours a week you could get away with in high school. You also have to remember that many freshman and sophomore level chemistry, biology and other lab courses require six to eight hours a week of lab time, often meaning a student will not just have sixteen or seventeen hours of class per week (the average course load), but twenty to twenty-five hours! Be prepared!

Once you are honest enough with yourself to know how difficult your curriculum will be, then you can decide if you'll have time for sports, job, love life, afternoon naps, shooting pool in the dorm rec room, and so on.

One very important source to consult is the school's curriculum catalog, which is separate from the school's general catalog. A curriculum catalog (sometimes each department will publish its own pamphlet) will tell you what courses you need to take to graduate with a degree in a particular area. The catalog will usually list the names of the required courses and the number of credits necessary. This varies significantly from subject to subject. For instance, someone who wants a degree in engineering or education may be required to take many more credits than someone in history or biology. It differs from school to school. And in most cases, you not only have to consider what courses are required by the department but also what general courses are required by the school to graduate.

Sample programs for the first two years of study are shown in the Freshman Year and Sophomore Year tables to provide an idea of an "average" student course-load. Note that individual programs may vary according to each student's placement scores, interest, and course work-load capacity.

Freshman Year

Course	Term		
	F	W	S
College Algebra, 4 cr	Mth 101	—	—
Calculus, 4 cr	—	Mth 207	Mth 208
General Chemistry, 3 cr	Ch 104	Ch 105	Ch 106
Chemistry Labs, 2 cr	Ch 107	Ch 108	Ch 109
English Composition, 3 cr	(Wr 121, one term, according to priority)		
Social Science Elective, 3 cr	(During terms when not enrolled for Wr 121)		
Arts & Letters, Elective, 3 cr	(One course each term)		
Physical Education, 1 cr	(One course each term)		

Sophomore Year

Course	Term		
	F	W	S
Organic Chemistry, 3 cr	Ch 331	Ch 332	—
Calculus, 4 cr	—	—	Mth 209
Animal Diversity, 5 cr	Bi 301	—	—
Cell Physiology, 5 cr	—	Bi 302	—
Plant Physiology & Div., 5 cr	—	—	Bi 103
English Composition, 3 cr	(Wr 122 or 123, one term)		
Social Science elective, 3 cr	(One course each term)		
Arts & Letters elective, 3 cr	(During terms when not enrolled in writing)		
Physical Education, 1 cr	(Two terms)		

Another major concern of the prospective college athlete should be, "Will I be allowed to take lighter loads during my athletic season?" Many college athletes claim this is the way they made it through school; they knew that there were fewer and less demanding courses they could enroll in during their seasons and that they could concentrate on their studies more in the off-season. However, to remain eligible for sports, one must be a full-time student.

For the high school athlete who played field hockey in the fall, basketball in the winter, and softball in the spring, a major adjustment has to be made. The all-around athlete will undoubtedly have to choose two of the three—or, more likely, one of the three—so she will have enough time for studying and other activities. It's totally unrealistic to think that the amount of studying you did in high school will suffice in college. It's likewise ridiculous to think training for and competing in a college sport will take no more time than a high school sport.

There's a growing trend, especially among male athletes toward specializing in one sport. This is not because coaches urge their players to take more time out to study; rather, it is because some coaches don't want their athletes to think about any other sport or be injured in another sport. A high school athletic director criticized this trend, saying, "We're not in the business of turning out professional athletes. This business of coaches playing tug-of-war with athletes is ridiculous."

However, some women's coaches still believe that, if the student has the time, she should participate in more than one sport to keep in condition. One Michigan coach encourages her softball team to take up field hockey in the fall, not only to stay in shape but also to help maintain enough student interest in that sport so that it will not be cut from the program. Her situation is not uncommon. Yet, one volleyball coach demands a rigid daily training program throughout the school year, virtually eliminating the possibility that her players will take up an additional sport.

Attitudes toward the number of sports an athlete should adopt vary from school to school, from individual to individual. Still, you will find those who can easily handle two sports plus an engineering or premedical program, while another will be struggling with one sport and a less demanding academic program.

Tennis player Claire Roehm of Houston found that tennis at Northwestern University was really a year-round concern for her. In the fall she had her regular season; during winter months she was expected to keep up with tennis indoors and also to participate in tournaments hundreds of miles away; and in the spring and summer there was more interscholastic competition, more practice, and the expectation that she would teach tennis at the local club.

Janet Haberkorn of Eastern Illinois University found plenty of time to play on highly rated badminton and tennis teams while keeping her grades high.

Joyce Schiltz of Chicago said she didn't have enough time to work on art while playing field hockey and badminton at Northern Illinois University, so she dropped out after three semesters. "I tried to double major in art and PE, but I never could get out of the PE building long enough to work on art."

If academics really comes before athletics in your mind, then what will you do if you're required to do an internship or semester at another campus or to student-teach in some out-of-the-way place? Can you arrange to do that work during the off-season? If not, are you willing to give up your sport for that year or however long it may be?

After three years on a nationally acclaimed Northwestern University basketball team, Alinda Cox decided not to play during her senior year because her fourth year in premed study requires her to be taking courses at the downtown Chicago campus, twelve miles from the main campus. "I came to Northwestern to study medicine, not to play basketball," says Cox, who tried out for the team when a couple of the team members encouraged her after seeing her goofing around on a gym court with a couple of guys she knew.

Other athletes have been known to quit sports when student-teaching or when really rigorous courses came up their senior years.

Then again, if you don't mind taking longer than four years to complete your education, or if you know that staying for summer school is a distinct possibility, then perhaps you'll be able to concentrate on sports as much as you might want to. Again, remember that your eligibility lasts only four years.

Each individual's case will differ. You need to decide what is best, based on your financial situation, the nature of your curriculum, and the amount of leisure time you'd like to have left.

In many cases, you might have to debate your parents about continuing athletics in college. Although men are not usually questioned when they decide to stick with sports on the college level, many parents are surprised to discover their daughters are serious enough about sports to compete beyond the high school level. Some even discourage their daughters from continuing in sports.

For women as well as men, however, there have always been two sides of the question: does athletics contribute to one's education? Is it worthwhile to have intercollegiate sports programs? Or are sports too important, overemphasized at the college level (particularly the revenue-making sports of football and men's basketball)?

> . . . Particular sports such as football, physical strains and dangers, the varying influences of the coaching system, sportsmanship standards such as amateurism and near-professionalism, commercialization centering around large gate receipts, the coordination or lack of coordination of athletics with educational aims and educational control, have been matters of discussion at various times. . . . many of the undesirable tendencies that have been associated with athletics among undergraduates have been the direct outcome of this intense rivalry and competitive system.[3]

We tend to think the current popularity of sports is a contemporary trend, now that seemingly everyone is jogging, working out at Ys, and roller skating. Yet people of the Depression era thought the same thing. After all, sports really didn't become big until the turn of the century, when people felt a little more at ease about letting down their Victorian hair. The NCAA is only about seventy years old. The modern Olympic Games date back to 1896. Back in the 1920s, the increased interest in athletics was probably viewed much the same as it is today. Just as running shoes and warm-up suits are now being sold in unbelievable numbers, fifty or sixty years ago the fashions, particularly those for women, were changing to allow for easier movement and participation in sports.

The growth of sports in the late 1920s could be seen partially as a result of the Depression blues. In any case, it was a noteworthy trend, and the Carnegie Foundation conducted research to determine how legitimate a place athletics should hold in academic life. Its 1926 study proved inconclusive. The same is true today. Numerous arguments for and against sports are still heard. The result? Individual institutions, private and public, at all levels from elementary through college, have had to decide how large a chunk athletics will take of the budget, how vital it will be to the campus image, how much of a priority it will be within general campus life.

In summary, you must take time to decide where *you* stand. Which institutions have a philosophy of sports and academics that most closely corresponds to *your* view? Do those schools also have the academic programs you would like to pursue? If so, then find out more about those schools. Whether you intend to be in school for two, four, six or sixteen more years, you owe it to yourself to make an educated choice.

CHAPTER 5
HOW THEY'LL RECRUIT YOU

They just wouldn't leave him alone. Of course, there were letters, hundreds of them. And phone calls. Sometimes anonymous callers offered lots of cash. Some offered cars, some offered cars for him *and* his mother, others mentioned luxury apartments. They'd promise him anything. And, in most cases, they would deliver. If only he would play on their team.

The athlete mentioned above could be any one of hundreds of high school boys hounded by college recruiters each year, particularly in basketball and football. After all, those are the money sports that keep college athletic programs out of debt because the gate receipts are so great, especially when the team is winning. Football and basketball teams often have budgets of $1 million or more. But that's justified by the fact that they bring in millions as well.

Everyone seems to care where the high school hotshots are going. In 1980, when Dickie Beal of Kentucky decided to forgo an offer from De Paul to play basketball at the University of

55

Kentucky, the news made the sports pages of most metropolitan newspapers. And he's not the only one who made the headlines. Numerous stars find their decisions publicized the day they make them, the day they sign their letters of intent. Often they hold press conferences; sometimes parents or their coaches are by their sides.

When Russell Cross, one of Chicago's top public league players, made his momentous decision to go to the University of Illinois at Chicago Circle, he held a press conference amid much hoopla and attention from the press. Cross, who had previously announced his intention to attend Purdue, wore a shirt with "Purdue" printed on it as he made his announcement over a radio station. His decision shocked many, since UICC's basketball program is virtually unknown. But with Cross ready to sign, UICC was suddenly being considered a potential threat. Newspaper accounts also noted that there might have been some sort of deal involved since both Cross and one of his high school coaches were being lured to the same campus.

Allegedly, Cross's academic average was not high enough to get him into either Purdue or UICC. Yet officials assured the public that Cross was earning all As during his last semester, bringing up his average to meet admissions standards. How a student with a C/D average could suddenly get straight As during one semester, especially a semester that was half basketball season, no one could really tell.

To make matters even stranger, Cross made the headlines again a month later, admitting he had never even signed a letter of intent with UICC and that he would, in fact, go ahead with his original plans to attend Purdue.

The recruiting and subsequent retaining of male college athletes has gotten so out of hand that most don't ask, "Is there any cheating? Are there any under-the-table deals? Are the rules regarded?" Instead they ask, "How much cheating is there? How many deals are being made? How many transcripts are being forged?" Apparently a lot is going on, and lately some of the parties involved are being caught, as was the case in 1980 when five Pac-10 schools were banned from postseason tournament action because of fraudulent practices. Public reaction to the case was divided: some people felt the schools got what they deserved; others said the punishment wasn't harsh enough.

Sports Illustrated exposed the scandals not in recruiting but in maintaining the star athletes' academic eligibility in the May 1980 cover story mentioned earlier. The article focused on how athletes are kept eligible—having transcripts forged, enrolling in easy classes, having others take their tests, and so on. These practices are often necessary when a coach recruits a star who can't keep up with the academic requirements. Often the athlete is black. Often the athlete is the one cheated in the end; he may be the star, but he neither graduates nor signs a pro contract. Lacking both of those pieces of paper does not exactly signal the end of the world, but by the time you are twenty-one or twenty-two, your chances of employment are mighty slim if you do not possess a marketable skill or you are not training to obtain some skill. "Playing" for several years may allow the student-athlete to develop psychologically and socially, but that kind of growth and development is probably not enough to ensure employment in any business besides a fast food chain.

Recruiting on the women's side is significantly different, although many coaches and players testify to the fact that it is going in the same direction as men's recruiting. Women *are* getting sizable scholarships, although cars and luxury apartments are seldom, if ever, part of the deal. One basketball coach at a Pacific 10 university did say, however, "It's starting to happen with women, too. I know it's going on, especially at some of the big schools. I've even heard of offers to move a girl's entire family so they could get her to attend their school."

A Midwestern softball coach said, "I know this one coach in our state has committed a number of recruiting violations. My girls tell me about it. And if I hear about one more, I'm going to report it."

Thus, scholarships for female athletes may not always be the blessing they appear to be. As mentioned before, women received only a handful of sports scholarships before Title IX of the Education Act of 1972. That law prohibits sex discrimination in any institution receiving Federal funding. The number of awards has been climbing steadily, and today more than $10 million is granted annually to more than 10,000 female athletes.

With so much money going to women's sports, the women's coaches undoubtedly are facing some of the same pressures to win and build programs that the men's coaches have dealt with for years. Some coaches readily admit there are recruiting violations. Even parents are wise to the game some recruiters play; in many cases, they have been the ones to ask, "How much money can you get for my girl?"

The potential for scandal within women's athletic programs is also great. Many coaches and athletic directors are out to prove that money spent on their programs has been well spent. They try to prove this by winning; consequently, they'll do anything to win. Because many colleges have had to trim their budgets in the face of rising costs and in some cases, lower enrollments, winning justifies the allotment of funds for athletics.

For the most part, the recruiting process for women athletes does not currently involve under-the-table dealings, anonymous phone calls in the middle of the night, or promises of four years of affluent living and automatic, guaranteed eligibility.

As one women's athletic director said, "We'd like to think of ourselves as being above the men's programs in not getting caught up with all the scandals they're seeing."

And, as a high school coach pointed out, "You're not going to see as many recruiting violations among women— our rules are different from the men's. They're stricter."

Basketball coach Mary Di Stanislao, who left Northwestern to build a program with Notre Dame women in 1980, has felt limited in recruiting because of the high admissions standards at both those institutions. She said, however, that she can still find super athletes who are also scholars. "I like motivated athletes with very strong self-images. I expect them to be perfect. I'm not very easily satisfied. And I'm not very easily satisfied with myself, so it's not like there's any kind of double standard."

Speaking of double standards, you might be curious to know that separate recruiting rules exist for male and female athletes. Bill Serra, who runs a college placement service for athletes (See chapter 5), said admissions offices will lower their standards for a male athlete and even extend their application deadlines. "All the standards and deadlines you read about in the Lovejoy and Barron's college guides are worthless when it comes to men. If the application deadline is February 15, the girls better get in their stuff by then. But for football players, admissions never close."

However, some institutions allow coaches to "sponsor" students who cannot meet admissions standards. One field hockey coach who tried this just once said, "I really tried hard to keep this gal in school—tutoring and all. But she ended up dropping out. Usually I can keep real close track of my teams and I'll have no problems."

It might be interesting to note just how vast a difference there is between AIAW (women's) and NCAA (men's) regulations for campus visits. Whereas the women's programs are allowed to subsidize the high school athlete's visit only as far as meals and accommodations go, the men's rules allow for much more—they can pay for round-trip transportation. And until a 1976 ruling was made, campus visits had been unlimited for men. Now the limit is three. University of San Francisco basketball coach Bob Gaillard wrote:

> We feel that there is no way to show in three visits that you are that much different from any other recruiters around the country. We just cannot give the attention to detail that we could in the past. James Hardy, one of the best athletes in the country, went to Jordan High School

in Long Beach, California. I personally made approximately twenty-five trips to Long Beach to visit with him or members of his family during the recruiting season. James Hardy's stepmother, Willie Mae Hardy, looks upon me as one of the family. She invited my wife, Sally, and me to her home for Sunday dinner and taught Sally how to cook soul food properly. Later, when James ate at our house in San Francisco, we were able to offer him something closer to home cooking.[1]

Gaillard, disappointed that this rule no longer permits him to "build up much more trust in" the players he recruits, said, however, that there is a way of getting around the three-visits rule. It's called "bumping into" a recruit. As Gaillard explained:

The NCAA does not say you must ignore a prospect if you run into him by chance, and such things have come to be known as "bumps." With the new rule, we now have what we call professional bumpers. They time how long it takes an athlete to go to the bathroom and they happen to be in the corridor when he comes out. They learn his route to school and manage to be in the intersection at the same time. It becomes quite a game to see how many times one can "accidentally" run into a player and get across one or two more points without using up one of the three visits.[2]

Because there is less funding for women, such "professional bumpers" are not used to recruit female athletes from high schools. But then again, maybe you should feel relieved that you're not going to bump into some stranger every time you come out of the john.

While some see the women's recruiting standards as too stringent and restrictive, others see them as giving high school girls a chance to remain free of many of the decisions and pressures of recruiting until they are seniors.

The following is summarized from the 1980–81 AIAW

handbook which is available for $6 from AAHPERD Publications Sales, 1201 Sixteenth Street, NW, Washington, DC 20036. Copies of the recruiting section may be obtained for 25¢ from the same address.

Definitions

Prospective Student-Athlete: an individual who, because of athletic ability, would be desired on an intercollegiate team and who previously has not attended an institution of higher education.

AIAW Letter of Intent: a statement of intention of a prospective student-athlete to attend the named institution and of the named institution to award the prospective student-athlete financial aid based on athletic ability. The Letter of Intent may be used by an institution whenever a prospective student-athlete is offered financial aid based in whole or in part on athletic ability. An AIAW Letter of Intent must be honored by all member institutions, and other AIAW member schools are required to cease all recruiting activities with respect to any prospective student-athlete once she has signed a Letter of Intent.

Auditions: sessions designed to give prospective student-athletes a chance to have sports talent assessed. Any institution may conduct auditions. An audition is not a tryout and does not guarantee team membership.

Financial Aid Based on Athletic Ability: financial aid awarded to a student-athlete where one of the criteria used to determine the amount or the recipient is athletic ability or sports performance skills. Such aid may be awarded for one year, and must be renewed if the student-athlete participates on the team for which financial aid for athletes is awarded. Such aid may be renewed for a maximum of four years. Athletic aid may not be given for summer school. A student-athlete who is injured or becomes ill, and as a result cannot participate in the sports season for which athletic aid was awarded, but is otherwise eligible, cannot be denied athletic aid for that year.

Signed Student-Athlete: a prospective student-athlete who has signed a valid AIAW Letter of Intent and/or an institutional agreement covering financial aid based on athletic ability.

Talent Assessment: the process of determining the athletic ability of a prospective student-athlete. This may be accomplished through observation of the performance of a prospective student-athlete who is participating in a scheduled athletic event off-campus or through an on-campus audition.

A. Recruitment Regulations That Apply to Colleges and Universities

1. A College or University **MAY**
   - Circulate brochures or flyers promoting the institution.
   - Initiate contact with prospective student-athletes, parents and coaches through letters or telephone calls.
   - Review films and videotapes provided by the prospective student-athlete.
   - Conduct special high school events such as high school contests, tournaments, or invitationals (if approved by the respective high school association).
   - Permit coaches to speak at high school banquets or teach at clinics or sports camps for high school athletes.
   - Conduct group or individual auditions on the college campus.
   - Send athletic personnel, at the institution's expense, to scheduled off-campus events for the purpose of assessing the talent of prospective high school athletes and eligible prospective junior college athletes. (Collegiate coaches or athletic representatives may not, however, enter into any discussions with any prospective student-athlete or

member of her family while in attendance at such events.)

- Permit a prospective student-athlete to visit the member institution's campus at her own expense.
- Permit a prospective student-athlete to work out with (or practice with) a collegiate team during an audition.
- Issue an AIAW Letter of Intent to a prospective student-athlete who has completed her junior year in high school (or who is completing her second year of normal progress as a full time student at a junior/community college) on or after the first Monday in March.
- Offer a prospective student-athlete financial aid for athletes, provided the aid does not exceed tuition, fees, room, board and loan of books, and is properly administered by the institution.

2. A College or University **MAY NOT**
   - Actively recruit a prospective student-athlete until she has completed her junior year in high school.
   - Contact in person any prospective student-athlete off-campus under any circumstances (such as at the student's home, school, or site of competition). If an accidental contact occurs because the prospective student-athlete or her parents/guardian approach a collegiate coach or athletic representative, the coach or representative must indicate that she cannot carry on a discussion of any kind with the athlete or her parents because of AIAW recruitment regulations.
   - Provide money and/or transportation for any prospective student-athlete to visit the campus.
   - Permit athletic department personnel to arrange off-campus meetings with prospective student-athletes even at the invitation of the student-athlete, her parents or coach.
   - Allow their coaches to train selected high school students using collegiate facilities.

- Offer gifts, money, or inducements to a prospective student-athlete or her family.

NOTE: To Prospective Student-Athletes, Parents and High School Coaches
If an official representative of an AIAW member institution violates these recruitment regulations, please report the matter to the AIAW. Allegations of violations may be reported by high school personnel, parents, and prospective student-athletes. Address your letter to: Ginny Hunt, Chairperson, AIAW Ethics and Eligibility Committee, Women's Athletics—Fieldhouse, Montana State University, Bozeman, Montana 59717.

3. The prospective student-athlete **MAY**
   - Visit a college campus any number of times at her own expense.
   - Participate in only ONE audition per sport at a given institution during an academic year. The audition may be either a group or individual audition. (Check with your state high school association before auditioning, since some states do not permit auditions.) An audition must be completed within one day.
   - Visit a given college once and receive free meals, housing and complimentary tickets to campus events and local transportation.

B. *The Letter of Intent*

1. The prospective student-athlete **MAY**
   - Sign only one AIAW Letter of Intent. The Letter of Intent may not be issued before the first Monday in March, and any Letter issued must be accompanied by a financial aid agreement or written statement of the amount, duration, conditions and terms of the athletic aid which is offered.

NOTE: Once a prospective student-athlete has signed an AIAW Letter of Intent, she may attend another institution but she may not receive athletic aid at any institution other than the one for which she signed a Letter of Intent unless she is granted a release from the Letter of Intent by the AIAW Ethics and Eligibility Committee. If a prospective student-athlete fails to meet admissions requirements, she must write to the Ethics and Eligibility Committee requesting a release from the Letter of Intent; the release will be granted if acceptable verification of this fact has been provided.

- Receive financial aid based on athletic ability up to the amount of tuition, fees, room and board at that institution. In addition, she may be given a book loan and tutoring services. The aid must be awarded through the institution's financial aid office.
- Receive financial aid based upon criteria OTHER THAN athletic ability.

NOTE: Financial aid which is awarded through the university and which is NOT, in any respect, based on athletic ability does NOT require the signing of a Letter of Intent.

2. The prospective student-athlete **MUST**
   - Sign the AIAW Letter of Intent at home. (It may not be signed on the college campus or with collegiate athletic personnel present.)
   - Sign an AIAW Letter of Intent within 14 days of its issuance by the college or university, or it becomes void.
   - Voluntarily inform all institutions that attempt to recruit her that she has signed an AIAW Letter of Intent, if that is the case. If she does not do so, she may jeopardize her collegiate eligibility.
   - Participate in the sport for which financial aid for athletes is awarded.

- Receive a Release Pending Notification from the AIAW national office if she wishes to attend any other institution than that named on the AIAW Letter of Intent, regardless of whether she wishes to receive financial aid based on athletic ability. No discussion with athletic personnel at any institution other than the one with which the student signed an AIAW Letter of Intent may occur until the student has received the Release Pending Notification.
- Settle her contractual obligations with the institution if she does not attend the institution.

3. The institution **MUST**
- Hold the funds intended for a signed student-athlete until she specifically requests a release from the FINANCIAL AID AGREEMENT she has signed or does not attend the institution or has been granted a release from the Letter of Intent by the AIAW Ethics and Eligibility Committee. This is true even if she has requested a Release Pending Notification.

C. *Eligibility Regulations for the Student-Athlete*

1. The student-athlete **MUST**
- Be enrolled at a college or university and must maintain the academic average required for participation in intercollegiate athletics at that institution.
- Be a full-time student as defined by her institution.
- Be making normal progress toward a degree in an established program, if she is a returning athlete or a transfer.
- Have amateur status in the sport in which she participates.

NOTE: For eligibility regulations for non-collegiate competition, consult the respective sports governing bodies.

2. The student-athlete **MAY**, with no effect on eligibility for AIAW events

- Accept officiating and coaching fees in excess of expenses.
- Receive expenses, including lodging, meals, transportation and entry fees for "open" events.
- Participate on an outside team or league if her institution's regulations permit.
- Practice with the college team after she graduates from high school and has been admitted to the institution she shall attend.
- Compete with the college team after she has graduated from high school when classes for the regular term preceding her enrollment have ended at the collegiate institution.

3. The student-athlete **SHALL NOT**
   - Have agreed to compete professionally in the sport for which she wishes to retain collegiate eligibility.
   - Accept payment or cash prizes for athletics-related activities in that sport or for commercial ventures based on her athletic skill or reputation.

D. *Financial Aid Based on Athletic Ability Regulations for the Student-Athlete*

1. The student-athlete **MAY**
   - Work and receive loans or general financial aid available to any other student on campus.
   - Receive financial aid based on athletic ability for all or any part of four academic years of study.

2. The student-athlete **MUST**
   - Try out (and participate if selected) for the team in the sport in which she participated the previous year in order to receive financial aid based on athletic ability.

3. The institution **MUST**
   - Attach the complete AIAW regulations governing financial aid based on athletic ability to any agreement for athletic aid.
   (The agreement may specify expected behavioral conditions

which apply to all teams. If a condition is not met, a student-athlete may have her financial aid based on athletic ability withdrawn, but she must also be removed from the team. Only funds not yet received may be withdrawn: no retroactive withdrawal of funds may take place. Financial aid may not be withdrawn on the basis of skill performance, reasons not stated in the agreement, or illness or athletics-related injury.)

- Inform a student-athlete whose financial aid based on athletic ability has been withdrawn or not renewed of her right to a timely campus review, and provide such a review if she requests one.
- Send out renewal agreements by July 1 of each year.
- Award the student-athlete at least the same amount of financial aid based on athletic ability specified in her athletic aid agreement of the previous year.
- Inform the student-athlete of exactly which monies are renewable and which are not renewable in case she has been awarded a one-time-only athletic grant or is receiving general aid from the institution to replace athletic aid.

Further information may be obtained from the person in charge of the women's intercollegiate athletic program at an AIAW school or:

ASSOCIATION FOR INTERCOLLEGIATE ATHLETICS FOR WOMEN
1201 Sixteenth Street, N.W.
Washington, D.C. 20036

Notes on AIAW Recruiting Regulations

While AIAW rules might seem rather restrictive at a glance, note the following points:

- Although college recruiters may not contact you before you finish your junior year, *you* may contact them at any time prior to your senior year.

- While recruiters may not speak to you directly, they may ask your coach about you before you become a senior.
- You may, at any time, request a school to send you information (brochures, catalogs) about their programs. This is not only allowed but recommended. Just as many juniors and even sophomores begin sending for college catalogs, it is highly advisable to request information on athletic programs as soon as you start considering colleges. Some colleges have no brochures or information about their women's athletic programs. In this case, it is wise to contact the coach or coaches involved in your sport(s).
- Once you're in college, if you wish to transfer and inquire about athletics at another school, that school's women's athletic director must report your contact to your current school and to the AIAW Ethics and Eligibility Chairperson. For your own good, you should be certain your contact is reported within ten days. However, if you are at a two-year institution, you don't have to make sure this procedure is followed. Or if you only contact another school's admissions office, you need not be concerned about having the contact reported.
- It is of particular note that a college student may not audition for a team at another institution unless she is finishing up a program at her school (most likely a two-year institution) or if the school to which she wants to transfer requires her to show her athletic ability in order to be eligible for financial aid.
- Even though it is uncommon for a female athlete to be offered money or gifts, it does happen. Obviously, all such offers should be refused unless you want to jeopardize your eligibility.
- You may not negotiate a scholarship package through another person. You must act as your own agent.
- While it is common for boys to be flown here and there to be interviewed by coaches and to visit campuses, prospective female athletes must pay for their own transportation

to and from a school. However, the institution may provide *for one first visit only of no longer than two days,* including room and board at on-campus facilities only plus free passes to campus activities. Schools can also pay to bring you to and from a bus depot or airport. However, do note that a school *may* pay for transportation to and from campus if that is the common practice for students in all disciplines at that school. Some coaches are trying to change this AIAW rule for the future.

- You can audition for a team, but you must pay your own way there.
- A representative of a college—whether it's the coach or someone else—may *not* speak to you or your family while you are attending a scheduled athletic event in which you are participating. However, the coach or rep may talk to your high school or junior college coach.
- A college coach is free to contact your current coach under any and all circumstances.
- College reps may discuss their programs at public meetings—college days, athletic banquets, etc.—but may not make the first move in recruiting athletes.
- Off campus, be careful not to have (and not to let your parents have) any contact with college coaches or reps— other than telephone calls and letters, that is.
- If and when you audition for a team, be aware that it is not the same thing as trying out for that team. You will still have to participate in the regular tryouts at the beginning of your sport's season. You are not guaranteed a spot on the team, *even if you receive an athletic scholarship.* Also, you are allowed only one audition per sport. Your audition may not consist of playing in an actual collegiate competitive event, but you may audition by playing with or against members of that school's team. The audition might be during one of the team's practices. It might also be a group audition or an individual audition. If it is a scheduled group audition, any prospective athlete must be allowed to participate. Expenses of

the audition are to be borne by the school but may include no more than a "social hour." Also be careful to note that the audition may or may not be the one allowable visit to a campus that may be subsidized. In other words, the school could pay for your meals and room (both on campus, as noted previously), but only if the audition counts as the one campus visit. If the audition is at a time other than your paid-for visit, you must find your own accommodations and meals. The exception is when the school pays for visits for all prospective students in all disciplines.

- Your high school team cannot compete against or with a women's intercollegiate team. Nor can you or any other high school athlete be allowed to work out with a college team.
- You may not be coached in any way by a college coach at a college's facilities unless the facilities are open to the public and all high school students receive the same training. This might be a concern when tennis, swimming, and gymnastics facilities at a campus are used by the community.
- While a college cannot pay for you to attend a sports clinic or camp, other organizations or groups may provide the necessary funds for you to attend. But the college may not select you to be given support or a scholarhip from any group.

Perhaps now that you know what you and the college coaches and representatives are permitted to do, you will better know what to expect from the recruiting process. The fact that a college coach does not talk to you doesn't mean that she or he is not interested in you. Remember, *you* have to initiate contact until you complete your junior year. After that time, colleges are free to shower you with letters and telephone calls. They may not visit you personally. There are limitations, such as the rule that prohibits college recruiters from talking to you or your folks when they come to observe you in an athletic event. In any case, your parents and your high school coaches may be valuable in the recruiting process. Both coaches and parents should be aware of AIAW regulations. Parents and coaches differ widely in how they handle recruiters. You should know what they can do to help you the most.

How Your High School Coach Can Help or Hinder the Recruitment Process

What Your Coach Can Do to Help

Probably the best thing your high school coach can do for you is know you, really know what your goals are in life and what your capabilities are, not only athletically but also academically, socially, and emotionally. That's asking a lot. Few coaches can get to know their players that well. But some do, especially if they have worked with them for four years in one or more sports. To be sure, what your coach knows about you depends on how open and honest you have been with your coach and how interested in and perceptive your coach has been about you.

If you want your coach to be instrumental in helping you make the right choice of a college (although sometimes several choices may be equally good), and to get the best financial aid package possible, here are some pointers:

1. Make an appointment with your coach or arrange to get together with your coach. Let your coach know that you plan to have a serious chat, that it might take more than a few minutes, and that it concerns your future.

2. Plan some questions for your coach. The following are some examples.
- How good does your coach think you are? Does he or she see you as being competitive past the high school level? Does your coach think you'd do better at a high or low level of competition?
- Does your coach anticipate any problems for you in participating in a college sports program? What might

these problems be? Is there some way of working them out? Be open to criticism.

- How does your coach suggest you go about finding a college that has a suitable academic and athletic program for you? How does your coach feel about the role of sports on the college level? Does your coach feel academics or athletics is more important? Why?

3. Be prepared to tell the coach a thing or two about yourself, such as the points below.

- What are your academic capabilities? Where do you stand in class rank, with test scores, and so on? Have you taken college preparatory classes? Do you want a challenging academic atmosphere or not? Is there a particular curriculum you wish to study? How much emphasis do you want to place on academics? How much time is required for you to do well—are you a fast or slow learner, a conscientious or an irresponsible student? Be honest. Perhaps, your coach will be aware of the different demands various schools place on students.
- How large a part do you want athletics to play in your college life? Do you foresee yourself playing one, two, or three (almost impossible in college) sports? Which sport(s) would you give up?

While talking with your coach, be honest about the role you would like the coach to take in helping you out. Perhaps you merely want your coach to be aware of your intentions to pursue college athletics. Perhaps you want your coach to know and be concerned about your plans; that is, you want your coach to take an active, personal interest in helping you find and get into a program that will benefit you. Perhaps you want your coach to know of your intentions but would prefer as little advice or intervention as possible.

How much your coach will help you depends on your coach and how you see your coach after your special meeting. You might judge the situation on the basis of your past experiences with the individual. A coach who has never taken much of a personal interest in you or the other players cannot suddenly be expected to become an immediate confidant and advisor concerning your college situation. On the other hand, your coach might be quite happy to help you. Sometimes you never know until you ask.

Be sure to consider what you'd like your coach to do for you and then be very direct in asking for it. The help you will want obviously will depend on what you think the coach is capable of giving and doing effectively for you. In most cases, you will want reassurance that your coach will write you a recommendation and fill out any necessary statistics or evaluation forms; an agreement to videotape or film your performance for audition or evaluation purposes; an agreement about how much your coach will speak to recruiters or college coaches when they visit, telephone, or otherwise contact your coach; and an agreement about how much your coach will or will not collaborate with your parents in handling your choice of a school and the recruiting process.

Now, can you expect your coach to come through for you? That depends on several factors: the coach's personality, your personality, your athletic and academic records and potential. Some coaches are willing to go out of their way for anyone; some are more picky about whom they will help; others won't do a favor for anyone. Some are agreeable but really would prefer not to become too wrapped up in the recruiting game when they've got a lot of other games, not to mention other players, to be concerned with.

And what about yourself? Do you find that you've been afraid to talk to your coach and now you suddenly find it necessary to level with this person? Have you been cooperative on the team? Have you put enough effort into sports to show that your interest in college athletics is sincere and not just a passing phase in your life? Have you proven yourself academically (that is, you're not constantly worried about eligibility, so that college does seem like a realistic and desirable goal?)

Let's assume positive answers to all of the above: you're

comfortable talking to your coach; you've been cooperative and have contributed to the team; you've shown enthusiasm for, and effort in, sports; you've kept your grades up and proven you are college material. All you need to do is go ahead and talk to your coach, hope for the best, and do your utmost to send out inquiries and make college visits on your own behalf. Being recruited is wonderful, but it does not happen to many female athletes. Be prepared for a letdown unless you are a truly top-notch competitor on a visible, top-notch team in a competitive conference in a populous state. In most cases, *you* will be the one recruiting the college to recruit you. If it works the other way around, fine. But don't count on it.

Now let's assume that you don't get along too well with your coach, or you weren't the most cooperative player on the team, or maybe you haven't shown a real dedication to either sports *or* schoolwork. What then? First, you ought to question how likely you really are to change. How can you suddenly say you want to be a college student and a college athlete if you have not put much effort into competing or learning at the high school level? Is change possible? Probably. But you will have to be the first one to give yourself a chance. If *you* can begin to believe in you, if *you* have the desire, then maybe your coach can, too. But first you have to begin by showing a willingness to change, a willingness to improve, a willingness to put forth extra effort.

High school coaches are usually well aware that many students grow and develop quite a lot in high school. They're not going to cross you off their lists if you've started out poorly, if you've lacked motivation or exhibited a bad attitude in the past. Most are experienced enough to know that a D student one year can turn around and work her way up to Cs and Bs during the next year, that someone who couldn't break three minutes in the half-mile one year can work really hard and come back the next season clocking in at closer to two, or that a ball hog on the court can suddenly learn to play unselfishly and more effectively. If you're ready to change, start now and prove it to yourself. Then try to prove yourself to others.

How Your Coach Can Hinder You

There's a good chance that you can avoid having any recruiting problems with your high school coach. But it is worth becoming aware of some of the things that can and do go wrong while you are trying to make your college plans. Here's a short list.

Your coach may want to steer you to a certain school.
Be wary. Coaches have their reasons for thinking one school may be better for you than others. Perhaps your coach wants you to go where she/he went, mostly for sentimental reasons or out of a feeling of obligation. Maybe the coach wants you to go to a school that she/he wished to go to way back when. Be aware that some coaches will want to live their own fantasies through you.

Worse yet, your coach may want to steer you toward a certain choice because a recruiter or coach from that school is pressuring or even paying your coach to sell you on a certain school. That happens, though rarely.

Your coach may have very limited knowledge of schools.
Your coach might know only of the best in-state schools or those within 300 miles, so don't hesitate to do some research on your own to determine where there are better schools, both academically and in sports.

On the other hand, your coach may be new to your school and your geographic area and may not know of any nearby or in-state schools to recommend. In this case, be careful, because the schools suggested may be out of your price range and too far from home—unless, of course, neither money nor location is an obstacle.

Your coach may be using you to further her/his own career.

As much as we would like to think there is little or no corruption in recruiting women athletes, violations do occur. And as much as we would like to think that high school coaches would not be the ones to get involved in such dealings, they do. Your coach might be promised a financial reward or even a coaching position if certain players are recruited. Or the coach might not have any offers from a school but believes in staying on the good side of a college coach by giving that coach the school's best players over the years, in hopes of someday landing a position at that institution. Although nonexistent among girls' coaches, it has been common with boys' coaches for a long time.

Your coach may ignore you.

Be prepared for this. Your team's progress and the improvement of everyone on the roster are undoubtedly at the top of your coach's priority list. That may leave little or no time for your coach to be concerned with your college plans. A coach may have time to do that extra routine with you on the parallel bars or work on switch hitting, but may wish to leave all talk of college until after the season is over. And even then, if your coach becomes involved in a new sport with a new season, there may be little opportunity to offer you advice or assistance.

If this is true in your case be sure you get at least the bare minimum from your coach—usually a letter of recommendation and the filing of other forms. Good luck.

If you're the star of the team, the coach might be reluctant to assist you too much for fear of being accused of favoritism. So, in any case, especially if you're not the star, *don't monopolize the coach's time.* Be reasonable in your requests for conferences and in applying to different schools. Instead of applying to eight or nine schools and asking your coach to fill out ten or twelve sets of forms, narrow your choices to four or five. No coach will be pleased to write a dozen recommendations, no matter how many world records you've shattered.

Your coach may give you unrealistic hopes.

Be ready for this. Most coaches want you to improve, and one way of encouraging this is to keep telling you that you have the potential and that you can run faster, hit farther, and so on. Yet, even an overly confident coach must be able to give you an idea of how good you really are. You already know, to a great extent. You can tell by how well you do on your team and in district and state competitions (if you get that far). Maybe you're really not suited for Big Ten or Pacific Ten competition. But maybe your coach doesn't have the heart to tell you that you'd be great in a certain university's premed program but you couldn't make it on their swim team.

In some cases, your coach may not be aware of how rough competition at various schools can be. If the coach hasn't attended any intercollegiate competition lately, chances are she/he might remember what it was like five or ten years ago when women athletes weren't as well trained or as well treated. Even a couple of years ago the levels of competition and perfection were lower. Don't be misled. Check things out for yourself. Rate yourself honestly—especially if your coach can't. Remember, if you're the best at a large high school in a competitive conference or district, you'll be suited for a much higher level of competition than someone from a small school in a less competitive conference or district.

Your coach may hate you.

Yes, as bad as this sounds, this is a distinct possibility. And maybe your coach has good reason to dislike you— because of your misbehavior, lack of dedication and improvement, self-inflicted or phony injuries, or poor attitude. Well, best of luck. If the situation really can't be remedied by a talk and a firm resolution from you that you *will* change, then there are only a couple of options left. Instead of asking the coach for a recommendation or for help, ask your college counselor, an assistant coach, the athletic director, or a teacher—or all of the above—for encouragement and assistance, which you obviously need at this point.

Now, if you truly have improved and have the statistics and other teachers' word for it, and your coach still won't give you a recommendation, consider taking your case (along with your parents) to your high school principal. If a coach holds a grudge against you or has labeled you as an undesirable or a lost cause, and if you really have proved that reputation to be inaccurate, some pressure from the principal might persuade your coach to take a better look at you. However, caution is advised. Your coach may hate you even more once the principal gets into the act. Contacting the principal should be used *only as a last resort.* It would be wiser to ask another coach, teacher, or counselor—even another player—to speak with the coach first.

Note that your coach should be urged to give an honest evaluation of your performance. In the end, no matter how much of a pain you may have been on the team, most coaches have good hearts and faith in human nature, as well as in an individual's ability to change. If you're sincere, you can probably convince the coach to give you a chance by giving you a good recommendation. Most would hate to ruin your chances for the future. But don't expect a coach to lie for you. You're responsible for your past actions; don't try to erase them unless you want the coach to lose even more respect for you.

Now that you realize how important it is to have your coach's assistance in choosing a school, here are some pointers to follow once the recruiters start to come around.

The Dos and Don'ts of Being Recruited

What to Do If You're Being Recruited or Interviewed

1. Be honest, be open, be yourself. No college coach or

recruiter will want to get to know you unless you come across as honest and unaffected. They won't want to take a risk on someone who is too nervous or anxious to present her true image or personality.

Be honest about how much time you want to dedicate to sports in college. Be honest about what you and your family can afford. Tell the coach and recruiters exactly how far from or close to home you would like to be, what curricula you might be interested in studying, and so on. Let them know your needs.

2. Listen well. Take notes. If a recruiter calls you, be sure to copy down the recruiter's name, the name of the school, its location, and other pertinent details. You have to be your own reporter and record keeper. If a scholarship or loan is mentioned on the phone or in a personal interview or meeting, keep note of it. What a recruiter/coach tells you one day may not be the same story you hear the next day or the next month. Try to observe how consistent the offers are, assuming you get offers. If there are no offers, ask how likely it would be to obtain an offer in the future.

3. Know the AIAW rules well enough to protect yourself. If a recruiter/coach contacts you first and you have not yet completed your junior year, it is best to level with the person and say you are aware of AIAW rules for recruiting and do not wish to jeopardize your eligibility by communicating, and that if you are interested, you will be the one to make the first contact. Be firm. You will gain the respect of the recruiters and perhaps make them aware that you are a serious athlete who wants to go by the rules. In most cases, this is what the schools are looking for in women athletes—integrity. For many years male athletes have been faced with overzealous recruiters who phone them anonymously, offer sums of money against all NCAA rules, and even offer high grades and credit. Many students know how to deal with this problem. One young man who had been recruited by more than 400 colleges

said that despite the offers, he always had to check out how much a school could really give:

> Yeah, some of them offered me a lot of money and stuff just to get me to come to their school. But when I got down there, it was just the opposite.
>
> When they would first tell me that they'll give me some money and take care of me, I would get worried. I thought about getting down there and the coach that told me all these things might get fired. A new one would come in, and all that stuff the first one told me wouldn't mean a thing.
>
> One coach said he would get me a job during the summer that paid about $12 an hour. He also offered me a car to help my mother out.[3]

Although he and others know the cash offers are clearly illegal, they rarely, if ever, report the recruiters.

4. Ask intelligent questions, whether you have a short conversation with a scout on the phone or you spend two days visiting a campus. See chapter 7 for a list of questions to start with. Plan your campus visit carefully. Talk with your parents, your coach, your college counselor and be prepared not only to ask questions but also to answer some. Know your stats and review your experiences—academic and athletic. Try to remember what you learned at sports camps or clinics. Take along a notebook that lists your questions. Also carry a little information sheet—like a resume—that you can leave with the persons interviewing you (see chapter 6). Perhaps the school has a letter from you or your statistics on file somewhere. It is always best to have the information at your fingertips and to be able to provide copies, just as you would hand out resumes if you were looking for a job. It is best to be organized, assertive (don't be afraid to tell recruiters about yourself), and prepared.

5. Try to answer the recruiters' questions yourself. If your parents accompany you on an interview, ask them not to be your mouthpieces. Colleges want adults, not children. Sure, there are some things you will need to check out with your parents. For instance, will you be free to participate in summer clinics and competition or will you have to work at the family summer home? For the most part, however, you should be the one to answer the questions. After all, you probably won't have your parents by your side to help you answer questions and make decisions once you're in college.

6. Be prepared to discuss your career goals and your academic interests. Many coaches want to know how realistic you are being about participating in sports while studying. Many want and expect their athletes to be career-oriented. If you don't have a specific career in mind, don't panic. Think about what subjects you liked best in high school and mention several areas of interest. Make sure you and they agree on how important athletics and academics will be to you. (See chapter 4.)

7. Try your best. Whether your campus visit involves five interviews and one audition or just a single interview, make sure you are ready and have thought seriously about what you want to ask and how you will answer the coach's or recruiter's questions. Get a good night's sleep the night before the interviews. If you have traveled, try to settle down and relax so that you can cure any jet lag or the discomfort that might follow a ten-hour ride in the family station wagon. You would do best to allow yourself enough time to take it easy and stretch out after your journey. One of your first stops on campus probably should be at the track for a quick run or at the pool for a few laps to ease your body and mind. Inquire about guest day passes to athletic facilities (more information on this in chapter 7).

Above all, be well-groomed and be cooperative. Put forth your best appearance—without overdoing it, of course.

8. Show that you are motivated, both as an athlete and as a student. Be self-confident. Be energetic and enthusiastic. Show the recruiters that when you really want something you have the competence and desire to go for it. If you believe in yourself, show it; then the recruiters will believe in you, too.

What to Avoid When You Are Being Recruited

1. Don't lie. Know your statistics accurately. Know your exact grade point average. Just as you should take notes on what the recruiter/coach is saying to you, your interviewer will be taking notes on you. Times, distances, team and individual honors should be memorized. That's right, memorized. You need to be accurate about your abilities at all times. Any inaccuracies may be misconstrued as dishonesty, and, obviously, you don't want that to happen.

More important than getting your statistics straight is getting your head straight. Don't lie about what you can or cannot afford, where you will not go, and so on. If you really can't see yourself going to an out-of-state college, don't encourage out-of-state scouts. If you really cannot afford a small exclusive college that doesn't give athletic scholarships but still is trying to recruit you, don't lead its recruiters on. If the college doesn't offer marine biology and that's really your only interest, don't say you might still consider the school— unless you seriously think you might change your mind about marine biology. For another example, if the softball coach tells you that you would have to give up volleyball so you could concentrate more on her sport, don't lie and say you'd gladly sacrifice one sport if you really intend to play two.

It's not easy to determine what you really want. If you are confused about all the different possibilities, locations, academic fields, and sports you'll play, let recruiters know this. Don't say something is definite if it isn't. In the end, letting interviewers know about your uncertainties will pay off. It might even help you make up your own mind if you discuss your uncertainties with others. The only problem is that you may be uncertain about too many things. That's why it's highly advisable to talk things over with friends, coaches, counselors, and, of course, parents. Don't think you can get through life making important decisions without putting in your own thinking time. Writing things down often helps. List the advantages and disadvantages of each aspect of the school. Weigh the various possibilities. Don't make snap decisions. Give yourself time.

2. Don't present your priorities as demands. Sure, you'd like to be able to play indoor tennis during the winter. Sure, you'd like to compete with the best schools in your sport. Sure, you'd like to be assured of a good travel allowance and new shoes or leotards or swimsuits every season. But don't act like a brat. Not every school can provide the best equipment, the best competition, and the best off-season training. When you ask about these points, be prepared for the worst. Yes, women's sports have come a long way. Yes, women are finally receiving more funds. But, realistically, women's programs are still sorely lacking in many areas. Rarely will you find a program that meets all the standards you would like it to meet. In a few years maybe, but for now look for the *best* choice, not the *ideal* choice, or you'll be disappointed.

Chances are that the scout/coach will be happy to answer your questions and will respect your intelligence for even knowing what to ask. However, if you observe the scout/coach becoming uneasy or defensive during a conversation, consider the possibility that you are asking about too many things that cannot be provided. Rather than continue with your questions, be sensitive enough to stop the interrogation; you might be able to come back with more questions at a later time, if at all. After asking a few key questions, you may decide against the school altogether. Don't ask questions that are really not important to you. If you're not picky about the surface of the track, then don't make it seem like a big deal. In fact, why bother to ask about it at all? Use your discretion and good sense. Don't put the interviewers on the spot. No coach or recruiter will think you're smart if you make it seem like you are reporting for "60 Minutes" or putting them on trial.

3. Don't be cocky or presumptuous. No coach or scout will believe you are the world's greatest until you've proven it—with a world record. You might be the best in your school's history but only eighth on the list of nine players they are recruiting or auditioning. It's great to be confident, but to be overly confident, to be arrogant and boastful, will make you unbearable and undesirable. If you're stuck on yourself, you're obviously not going to help the team much. You're obviously not going to be easy to coach, either. No coach wants a player who is closed to criticism and oversensitive to ribbing. But if you *are* cocky, it's not too late to change, or at least try to change. Hopefully, you will be able to see the light before you miss out on too many opportunities.

Don't presume that just because a scout traveled halfway across the country to see you that half the kingdom will be laid at your feet. You just might have been a convenient stopover on the interviewer's way to see someone else in the neighborhood. In other words, don't count your points until you've scored them.

4. Don't pretend to know what you don't know. If you know your time in the butterfly is two-tenths of a second off the state record, which is three-tenths off the national record, then go ahead and say so. But if you're not sure, don't be afraid to admit it. Of course, it would have been useful if you had known, but if you don't know, don't fake it. Chances are the scout or coach is a walking record book. Otherwise, why would they be in the position they're in? Assume they're competent, knowledgeable, and impossible to fool.

5. Don't butter up the interviewers. Don't try too hard to impress them. Your high school and grade school teachers might have responded well to your browning, but scouts and

coaches will see through you in a minute. They're looking for performance, statistics, character, and motivation, to name a few attributes. You can't substitute your charm and good looks for those assets. Not that charm and good looks don't help. But allow your record to speak for itself. Your self-confidence, sincerity, and honesty will then be enough to interest recruiters.

6. Don't complain about the school's facilities, meals, dorms, or auditions. You don't realize all the complications involved in setting up these things. Don't be overly critical. There's a diplomatic way of expressing dissatisfaction, and if you're really disappointed with the facilities or accommodations, maybe you don't belong at that particular campus. Don't stay if you're on a campus visit and you immediately know you're not interested in the campus. If you stick around and express your gripes, you might be put on the recruiting blacklist. And you'd better believe that such a list does exist.

7. Don't be discouraged. Especially if any of the following situations occur:

- You find out the school doesn't have any money left to offer you a scholarship.
- You get nervous and don't perform well at your audition or at the event at which the scout chose to observe you.
- You find out the scout really came to see someone else on your team.
- You can tell that you're the least skilled one at the auditions.
- You learn that the team really doesn't need someone who plays your position, swims your stroke, or whatever. (Is it too late to become versatile and learn something new?)
- The team doesn't have a coach for next season.
- The college cannot assure you that the scholarship you are being offered will be renewed in the future.
- The interviewers don't seem to like your coach or your

parents.
- The recruiters tell you it will be months before they can guarantee you anything. (Actually, even if they can guarantee you money, they cannot guarantee you a team position because tryouts will still be required.)
- They forget your name or where you're from. (You're used to being known. Well, face it, you'd better get used to being an unknown.)

8. Don't make excuses. If you didn't do as well as you thought you could while the coach or scout was watching, don't worry too much. There are lots of considerations to be made in determining whether or not you will be offered an athletic scholarship. Keep cool. The more often you say, "Well, I could've done better, but . . ." the more it will stick in their minds that you didn't do well, or as well as they had expected you to. Just relax and hope for the best. Second chances are not that difficult to come by. And your record will not be ignored or forgotten.

9. Don't allow the recruiter or coach to recruit your coach or your parents instead of you. Some coaches and scouts can sign up a player becuse they have won over (or paid off, although that is much less likely) the high school coach or parent or both. The high school coach or parent can then apply an inordinate amount of pressure on the athlete, making the choice of any other school impossible. So be careful. Make sure they are recruiting *you*.

10. Don't cover up your weaknesses. This is the hardest thing to do. You want to present your best, of course, but in the final analysis, you're better off if you are honest about what you can and cannot do. If you can't play a certain position or haven't tried a specific strategy, say so. Otherwise, the recruiters will find out later anyhow and accuse you of the sin of omission. Or, worse yet, they won't accuse you of anything. They'll just ignore you.

What It's Like to Be Recruited

Now that we have considered all these dos and don'ts, what is it really like to be recruited? What type of experiences have women had recently and in the not-so-recent past? Here are several stories from women in various sports. Perhaps some of their experiences will give you a more realistic idea of what to expect and what not to expect.

When Fran started playing tennis in high school in 1970, she was elated to be the first freshman to make the team. It was an excellent team, usually placing third in her large Midwestern state. Girl's athletics had just been instituted in her high school. Since that school was large (more than 4,000 students), a sincere effort was made to start up interscholastic sports for girls; the school's size also provided for equality in facilities. By 1974 Fran looked into several colleges that ranged from small to large, but which were all academically top-notch. She wanted a school with a strong tennis program and a strong academic program. Her high school coach didn't know which schools were good in what areas, and, besides, women's athletics were just beginning to develop in colleges. She and her high school coach never discussed her plans.

Recruiting was more or less nonexistent back in '74, so Fran checked out several schools on her own. One school especially interested her. She heard that the women's tennis team was new but was promised a lot of money. She knew the school had already established a solid intramural program and had good men's teams. Fran was also assured that indoor tennis courts were to be built by the time she'd be a sophomore. That was a major factor in her decision.

Well, Fran went to this Eastern school, an institution that had admitted only men a decade ago. Some good incidents and some bad incidents took place while she was there. Because the school had recently become coed, extra effort was directed toward establishing women's programs. But the indoor courts never materialized and the tennis players continued to travel to courts an hour away. During the winter, transportation was really difficult. Other than that, however, Fran was pleased to be part of a team that won five straight state championships. And the school *was* committed to building women's sports. "We had a good women's athletic director. She wouldn't take no for an answer on a lot of issues. They even turned the men's baseball team into a club sport to get more money for the women's programs."

•   •   •

Sometimes recruiting can start at the time you least expect it or want it. That was the case with Alinda, who had never thought of playing college basketball until she was recruited. One day, as a freshman at a Big Ten university she had chosen for its premed program, knowing nothing of the basketball program, Alinda was doing what she usually did when she was bored and tired of study—play basketball in one of the open gyms with some men. And who happened to be wandering by but two starters on the women's squad, which happened to be one of the best in the nation! The two women watched Alinda, then approached her and asked her to come to tryouts. They ended up with a new teammate. Alinda played much of the time but then quit after her junior year, a year her team made it to the national tournament. She quit to enter the second phase of her premed program—a four-year program at another branch of the university. Alinda, by the way, played on her high school team only during her senior year—the first year the team existed.

•   •   •

Julie, another basketball player, was highly recruited within her own state, a large Western state. But she didn't like the basketball programs in the area—the schools were small, the teams weren't too good, and there wouldn't be much of a challenge. Yet Julie—at five feet, eleven inches—didn't feel she wanted to play with any of the national powerhouse teams with players who were well over 6 feet tall. Luckily, one of the state college coaches who had tried to recruit Julie went out of her way to help her. "My father gave this coach his credit card and she just started calling around to various schools and telling them about me. Then I followed up her calls; I would write to them and then call them." After visiting several schools and negotiating over the telephone with others, Julie made up her mind. She had thought all along she would go to a California college, but when it came to the best combination of academics, athletics, and a scholarship, she ended up in the Midwest, at a campus she had never visited. And she's been content there ever since. "I wanted to play with people who were as good or better than I was." Although she didn't start as a frosh, Julie played a vital role on the team and then obtained the chance to start as a sophomore on a nationally ranked team.

●   ●   ●

Perhaps one of the most common courses followed by athletes, both male and female, is to choose a school within your own state because the school offers the academic program you want, it's not too far away, you're familiar with the school's reputation, and perhaps you even know students there. In-state schools are also generally less expensive, which is a major consideration nowadays. Many athletes decide to remain in state. That was the decision Karen made when she looked for a school. And they were looking for her, too. Karen was a top tennis player in a large metropolitan area and also played on a state championship badminton team. Although Karen had a high academic average and could have been accepted by other in-state universities with higher academic standards, she chose a medium-sized state university and received a tuition scholarship. "I wanted to go to a good school, but a good one that had a good badminton team. I liked the campus. The other school I considered had a better academic reputation, but I figured I would get out of school whatever I put into it. And I think the other university may be better, but not by much; in fact, I'd say it's overrated. I really think I can do as well, learn as much at any campus, because it's the person, not the school, that really makes the difference."

●   ●   ●

They recruited her mother, not her. That's what Pam, a nationally ranked high school tennis player, claimed. Sure, she was sent letters from all over the country. And there were plenty of phone calls, too. But what really counted in the end were a number of calls a certain coach made to Pam's mother. "Everyone's mother remembers being recruited by our coach," Pam recalled. However, she did not resent her mother's pressure too much. She ended up liking the campus at which she enrolled and happily went on to grad school on the West Coast, where she also teaches tennis.

But since Pam was ranked nationally, she was being sought much more than other female stars were five years ago. One school was so intent on getting her to sign that she received letters from bankers in its area and the town's mayor. "It was a real good recruiting job," Pam said, "because they made you feel everyone there wanted you, which was true because everyone loves tennis in that place. It had a great tennis program, but it didn't have the academics. Anyone could get into that school—maybe even with straight Ds."

• • •

Because women's programs are still so new at so many places, a lot of coaching changes are constantly being made. This can often cause a lot of confusion with recruiting. What happens when one coach recruits you and you go to school that fall only to play for another coach? Well, for one tennis player, Stacey, the confusion was so great that she ended up transferring after her freshman year. A top prep player who made it to state competition each of the three years she played, Stacey was recruited by several area schools and ended up at a state university. "But the university didn't like the coach who recruited me, so they got rid of her and the next coach didn't know a thing about tennis. So when I was playing she had me at number eleven and it was real upsetting." It wasn't until the end of the season that Stacey was able to prove herself—she and her partner took the state doubles championship.

But after that year-long disaster, Stacey decided she needed a change. Having been valedictorian of her high school, she found a prestigious university was interested in her and could offer her an academic scholarship.

•   •   •

All of the stories above are about athletes who graduated from high schools in the mid-70s or late '70s. What about the current recruiting process? Has it become more intense? Yes. Much more money is available. More coaches are better qualified and more secure in their jobs, not to mention that they are paid better. Whereas schools were just beginning to build programs following Title IX in 1972, they are now at the point of further developing and enlarging their programs. Schools that started out with a couple of interscholastic sports for women are now boasting ten or eleven.

The building process continues, depending on the sport. But for the most part, programs are now better established. Five or six years ago there were times when a high school star would be promised the best of coaching and facilities in a first year program, only to come to the campus and find the team no longer existed—not enough players were recruited, not enough money was available, or no coach existed. That happened to one tennis star who ended up dropping out of the university with a hefty loan on her hands—the school couldn't even come through with half the scholarship they had promised. She then turned sour on the whole idea of college and turned to teaching tennis at park districts and racquet clubs.

CHAPTER 6

IF THEY DON'T RECRUIT YOU, GO OUT AND RECRUIT THEM

So. Your phone isn't ringing off the hook with hundreds of calls from scouts and college coaches. No one has bothered to scout you at practice or at an athletic event. And you haven't been skipping out of your classes constantly to answer invitations to auditions.

Sure, you might be good. In fact, you might be excellent. But unless you are really super, you probably won't be recruited unless you're visible. And to be visible you must live in a populous state, attend a fairly large public high school that has an established reputation and a well-known coach. In addition, it helps if you've played in at least district, and usually state competition.

Because women's programs still lag behind the men's programs in funding, and because the recruiting process is still fairly new to women, many top athletes are never recruited. Nor are average athletes recruited. But do not despair.

93

Your first step is to recruit the colleges of your choice to recruit you. Once you make yourself known to them, once you become a familiar entity, then you might get a few letters or phone calls. *You* must make the initial contact, though. *You* must be assertive, aggressive. And if you like to plan ahead, you don't have to wait until you complete your junior year. Yes, you may contact them. But they can't try to recruit you until you're a senior.

Once you begin your campaign to elicit a college's interest in you, you might start to hear that phone ring and you might begin to receive some mail. But, until you initiate the contacts, don't expect too many calls. Here, in short, is what you will need to plan and execute:

- Selecting the colleges
- Writing a resume
- Writing a cover letter
- Obtaining recommendations
- Typing, duplicating, and mailing your information
- Following up the letter with telephone calls and/or more correspondence
- Asking your coach for help in following up
- Arranging a college visit
- Trying to find other ways to become recruited—what are the alternatives?

Keep in mind that if you never are recruited, you won't necessarily be banned from intercollegiate competition! Many college athletes were never recruited. Many never even played on high school teams. All college teams *must* have tryouts. Even a scholarship athlete has to try out at the beginning of the season. Occasionally, walk-ons who show up to try out end up playing vital roles on a team. This trend, however, will probably change in the coming years as more and more girls participate in high school sports and become aware of the opportunities available to them in college sports. Perhaps walk-ons will become as outdated as play days and GAA within a couple of years. With the levels of competition becoming stiffer, it should be more difficult for the inexperienced, untrained young woman to earn a place on a college team.

Now is the time to become concerned about your future in college athletics. It's never too early to be placed on file, to make that first contact, to start familiarizing yourself with the college selection and recruiting process. The following pages describe what you will have to do in each step.

Selecting the Colleges

The number of schools you contact will depend on many things. First, consider what you want in academics. If there are only three schools in the nation that offer the program you want, your task will be easy. You won't have to write many letters. You won't want to contact schools that really cannot accommodate your academic needs.

However, if there are many schools that can serve your academic needs, your task will be more difficult. If you want to major in mathematics at a large state university and money is not a problem, then good luck trimming down the list of institutions that will fit those qualifications. Of course, there will be fewer in-state universities from which to choose.

In most cases, you will be somewhat limited by your preferences and choices of curricula, location, cost, size of campus, and academic requirements. Once you do your research or visit the campuses, you can eliminate additional schools. If you cross too many schools off your list and find that no single school offers everything you want, don't be too surprised. In such a case you will have to study your priorities. Perhaps you will have to sacrifice location or sports or the best possible academic program to obtain the other things you want. Perhaps you have an unrealistic image of what any one school can offer. Think things through. Read chapter 4 on academics vs. athletics, if you haven't already read it carefully. You should have already begun thinking about which things or how many of them you would give up if you had to sacrifice one or the other.

A dozen schools is a good number with which to start. If the response you obtain from these colleges is not great, you can begin again and add other schools to your list. But if you start with a dozen, your response should be pretty good. Depending on the amount of time and money you have to spend in your search for a school, you can decide which schools you want to visit for further research.

Once you have your first list of schools, go for it. You might end up with more lists as you begin to discover the results of this first endeavor. Begin writing resumes and letters.

Writing a Resume

This sounds like you're looking for a job. In a way, you are. College hunting is very similar to job hunting. If you have taken a business or personal typing course, perhaps you are already familiar with resume writing. However, the resume you will write for this endeavor will be different from any other you will ever write. It will be an inventory of your academic and athletic accomplishments. It should look something like the one on the following pages.

Explanations of Resume Items:

Education: Be sure to list, from the present to the past, all the schools you have attended, plus their addresses, enrollment, athletic conference (if any), and the type of school— public or private, academy, vocational, technical, magnet, alternative, or experimental. Also be sure to give the dates you attended each institution. If you went to very many grade schools, do not feel you have to list them all. Just list the ones at which you participated in sports programs.

Academic Achievements: List as many honors and accomplishments as possible. Even if you entered contests but

Academic and Athletic Data for Jeannie Athlete

PERSONAL INFORMATION: Jeannie Athlete
                          1234 N. Hartford Lane
                          Elsewhere, IN 47070
                          (811) 322-8089

AGE: 17, born Feb. 22, 1964

PHYSICAL DATA: 5′6½″
                          126 lbs.

EDUCATION: Washington High School (attended grades 11–12)
                          2020 W. Ridge
                          Elsewhere, IN 47070
                          enrollment: 1,200
                          conference: Northeast Suburban
                          type: public (vocational)

                          Luther Academy (attended grades 9–10)
                          1177 S. Main
                          Heartland, IN 47171
                          enrollment: 200
                          conference: none
                          type: religious academy

                          North Junior High (attended grades 6–8)
                          55 E. 38th St. NE
                          Heartland, IN 47171
                          enrollment: 840 (grades 6–8)
                          conference: none
                          type: public

                          Walnut Elementary
                          33 W. Walnut Ave.
                          Middleville, KS 66000
                          enrollment: 530
                          type: public, magnet school

ACADEMIC ACHIEVEMENTS: top third of class
                          grade point average: 2.9 (B-)
                          college prep classes
                          special vocational work in architecture
                          dean's list for two semesters
                          honor society—Spanish
                          architectural design fair, two years
                          qualified to enter mathematics contest
                          SAT scores: verbal, 419; math, 550

EXTRACURRICULARS:	Spanish Club, 9, 10
	Toppers (athletic club) 11, 12
	Campus Corner (religious) 10
	Band 10, 11, 12; president, 12

ATHLETICS:
FIELD HOCKEY 10, 11, 12
varsity 11, 12
junior varsity 10
positions: wing, fullback, center forward
Team placed third in state AA—1979–80

SWIMMING 9, 10, 11, 12
varsity 11, 12
junior varisty 10
freshman
events:
(1) 200-yard indiv. medley
    district time, 1981: 2:18.126
    state time, 1981: 2:19.214

(2) 100-yard butterfly
    best time: 1:05.735
team placed second in districts (1981)
team placed eleventh in state (1981)

RELATED HONORS:
voted "Best Sense of Humor" by Toppers
varsity letters in field hockey, swimming

ATHLETIC CAMPS, CLINICS:
T.S. Johnson Field Hockey Camp
Mount Glad, N.J. 08000
August 1979 and June 1980

Pro Swim Clinic
Elsewhere, IN 47040
July 1980

HEALTH:
excellent
had all normal childhood diseases
allergic to dust, animal hair

INJURIES:
twisted ankle, November 1978
pulled hamstring, October 1980
broken finger, November 1980

EMPLOYMENT HISTORY:
Park District
1010 S. 10th Ave.
Elsewhere, IN 47070
summer 1979 and 1980: lifeguard
spring 1981: soccer coach for fourth and fifth graders
supervisor: Anne Clark
(811) 321-1112, ext. 20

EMPLOYMENT HISTORY
(continued)

Elsewhere Memorial Library
22 W. Hickory St.
Elsewhere, IN 47070
September 1980 to present
checkout clerk
supervisor: Dana Thomas
(811) 322-5522, ext. 52

ACADEMIC REFERENCES:

E.C. Ernest, architecture teacher
Washington High School
(811) 322-2888, ext. 70
home: (811) 333-4444

Tanya Hopkins, counselor
Washington High School
(811) 322-2888, ext. 45
home: (811) 353-5353

ATHLETIC REFERENCES:

Cathy Simpson, field hockey coach
Washington High School
(811) 322-2888, ext. 15
home: unlisted

Donna Smith, assistant field hockey coach
Luther Academy
(811) 441-6600, ext. 22
home: (811) 442-6123

Lee Wilson, swim coach
Washington High School
(811) 322-2888, ext. 16
home: (811) 323-5100

Jay Martin, swim coach
Luther Academy
(811) 411-6600, ext. 22
home: (811) 451-7111

ACADEMIC INTERESTS:

major in architecture or business
minor in accounting or marketing

ATHLETIC INTENTIONS:

field hockey
swimming
intramural soccer or softball

PREFERRED INSTITUTIONS:

medium-sized university in New England or
on Eastern seaboard

CAREER GOALS:

architecture or business

did not place, list them. If you have few or no honors to list, just list the kind of training you have had—business, the arts, or whatever your special field was.

Extracurriculars: Just as many high school yearbooks list your activities, you should do so in your resume. List years of participation and any offices you held.

Athletics: List all sports in which you participated; the dates of participation; positions played or events entered; placement or honors in conference, district, or state competitions; times or distances, where appropriate.

Health: Give a fair assessment of your physical condition. List any allergies, asthma, bursitis, or chronic illnesses you might have.

Injuries: Be honest about when you were injured and what was injured.

Employment History: This section will give the coach an idea of how busy you were outside of athletics and school.

Academic References: List only those teachers with whom you have spoken about providing references. Obtain home phone numbers if possible, but don't insist on them. Most teachers would prefer to take care of school business at school.

Athletic References: Handle these in the same way as academic references. Inform your high school coaches of your plans to contact schools. Your coaches might then be motivated to help you find a school. List all coaches, assistant coaches, the athletic director (if you really know that individual well enough), and any other coaches you may have had at clinics, workshops, or camps.

Academic Interests: This is where you need to give the coaches an idea of the curriculum choices you will make. List as many as you think you might consider. If you are very uncertain, list a general area, such as engineering, the performing arts, or liberal arts.

Athletic Intentions: Here you have to give the coaches an honest idea of how many sports you think you will want to handle. Don't be naive. Remember that the two- or three-sport athlete often cuts her participation to one sport on the college level. Some sports require more intensive year-round training and competition. Make sure you are aware of this in letting your intentions be known.

Preferred Institutions: You must make sure you don't send a resume to a small Northeastern liberal arts college saying that you want to go to a large Western state university. If you have real preferences for size or type of institution or location, do list them. And then make sure you send the resumes to only those types of institutions. If you're uncertain of the general type of school you want, leave this section out of your resume. Decide later.

Other Data: There's a good chance that you will want to list other things on your resume. If you intend to go to a religiously affiliated school, then you might want to add a slot for your religious affiliations and organizations. If you have done extensive volunteer work, you may wish to include a section on this topic. Use your head. What else is there that you would like a would-be coach to know? If you have some interesting hobbies—like hang-gliding, piano playing, or jewelry making—you would do well to include a section on your hobbies.

Writing a Cover Letter

Your cover letter should be simple, direct, and brief. If you are creative and would like to liven it up, do so. If you have some personal experience you would like to relate about having seen the school's team compete or knowing someone on the team, go ahead and write about it. But if none of the above is applicable, just write a short note to go along with your data sheet.

Here's an example of what your letter should look like:

1234 N. Hartford Lane
Elsewhere, IN 47070
May 2, 1981

Coach Judy Miller
Athletic Dept.
State U
Hartley Gymnasium, Office 202
Midtown, PA 33333

Dear Coach Miller:

Enclosed is a resume, a recommendation from my coach, and my personal statement of goals. I am finishing my junior year at Washington High School and am very interested in playing field hockey and swimming while studying at State U. I have already requested catalogs and an application from the university's Office of Admissions.

I would apreciate it if you would send me any information, applications, or brochures concerning field hockey and women's athletics at State U. I have also written to Coach Busby for information about swimming.

Also, please let me know if you conduct auditions, and, if so, when they are and how I could take part.

Thank you.

Sincerely,

Jeannie Athlete

Jeannie Athlete

Obtaining Recommendations

When a school sends you applications and information about its athletic department, you will often also receive a special recommendation form for your coach(es) to fill out. However, if you can ask your coach(es) to write a single recommendation that you can then duplicate and send out with all your letters, any additional forms you ask for might not seem as difficult to fill out because you will be able to provide the coaches with copies of the recommendations they wrote for your letter campaign.

One good approach to use when seeking recommendations is to write something for your coach. You should be the best judge of your personal assets. So write a short recommendation for yourself and give it to your coach. Say something like, "I thought I'd let you know that these are some of the things I hope you will include in my recommendation." This helps a coach in two ways: first, it gives the coach an idea of what you think your strongest points are; second, if you have been sufficiently thorough, your self-recommendation may bring up some data that your coach has overlooked or forgotten. After all, coaches have tons of responsibilities and many others to look after. So, if your coach is pressed for time or has an aversion to writing, your statement might be greatly appreciated.

Some things you might ask your coach to emphasize about you are listed below. It would also be a good idea to list specific examples to go along with each point you want to make.

- The amount of improvement you have made
- The effort you have expended
- The way you get along with the team
- How cooperative you are
- How easy you are to coach
- How quickly you learn new strategies, moves, techniques, etc.
- How you have helped and encouraged others on the team
- How you have contributed to the team spirit
- How receptive you have been to criticism
- Your sense of sportsmanship
- How unselfishly you play or perform

- Your leadership abilities
- The injuries you have had to overcome
- Your positive attitude
- Your natural ability and potential
- Your desire to better yourself
- Your ability to keep athletics going despite work and studies (or personal problems)
- Your willingness to help with team chores—cleaning up, picking up equipment, etc.
- Your role in establishing the team (often students are the prime movers in forming teams and starting club sports that eventually win interscholastic status)
- Your attendance at clinics, workshops, summer camps
- Your job coaching grade-schoolers at a park district
- The importance you place on keeping up with your grades

Of course, you should be able to think of other things to mention. Just be sure to remind your coach of your strongest points and to request that these points be made in your recommendation.

Sometimes a standard college recommendation form can be obtained from your college counseling office. You might select several forms and choose one that you would like your coach to fill out for you. When you do, have it typed neatly.

Typing, Duplicating, and Mailing Your Information

Once you have the data sheet, a cover letter, and at least one recommendation to send out, proofread them, have a friend or an English teacher proofread them, and then have them all typed letter-perfect. If you can't type, it's worth the cost to pay someone to do a perfect job. You might ask the typing teachers at school to recommend a student to do the job. Or ask a school secretary to do it for about $1 a page. Be picky about the kind of paper you use. Insist on thick, white bond. Insist that a good, clean typewriter be used. Make sure the type is legible (preferably not script), that the ribbon is dark, and that the keys are clean. Be sure the margins are set so that the information is easy to read.

When all materials have been typed and proofread, you are ready to duplicate them. Make twenty-five or more copies of each item so that you will have enough copies to send to one or two coaches at each institution you're considering. You will also need to keep some copies for yourself. You might wish to give your coach and counselor copies for their files.

Now you must obtain large enough envelopes to hold the materials (business size or six-by-nine envelopes should do). Be sure to type the addresses on the envelopes and make sure you address your inquiries properly. Incomplete addresses can be avoided if you look up the schools as listed in the annual *National Directory of College Athletics* (Women's Edition) available for $7 from Ray Franks Publishing, P.O. Box 7068, Amarillo, TX 79109. Your counselor or athletic director might have a copy. This directory lists telephone numbers, names of coaches, enrollment, and conference memberships of AIAW members, including two- and four-year institutions. Usually, college catalogs do not list college coaches' names. You will want to address your correspondence personally, so check out the names in a current directory.

Keep a record of all materials you send out. Use three-by-five-inch index cards and list each mailing, the date, and the coach to whom you addressed the information. Then wait for your responses. Keep track of any phone calls or additional letters you send to follow up your initial contact.

Following Up the Letters

Let's say the coaches you have written to begin to respond. What can you expect? In some cases, they will send you special athletics applications. You might find yourself rewriting everything you originally wrote (and more) on your resume. Don't be offended. That's standard procedure. You might also be sent more recommendation forms for your coaches and teachers to fill out. If this happens, just give your coaches and teachers copies of the recommendations they already wrote and ask them to transfer the information to the new forms. However, be aware that such forms vary considerably, so an easy transfer might not be possible. You'll see just how similar your original recommendation was to the one that was sent to you to be filled out by your coach.

If and when the colleges respond, be prompt with your reply. The easiest way to be forgotten is to be slow in returning forms. It also will indicate that you may not care very much about attending an institution if you wait a month or more to fill out its forms. One coach at a large West Coast university said her recruiting process involves eight letters (and forms) that go out to a prospective student. With so much correspondence necessary, your prompt replies will certainly be appreciated. Many times deadlines for applications and auditions necessitate prompt action.

Always type forms if possible or use a dark pen (not the type that tends to soak ink through to the other side of a form). Use the same pen for the entire application; don't switch in midstream. Print legibly and do not skip any items on any forms. If an item does not apply to you, write "not applicable." Read directions thoroughly.

If your letter-writing and resume campaign is successful, you will be deluged with forms to complete. If not, follow up your mailings with some telephone calls. Find out whether or not the coaches received your inquiries and ask about their programs and how you can learn more about them.

If telephone calls yield no response or little interest, you will at least have a fair indication of what the athletic department is like at those schools. Perhaps they are too busy and understaffed to respond to your letters. Perhaps they are too busy with tournaments or finals. In some cases, you will learn that a certain athletic program does not offer what you want. At that point you can either pursue your interest in that institution for its academics alone or you can continue your search. The latter approach is recommended. If you've really been serious about sports—and you probably have been since you are reading this—then keep looking. There are thousands of institutions, many with growing and improving academic and athletic departments.

Perhaps the response you obtain will also tell you the objective truth about yourself. If you sent your resumes to schools with well-established, nationally ranked teams, these colleges might inform you that your experience and success in sports do not quite measure up to their standards. If that happens, do not despair. You will just have to reevaluate your choices and scale down your selections. It is quite common for a high school junior or senior to discover that either her grades or her athletic record fails to meet the standards of the institution she had her heart set on. So keep looking. You'll find a place you like that's best suited to your abilities and interest. Just continue your research. Pick out some other schools.

You might be encouraged to know that at least one coach of a top basketball team said, "I'd rather have someone who really *wants* to play than a star who wants to sit back and be told how great she is."

Asking Your Coach for Help in Following Up

This is not a necessary step, but if you have good rapport with your coach and know the individual has the time and is willing to help you, ask your coach to make some calls for you.

Arranging a College Visit

Depending on the responses you receive, you might be able to narrow your choices to five or six schools, perhaps even three or four. Then you can decide which schools are worth visiting, which ones seemed receptive to you, and which ones would be realistic to attend.

So your next step would be to return any applications or forms to the college coaches and request meetings with them.

Say that you intend to visit a particular college to confer with academic advisers and to check out athletic opportunities. Your letter informing a coach of those intentions might look like this:

> 1414 Decker Drive
> Rock Springs, MI 49999
> January 14, 1981

Coach Mary Lou Adams
Athletic Department
Big State U
Hudson Gymnasium, Office 101
University City, CA 94444

Dear Coach Adams:

Thank you for sending me the materials I requested about your track and field and cross-country programs. Enclosed are the completed applications. My coach will return her recommendation form in the near future.

I would like to visit the Big State U some time in February to confer with a counselor in the College of Engineering and to look over your athletic facilities. I would also be interested in talking to you and perhaps observing an indoor track meet.

Could you please write or call to let me know when you would be available for such a conference? Thank you.

> Sincerely,
>
> *Ginger Fleetwood*
>
> Ginger Fleetfoot

Recruiting Alternatives

If you like to gamble, you can lay $250 on the line and almost be assured of finding a school that will pay you to play for them, in the case that the previously described approach leaves you unrecruited. The $250 fee goes to Bill Serra, who runs the College Athletic Placement Service (CAPS) in Asbury Park, New Jersey. CAPS was able to find athletic scholarships for about 90 percent of more than 1,000 clients in 1980. The enterprise also has a branch office in Youngstown, Ohio. Serra works on the principle that "Certain kids belong in certain kinds of schools." Through his contact with college coaches and his ten years of experience in knowing what campuses have to offer, Serra said he interviews the prospective college athlete and her parents and then suggests schools. Serra even arranges to have audition films sent to colleges. He will also arrange college campus visits.

Serra said it's easier for him to place women than men. And speaking of all the recruiting scandals among the men, Serra said, "Morals are considerably higher among the women. Whew! I'm used to dealing with men's football coaches. They're not educators—they're there to win or else they know they'll lose their jobs."

When a coach is having a difficult time finding in-state players for a team, that coach will often contact Serra. Many coaches have worked with him to obtain players. A Michigan coach said, "You know there aren't too many high schools with field hockey teams in Michigan, so Serra got me several players from the East."

Although coaches and players alike have had mixed reactions to Serra's service, CAPS might still be worth checking out. Further information can be obtained by writing: College Athletic Placement Services, Inc., 1506 Main St., Asbury Park, NJ 07712. Or call (201) 775-3200.

At this point what can you do if you still have not been recruited? Should you decide that you belong on intramural not intercollegiate teams? Perhaps you should examine the way you sent out your resumes and letters. Was there insufficient postage on your mailings? Were there misspellings in your mailings? Maybe you should have been neater. Recruiters and coaches can be turned off by the littlest things. But if you did a commendable job on your mailings and still obtained few or no responses, consider the following possibilities:

- The schools you contacted did not have the resources, the time, or the desire to pursue you. Some coaches do not believe they have to go out of their way to recruit.
- Personnel changes—the coach was fired or there is no coach at all—made it impossible for your inquiry to be answered. Maybe you should try again later.
- You are not college athletic material. Hit the books and look into intramurals. Your record is too weak for college competition.
- The caliber of the schools that interest you is too high for your ability. Look for other schools with less competitive programs or with lower academic standards.

Let's assume that you do, after all, get a decent response, and that you have narrowed down your choices and are ready to make your first college visit.

What should you look for? What should you expect? Before you look at the next chapter for details, it would be wise to review the following AIAW Code of Ethics for Players. Perhaps the code can best describe the type of athlete every coach would like to recruit.

Code of Ethics for Players

The purpose of intercollegiate athletics is to provide an opportunity for the participant to develop her potential as a skilled performer in an educational setting.

As education seeks to provide ways in which each may know herself and grow emotionally, socially and intellectually, so does the intercollegiate athletic program. In addition, the participant has the opportunity to travel, represent her school and learn the art of being a team member. All this gain is not without sacrifice, for the player may lose some individual rights and privileges as she accepts the policies of the program when she becomes a member of the team.

Ethical considerations for the player:

1. Maintain personal habits which enhance healthful living.
2. Objectively acknowledge one's own strengths and weaknesses. Recognize that each person has her own strengths and weaknesses—praise the strengths and help to strengthen weaknesses.
3. Value one's personal integrity.
4. Respect differing points of view.
5. Strive for the highest degree of excellence.
6. Willfully abide by the spirit of the rules as well as the letter of the rules throughout all games and practices.
7. Uphold all standards and regulations expected of participants.
8. Treat all players, officials and coaches with respect and courtesy.
9. Accept victory or defeat without undue emotion.
10. Graciously accept constructive criticism.
11. Respect and accept the decisions of the coach. When ethical decisions are questionable, the participant should direct her questions to the coach in private and follow appropriate channels to voice her concerns.
12. Be willing to train in order to achieve one's full potential.
13. Respect the achievements of the opponent.
14. Extend appreciation to those who have made the contest possible.
15. Be grateful for the opportunity afforded by the intercollegiate program and be willing to assist in program tasks as evidence of this gratefulness.
16. Assist in promoting positive relations among all participants who are striving to achieve athletic excellence.
17. Exhibit dignity in manner and dress when representing one's school both on and off the court or playing field.

18. Respect the accomplishment of one's teammates.
19. Expect fans to treat officials, coaches and players with respect.
20. Recognize and value the contribution of each team member.
21. Keep personal disagreements away from practices and contests.
22. Keep the importance of winning in perspective with regard to other objectives.
23. Contribute to the effort to make each practice a success.
24. Exert maximum effort in all games and practices.
25. Seek to know and understand one's teammates.
26. Place primary responsibility to the team rather than to self.
27. Refrain from partaking of drugs which would enhance performance or modify mood or behavior at any time during a season unless prescribed by a physician for medical purposes.
28. Refrain from partaking of alcoholic beverages while representing one's school.

CHAPTER 7

WHAT TO LOOK FOR ON YOUR COLLEGE VISITS

A lot of college freshmen see their campuses for the first time when they register for classes in August or September. It's almost incredible to think that many students enroll in schools halfway across the country that they have never seen before. But it happens. Sometimes the results are good. Sometimes you're not that lucky. You might end up wishing you had made a preliminary trip to check out the campus.

This chapter is based on the assumption that it is better to know exactly what you're getting into than to make a choice based on college catalogs, reputations, and so forth. Visiting a campus can give you an entirely different view of the place—perhaps one that does not coincide with its image or reputation according to your best friend's older sister or your parents.

On the other hand, there's still a chance that you can be very thorough in studying a campus and quite certain that you want to attend it, only to arrive and suffer disappointments in grades, classes, friendships, or sports. Transferring, of course, is always an option. However, you might desire the continuity of attending one institution for four or more years. In either case, you can better your chances for making a solid choice by reading this chapter and then visiting your top choices.

When Is the Best Time to Visit?

When you make your college visits will depend mostly on how soon you want to make a decision. In any case, do not visit a campus during the summer if you can avoid it. If you do, you will miss finding out what the campus is really like in action. There are fewer students attending summer sessions, fewer classes to observe, and no sports programs in progress. Faculty members and coaches you may wish to see might be on vacation.

Some students like to start looking for a college during their sophomore year so that they will know where they will be going by the time they are juniors. Toward the end of your junior year, or at the beginning of your senior year, you take college aptitude tests (SAT, ACT). On your test sheets you have to designate to which schools your test scores should be sent. Since the College Examination Board will send your test scores to three colleges of your choice, you may as well designate some realistic choices. However, if you are uncertain at the time you are testing, don't worry too much. You can, at a later date, write to the college board and request them to send your scores to other schools. This will cost you your time, a stamp and envelope, and $2 per school.

Some students wait around until halfway through their senior year before deciding on a college. Many of these students are disappointed, however, because college application deadlines are often in the fall. This is particularly true of Ivy League and other prestigious private universities. Some very highly rated state universities also have fall application deadlines. Other colleges accept students right up until a week or two before fall registration. This does not necessarily reflect the academic competitiveness, or the lack thereof, at an institution. At times it may reflect the fact that high school enrollments have been declining sharply over the past decade and colleges are being affected by the dwindling enrollments. Although most do not want to lower their academic requirements to allow in more students (and avoid going broke), many have been doing that.

As mentioned in chapter 3, there are some large universities with different application deadlines for different colleges within them. For instance, liberal arts and sciences students might have to have their applications in by November 1 of their senior year, while fine arts students might be accepted through January 1. Check college catalogs to be sure. What this implies, then, is that if you have procrastinated or made a last-minute choice of schools, you still may have a chance at enrolling in the university of your choice if you can make the latest deadline. Sure, you will be stuck in, say, the college of engineering when you really want to be somewhere else, but in most cases you will be able to transfer to the college of your choice within a semester or so. Actually, you're not really wasting much time, because most university students must fulfill general requirements during their first two years.

If you want to make an early decision concerning schools, consider visiting during the early part of your junior year or even during your sophomore year. Don't be surprised, however, when the coach informs you that no discussions on athletic aid may take place *until you have completed your junior year.* Coaches can send you all the brochures and information about their programs that you request, but they will ask you to come back during your senior year, when they will sit down to talk about scholarships with you. Before you are a senior, schools are prohibited from asking you for any information about your athletic abilities. They can scout you, but they may not talk to you. One thing they *can* do, if they are interested, is to obtain information from your high school coach about you.

If your finances are going to limit you, you may wish to put off your visits until the last possible moment. But if you have the money, go ahead and visit the colleges early and then perhaps again after completing your junior year. You'll undoubtedly be able to accomplish a lot more as a senior than when visiting earlier. In fact, you might not consider it as beneficial to visit before you're a senior. This is not necessarily so, however, since there's a lot more to college than a sports program.

Remember, unlike the top-notch males, the best female athletes do not get to take a lot of free trips around the country to visit college campuses. Whereas the NCAA allows the schools to subsidize fully three campus visits per recruit (including transportation to and from, room and board for forty-eight hours), the AIAW allows only one partially subsidized visit. For female recruits, room and board for forty-eight hours is provided, but only transportation to and from a bus or train depot near campus is paid for.

When a female athlete visits a college for an audition, this may be considered the one subsidized visit, but it doesn't have to be. If other visits are involved, one of them can be counted as the subsidized visit. Obviously, since you cannot be recruited until you're a senior, your audition won't be until then. Not all schools require or desire auditions. Not all sports necessitate them. Limited funds or lack of time on the part of the coaches may prevent a school from having auditions. Many coaches will accept a video cassette or film of your performance as an audition or for the purposes of evaluating you for a scholarship.

What Should You Look for in a School's Academic Programs?

The main purpose of this book is not to aid in choosing a college on the basis of academics. It is assumed you have already undertaken that task and have a good idea of where you want to go based on what you want to study. There are many self-help books, college catalogs, and guides that can help you make this decision. College counselors and teachers generally know what the best colleges are in certain subject areas. However, they are usually most familiar with the in-state schools. This will facilitate you if you want to go to a nearby or state campus. If you don't, the Peterson's, Barron's, and Lovejoy's guides to colleges will be helpful.

To give you an idea of the factors that are important to look for in using the above references, consider the following:

- Does the school offer the majors and minors in which you are interested?
- If you are uncertain of your career goals, do you at least see several possibilities in the majors offered at the school?
- How good are the school's departments?
- Does the college have the facilities you want—labs, libraries, computer systems, recreational facilities, theaters, work areas?
- Can you meet the academic requirements and maintain them?
- Do you have half a chance of being accepted at the school? (Don't expect them to lower their standards because you're a star on the volleyball court—that may happen with men's athletics, but this is rare in women's programs.)
- Are foreign study programs or internships offered? Special five-year programs leading to a masters? Honors programs? Remedial programs? Six-year premed programs?
- How easy is it to switch majors? Do you even have to declare a major before your junior year? (In many schools, if you are not entering a technical, artistic or engineering program, your first couple of years of courses will be very general and will allow you to change majors about as often as you would buy new sneakers.)

A prime concern that should not be overlooked is the attitude of the faculty, the student body, and the town or surrounding area toward athletics, particularly women's athletics. In the last chapter, a tennis player related that being recruited by the mayor and business people near one Southern university made her realize the importance the town placed on athletics. She realized its citizens would be supportive.

The father of a swimmer who was being recruited by an Arkansas university noted that the town's attitude can make a huge difference in the athletic program. He said, "When we visited the campus, we didn't even see the swim facilities, but we could feel the spirit of the place. In every place in town you could see something about the campus. In the shopping centers, instead of hearing Muzak over the PA systems, you'd hear the football game. And the local TV stations have good coverage and good interviews of athletes, male and female alike. In that town everything revolves around the campus and a lot around athletics."

But the town's attitude may not nearly be as vital as the faculty's attitudes. If you are going to need to miss Thursday and Friday classes to participate in regionals, what sort of response will your profs have? If you want to arrange your schedule so that it is the lightest and easiest during your sport season, how possible will that be? How understanding and accommodating will your adviser or the deans be? These are things that are difficult to check out. Asking athletes and other students will help you find out. The coaches should also be aware of the faculty's attitudes toward sports.

Schools commonly make athletics one of their highest priorities. Some will criticize these campuses for being too interested in winning, too concerned about their national reputations, too greedy for the millions in gate receipts that they can get with a team that is a national contender, too little concerned with the education of their athletes and the academics in general on their campuses. Many of these schools have also built highly competitive programs for women. But that is not always the case. Sometimes women's sports are overlooked at institutions boasting the best men's teams. Sometimes women's sports programs are strongest at institutions whose men's teams are not perennial powerhouses.

On the other hand, some schools have made athletics important but not an obsession. Many schools are proud not so much of their teams' national rankings, but in providing athletic programs that stimulate maximum participation. Many schools can boast that 70 or 80 percent of their students are involved in team, club, and intramural sports. What these schools aim for is allowing as many students as possible the opportunity to keep their bodies in shape and to gain all the positive aspects of athletic involvement. At times you will be able to tell how important this is just by seeing who uses a school's athletic and recreational facilities. Examine their main facilities. Even if they look wonderful to you, do the women get their fair share in using them?

Check out the bulletin boards in the sport facilities. Find out how extensive the intramural programs are. Does it seem that the tracks and pools are used extensively? Or are the facilities, in fact, overcrowded because the campus has too few recreational facilities or too little concern for athletics?

On some campuses the interest in physical education and involvement is so great that students and faculty alike participate in large numbers. One small Colorado college has sponsored a dean's race each fall for the past several years. The event is fast becoming a tradition. The college's women's athletic director explained: "Every dean and assistant dean— and there are five—is a marathon runner. And even their secretaries run a couple of miles a day. So they decided to have a dean's challenge race. Unfortunately, the deans haven't been winning." But the race does tend to indicate the administrator's interest in fitness. The athletic director added, "On this campus you'll have a very difficult time finding an overweight student." That's another indication of the attention paid to recreation and athletics, she said.

What Is the Campus Like?

College catalogs and campus maps can be invaluable in determining how well a campus will suit your needs. Things to consider include the following.

Do you like the size and location of the campus? Some universities are large, with 30,000 or 40,000 students. Some colleges are tiny and have only 500 or 600 enrolled. Some are spread out, while others are compact. Some are within cities and not contiguous. Others are like little villages or towns and are fairly distant from any town or city.

What kind of housing is offered? Is there every price range—from exclusive dorms with kitchenettes and pools to co-ops where the cost of living is halved because everyone living there contributes to making meals and cleaning? Are apartments available? If so, are they more or less costly than the dorms? Are freshmen and sophomores required to choose campus housing rather than their own apartments? Are athletes required or encouraged to live in any particular dorms? Are they prohibited from living in apartments? How close are living facilities to the athletic facilities and classroom buildings? Are there sororities? Could you live at home and still comfortably commute to school? If you have to commute, what is the public transportation like?

What is the parking like? Are permits required for bicycles, motorcycles, cars? Are the permits costly? How much does it cost to rent a campus parking space?

What kinds of vehicles are allowed on campus? Can freshmen have cars? Are bicycles popular? Stolen often? Are motorcycles allowed and, if so, can they be stored easily?

What is the climate like and how will it affect your studying, your recreational activities, your training? Do you like to run outdoors and, if so, do weather and geographic conditions at the school permit it year-round?

What types of students attend? Are there students of only the seventeen-to-twenty-two age bracket or does the campus attract a lot of older students? Are there many foreign students? Are many of different races, from varied geographic locations, or of the same socioeconomic background? How diverse is the student body? How diverse do you want it to be to feel comfortable? Do you want to go to college with the same type of students you knew in high school or do you want to meet new and different kinds of people?

Are there enough athletic facilities and can you use them

at any time? Are the facilities too crowded? Are they clean? Is the equipment maintained? Is the equipment new enough? Are there enough indoor and outdoor tracks, pools? Are there sufficient gyms for both competitive and intramural athletics? Are enough weight rooms provided, with decent equipment?

Obviously, the above questions are just a few you may consider. Self-help books and catalogs can give you more ideas on the various aspects of campus life that you need to examine.

What Kind of Financial Aid Is Available?

Financial aid based on your need or academic ability is definitely worth investigating as you look for a school. Just remember you cannot find out about any athletic scholarships you might be offered until you have completed your junior year. Do not bother to ask about the possibilities until that time. College coaches or recruiters who will discuss athletic scholarships with you before you are a senior are violating AIAW rules. But, while you are a junior, you can find out how many athletic scholarships are available, often just by learning whether or not the school competes in Division I, II, or III. These divisions will be explained in the next part of this chapter.

Financial aid applications, you should remember, almost always have earlier deadlines than admissions applications. So, if you know you will need a scholarship, a loan, part-time employment, or all three, you would do best to plan well in advance.

Most information about financial aid can be found in a college catalog. Applications for financial aid can usually be found in your high school counseling office. Many colleges use the standard parents' confidential statement applications. You should also write to the school for more information about aid. Multiple applications for financial aid are often required because so many different types of loans and grants are available.

Three major types of loans are usually available: federal, state, and college loans. A parents' confidential statement is likely to be required for each. However, students who can prove that they have been self-supporting for a given number of years, depending on the source of the loan, can often apply for aid on the basis of their own resources.

Just to give you an idea of the number of loans that are available, here is a list from a large state university's catalog: National Direct Student Loan Program, United Student Aid Funds, Inc., Federally Insured Student Loan Program, State Guaranteed Loan Program, Nursing Student Loan Program, and Short-Term Loan Program.

Available scholarships will also be listed in college catalogs. The lists are usually long and eligibility can be based on anything from the field you will be studying to whether or not you smoke or drink. Many are based on your ethnic origins. Nursing, ROTC, and even special education scholarships are common. Alumni, corporations, and foundations also provide aid. Some scholarships are not even based on need; in fact, most are based on academic achievement or on special talents such as music, dance, and science.

Grants are outright monetary awards that usually go only to those showing financial need. Grants are commonly offered by the state and federal governments and the college. The most widespread Federal grant is the Basic Educational Opportunity Grant (BEOG) offered to students enrolled in at least six credit hours. To qualify, you first must show need. You also must be a U.S. citizen or a permanent resident or intend to become a permanent resident. In addition, you must be enrolled in a degree program. BEOGs had a maximum value of $1,750 for 1980–81. More information can be obtained from pamphlets found in your counseling office.

Work-study programs and campus jobs are other ways a school can help you finance your education. These are usually based on need, but not necessarily, especially when campuses need individuals with computer programming, bilingual, clerical, or other special skills.

What Kinds of Athletic Aid Will Be Available? How Stiff Will the Athletic Competition Be?

These questions can be answered together because how strong and how competitive a team is happens to be related to the number of athletic scholarships made available.

Simply, the AIAW categorized its member schools not according to size or enrollment but according to how many athletic scholarships they are allowed to award in a sport. Division I schools can offer as many athletic scholarships as the AIAW rules permit. Division II schools can offer anywhere from 0 to 50 percent of the maximum limit of scholarships as stipulated in the AIAW rules. Division III schools can only award up to 10 percent of the allowable limit for each sport. It's important to note that the relative size of a school does not necessarily determine the number of scholarships it awards or the strength of its teams. Immaculata College, for instance, has just over 500 students, yet it has a powerhouse basketball team that has been ranked nationally in Division I for the last six years. Another Pennsylvania campus, West Chester State College, with 5,700 students, boasts a field hockey team that took Division I championships for four straight years (1975–78), the first four years that such competition existed.

Note that if a sport is in its initial year, it is probably not in any one of the divisions. A sport is commonly introduced first as a club sport, receiving little or no funding from the athletic department. Then, if the students prove their interest in a sport, team and division status may be established. No scholarships are available in club sports unless sources outside the school finance the aid.

If you're intent on obtaining an athletic scholarship, you'll find that most scholarships are offered at Division I schools where competition is stiffest. But it should be noted that a school could be in Division I for swimming, basketball, and gymnastics but in Division II for its other sports. This can happen because student interest and participation will vary from sport to sport.

Because Division I schools offer the most money, they are likely to recruit the best athletes and thus have a higher level of competition than Division II or Division III schools. However, some Division III schools have very respectable teams. If a team is in Division III, the implication is that the school does not place a very great emphasis on athletics (perhaps they fear athletes will lose sight of their studies) or that there is not enough money for women's (and possibly men's) athletics. As schools budget more funds for women's sports, more schools have been changing the status of their sports from Division III to Division II or Division II to Division I.

Top-notch athletes often choose Division II or III schools because they do not want the pressure of Division I competition or because their studies are more important than sports. One basketball player who was an all-state prep star in southern California dreamed of "going to UCLA and becoming the school's female Bill Walton." She was recruited by numerous large prestigious Division I schools. But she viewed the big schools as being too big, too awesome. She preferred to avoid the pressure of receiving an athletic scholarship and knowing she would have to perform to earn it. So she chose to attend a small liberal arts school in the West. "There was never any pressure," she said. "Classes could come first if they had to. I knew I could quit basketball if I really wanted to. I never skipped practices for academic reasons, but I knew if I had to I could have." Fortunately, her college attracted other similarly talented players and her team went to Division II nationals once and the regionals the next three years.

A tennis player who survived the pressure of Division I competition said, "When they're paying you $8,000 a year to play tennis, you play tennis." She said she regretted not having enough time to do anything except play tennis and study at her university.

If you are a decent athlete in high school, you probably will have to decide whether you should compete on a Division I team with an athletic scholarship or be on a Division II or III team with no scholarship unless your academic record or financial need can earn you a grant.

To give you an idea of how many scholarships are available, the following is a list of AIAW sports that have national championships and the corresponding maximum number of scholarships allowable according to AIAW rules:

Sport	Maximum per year	Sport	Maximum per year
Badminton	8	Slowpitch Softball	13
Basketball	12	Softball	15
Cross-Country	8*	Swimming	15
Diving	3	Synch. Swimming	12
Fencing	5	Tennis	8
Field Hockey	14	Track & Field	20*
Golf	8	Volleyball	12
Gymnastics	10		
Lacrosse	14		
Skiing	12		

*A student-athlete participating in both cross-country and track and field is counted in both sports against the financial aid limits.

Here is a listing of AIAW sports that do not have national championships and the corresponding maximum number of scholarships allowable:

Sport	Maximum per year	Sport	Maximum per year
Archery	6	Riflery	5
Bowling	6	Sailing	6
Crew	16	Soccer	14
Ice Hockey	15	Squash	9

Thus, if a school has Division I status, it may elect to award up to the maximum number of scholarships as designated above. However, a Division I school does *not* have to offer the maximum. Theoretically, a Division I school in skiing, for example, can decide to award no scholarships in that sport although AIAW rules allow them the option of awarding up to twelve scholarships. It is possible, then, but not likely, for a Division I school to offer few or no scholarships in a given sport. However, the usual case is that a Division I school will offer at least half the maximum number of grants allowed. In fact, to be really competitive, as noted previously, a Division I *has* to offer the scholarships it's allowed to attract the best athletes.

According to the above maximums set by the AIAW, a Division II school could offer anywhere from zero to four scholarships in badminton, zero to five in gymnastics, zero to ten in track and field, and so forth.

Since Division III schools are allowed up to 10 percent of the maximum allowable, they can award up to 1.2 in basketball, 1.5 in swimming, and 1.4 in lacrosse.

Again, the percentages set are maximums allowed, so theoretically three separate schools—each in one of the divisions—could each offer only 1 scholarship in gymnastics, 1.3 in softball, and 1.4 in soccer. Yet that is highly unlikely.

How are fractions of a scholarship available? How can a school award 1.5 scholarships in ice hockey, 0.8 in golf, or 1.2 in basketball? It is all calculated by the following regulation from pages 43–44 of the AIAW handbook:

Note: In no case shall the number of athletes on aid in any sport in any division exceed the AIAW maximum permissible head count for that sport.

Given X institution where the following financial values for in-state tuition, fees, room and board equals $2000 and the values for out-state tuition, fees, room and board at the same institution equals $4000.

An in-state student at this institution who receives an athletic grant of $1000 would calculate at .50:

amount of award = % equivalencies,
maximum possible

Therefore $1000 = .50;
$2000

An in-state student who receives a "full ride" would calculate at 1.00;

$$\frac{\$2000}{\$2000} = 1.00$$

An out-state student who receives $1000 would calculate at .25;

$$\frac{\$1000}{\$4000} = .25$$

An out-state student who receives a "full ride" would calculate at 1.00:

$$\frac{\$4000}{\$4000} = 1.00$$

If the 4 individuals mentioned above were on the same volleyball team, their "equivalencies" would be added together to equal 2.75 (that is, .50 + 1.00 + .25 + 1.00 = 2.75). Therefore, X institution would have 3.25 equivalencies remaining if they chose to declare that team to participate in Division II competition (because Division II is restricted to sports in which no more than 50% in financial aid equivalencies are awarded based on the maximum amount of aid permitted in that sport). They also currently have four individuals on aid and could not exceed the maximum head count of 12 in awarding the 3.25 equivalencies they have left.

If X institution chose to align itself with Division I, it would have 9.25 scholarship equivalencies remaining—utilizing the maximum numbers of athletic grants permitted by AIAW. They could not exceed the maximum head count of 12 in awarding the remaining 9.25 scholarship equivalencies.

It is best to find out, if possible, how many scholarships are available to freshmen only.

The AIAW specifies that aid to be given on the basis of athletic ability "may not exceed the accepted educational expenses for tuition, fees, room and board at that institution; however, less than that amount may be awarded. Partial awards may be given for tuition, fees, room and/or board."

If you obtain an athletic scholarship, what are the chances that you will be able to renew it for all four years? This is a very good question, since you undoubtedly would not want to go to an expensive institution for only one year and then find the aid nonrenewable. Your chances of renewing an athletic scholarship are very good unless you really foul things up. Whereas many academic scholarships are one-year, one-shot awards, athletic scholarships are renewable, as AIAW rules state:

E. GENERAL POLICIES FOR RENEWING FINANCIAL AID BASED ON ATHLETIC ABILITY FOR STUDENT-ATHLETES

1. *Conditions of Renewal*

   Financial aid based on athletic ability shall be renewed yearly for a returning student-athlete if the student meets the following criteria:

   a. maintains academic eligibility
   b. makes normal progress in a degree program as determined by the institution
   c. observes conditions specified in the financial aid agreement
   d. has been included on the current AIAW Affidavit of Eligibility in the sport for which she is receiving athletic aid
   e. tries out for the team in the sport for which financial aid was renewed.

   Notes:

   1) Financial aid based on athletic ability may be withdrawn following a year of non-participation.
   2) Athletic aid must be renewed if the student-athlete made the intercollegiate team the previous year.

2. *Date of Renewal Agreements*
   Returning student-athletes must be issued agreements for renewal of financial aid based on athletic ability which, if mailed, are postmarked on or before July 1, but not before the end of the competitive season, prior to the academic year for which it is to be effective. If the agreement is not signed within two weeks, the university is not obligated to renew the financial aid based on athletic ability.

3. *Signing Renewal Agreements*
   Financial aid agreements for returning student-athletes may be sent to the student's home for signature or may be signed on campus.

4. *Student Not Returning*
   If a student-athlete does not return the following academic school year, the institution is not obligated to the student to renew financial aid based on athletic ability at any later date.

5. *Student Not Making the Teams*
   A student-athlete whose financial aid based on athletic ability was not renewed because she did not make the intercollegiate team the previous season may immediately become eligible for financial aid based on athletic ability at a second institution provided a statement to that effect has been filed with the Regional Representative, Regional Ethics and Eligibility Chairperson and AIAW national office.
   Note: A student-athlete may transfer and receive aid following an academic year of non-participation due to not making the team.

6. *Amount Not Decreased*
   The amount of the financial aid based on athletic ability for a returning student-athlete may not be decreased. The amount must be the same or greater than the amount received the previous year.
   Notes:
   1) Institutions whose source of funds is not renewed

may appeal for approval to decrease the amount of the award. All students on financial aid based on athletic ability must be affected in equal proportion in any cutback.

2) The total amount of financial aid may be changed if aid is given completely on the basis of need, but the Regional E&E Chairperson, the AIAW E&E Chairperson and the AIAW national office must be informed of the change.

7. *Change of Sport*

In renewing a student's financial aid based on athletic ability, an institution may, on an annual basis, change the sport for which the aid is designated provided that the student-athlete ceases to participate in the sport for which financial aid was originally awarded for as long as she continues to receive aid in the new sport and participates in the sport for which financial aid is currently to be awarded.

Notes:

1) The amount of financial aid involved and the duration of financial aid agreement may not be decreased and the student must sign a new agreement each year. In addition, the student must actually participate on the team of the second sport for which financial aid shall be given.

2) If a student-athlete previously received financial aid based on athletic ability in two sports, and the institution wishes to award the total amount in one or the other of those sports, the athlete may accept the aid in one sport and she may still participate in the other sport; she is not considered to be *changing* the athletic aid from one sport to another. (NOTE: A Division III institution would have to count the amount in all sports in which the athlete participates.)

8. *Renewal in Case of Injury*

If the injury occurs as a result of participation in an

institutionally sponsored athletic program or activity
during the try-outs or the season for which financial aid
based on athletic ability is awarded, the financial aid
agreement must be renewed the following academic year.
9. *Renewal in Case of Illness*
    If the illness occurs during the try-outs or during the
    season for which financial aid based on athletic ability is
    awarded, the financial aid agreement must be renewed
    the following academic year.

No matter what the circumstances, it is best to ask some
college players about how difficult it has been to retain
scholarships. Depending on the school, the division, and how
the coach doles out the funds, you might find athletes are
under too much pressure to perform in order to retain their
scholarships. This is not usually the case, though.

There is a possibility, however, that you can obtain a
scholarship one year and not be good enough to make the
team the next year. AIAW rules dictate that you will lose the
athletic scholarship in this case but still be eligible for an
academic one.

Many coaches are pleased when their athletes are either
needy enough or intelligent enough to obtain grants or
scholarships. If enough good athletes obtain funds through
nonathletic aid, the coach can grant the allowed number of
scholarships to other good athletes. Frequently a team from a
school with high entrance requirements and a stiff academic
program will have a team whose members are all on financial
aid—academic scholarships, athletic awards, and grants. This
is especially true when the university charges tuition of more
than $2,000 or $3,000 a year.

What Range of Competition Should You Expect?

Generally, you will find that Division I and II schools
schedule more events in any given sport because these institutions have more money available for travel. One school might

schedule twenty basketball games, another twenty-eight. And if the school has been making it to regionals and nationals, count on more than thirty basketball games a season. This is something you will want to check because you will need to know how long your season is and how much time and travel will be required.

Find out how far away you will be traveling for events. Will you have to take a lot of long weekends or miss classes during the week to get to schools for competition? How large a chunk of time will be required? How much can you expect to study on road trips? Would you be better off playing intramural sports because the schedule involves too much traveling and too much time away from your books and lab work? Some academic subjects require using laboratories, self-teaching computer programs at scheduled times (hopefully not during practice or game times), and computer programs—if you have never witnessed chaos, try visiting a school's key-punch and computer terminal rooms.

If you are looking for the toughest competition possible, you will first want to look at Division I schools; then you will want to examine their schedules. Some Division I schools have enough funds to play a couple of contests at distant schools. Often this competition is valuable when the teams you're playing are the ones most likely to end up in the nationals. If your team has hopes of reaching the nationals, your coach will want you to get a taste of that type of competition.

Will Your Team Be Allowed to Participate in Regionals and Nationals?

Unfortunately, it is not uncommon for a women's collegiate team or an individual to qualify for nationals, regionals, or an invitational—only to learn that there are not enough funds to attend or that the team will not be allowed to participate for academic reasons.

One such case involved the basketball team of a large prestigious private university. After losing in the opening round of Division I nationals, the team learned that it had been invited to a tournament in Texas. "Our coach didn't want to tell us about the invite because then she figured that we wouldn't play as well in the nationals if we knew we still had a crack at another tournament. But the way it turned out, the university told her we couldn't go regardless, that we were missing too many classes and that finals were approaching. So we didn't get to go. And we didn't feel it was right because no one on our team has had any problems with academics."

Perhaps her team's academic success resulted partially from the fact that "You'll always see us bring our books along on the road trips."

In another case, a badminton team at a mid-sized state university discovered that it would not be able to attend nationals because the athletic department didn't have sufficient funds. Well, the coach complained loudly enough and the department came up with the funds. Schools generally do pay for hotels, meals, and transportation, but in this case the badminton team had to pay for its own room and board on the trip. During a previous season the team had also qualified for nationals and was able to attend only because it had money left over from two snowed-out meets during the season. However, instead of getting plane tickets to the nationals, the team ended up in a university station wagon, traveling for more than sixteen hours to the tourney and sixteen back. Part of the financial problem at that university stemmed from the fact that the men's athletic programs had run up a $100,000 deficit, resulting in some cuts to the women's programs. After qualifying at regionals, the women's tennis team couldn't even obtain partial funding to attend nationals 2,500 miles away.

What Do the Athletic Program's Funds Cover—Travel, Equipment?

Caroline Kriz, a tennis player at Purdue University in the late '60s, recalls that all her team had on road trips was "a beat up old station wagon to travel in and a bag of oranges to snack on." Chris Marshall, who played four sports at Northern Illinois University during Kriz's era, noted, "On trips we'd get 75¢ for breakfast, $1 for lunch, and $1.50 for dinner. The guys would commonly get $5 and $6 per day. We'd end up eating at Mac's all the time. Usually with the guys, their moms would pack 'em with food for their trips, so if they had money left over, they'd keep it. We had so much integrity that if we didn't spend all our allowances, we'd give it back."

And so things changed, as you may have read already in chapter 3. Yes, following Title IX, women were able to ask for and obtain more funds, more equipment, higher daily allowances for food, and better hotel accommodations. But it is still wise to determine for yourself just how much progress has been made at the institutions that interest you. Some women's programs still receive minimal support. Some road trips are disastrous because of old vehicles, cramped quarters in hotels, and too little money for meals. Some schools expect you to equip yourselves; others are generous providers.

Regardless of the sport, the following questions should be answered during your college visit:

- What kind of transportation is available for road trips? Are the school vehicles, if used, in good shape? Will you be cramped?
- What are the usual types of hotel accommodations arranged on road trips? How many athletes per room?
- What is the daily allowance for meals?
- What expenses will you be expected to absorb on road trips?
- What equipment does the school provide—mitts, racquets, athletic shoes, practice uniforms, sweat suits, shorts, T-shirts, socks, to name a few?
- How often does the school replace equipment?
- Is the equipment in good shape? If not, will it be a struggle to get the funds to replace it?
- Are the facilities in good shape or are the gym floors warped and the swimming pool in need of a paint job?

Do you have to go to a nearby school or community center to share facilities?

- Are the practice fields the same size as the playing fields?
- Are the courts close to campus? In decent shape? Proper size, surface? Are they kept dry following a rain? How close to campus are indoor courts for use in inclement weather? Who pays for you to get to and from the indoor courts? Who pays for your court time?
- Are your practice times convenient or are they arranged around the men's schedules and intramurals because facilities are limited?
- If practices are at night, how safe is the campus? Are there any arrangements to provide transportation home from night practice?
- Is tutoring provided for free? Can you use the tutoring services as much as you need to or is there a limit?
- Does the school have a book exchange specifically for athletes so they can either buy their texts at reduced rates or borrow texts without ever having to pay for them?
- Have there been any formal complaints of unequal opportunities in the women's programs? And if there have been complaints, was anything done to change the situation? You might ask a school's athletes about this, but more often than not, a coach or athletic director will not admit any problems of this sort. You might check with the Department of Education, which now handles Title IX complaints (See chapter 3.) Or you can telephone the year-old hotline called SPRINT, funded by the Women's Equity Action League Fund and intended to answer questions and complaints about inequities in women's athletic programs. The toll-free number is 800-424-5162.
- Will the school pay for tournament play? Do they expect you to attend tournaments in the off season? At your expense? Are you expected to attend clinics, camps, workshops at your own expense? Are there any funds available if you find a workshop or camp you would like to attend but cannot afford?
- Does the women's athletic program find itself constantly

begging for funds or does the school sincerely try to accommodate the women and really build, develop, and continue women's programs? Are the women coaches themselves resistant to change?

You will come up with many more questions, particularly once you visit a campus and start to speak to coaches and athletes. Because the men's organization, the NCAA, pays for the accommodations of all men's teams at national tournaments, they do not have the same problem with sending teams to tourneys. In the spring of 1980 AIAW officers and many coaches were upset to learn that the NCAA had voted to sponsor women's nationals for Division II and III schools. This action stirred much controversy, with some women's coaches welcoming the move and others decrying the move as an NCAA attempt to take over the AIAW. The controversy continues as the NCAA plans to sponsor women's nationals in two divisions.

Are the Services of Trainers and a Team Doctor Available?

Ann Meyers, one of the best collegiate basketball players ever to enter the pro ranks, once said as a student at UCLA, "One thing I've learned is that going through pain and anguish to win is what sports is all about." Yes, pain and injury are givens in any sports, yet you have to believe, as Ann put it, "You only have one body, so you might as well feel good about it." So you ought to study seriously how much is done for ailing athletes.

Injured athletes do not always obtain the medical attention they need. In 1976, 188 out of South Dakota's 189 high schools were without the services of a certified athletic trainer.[1] Many other high schools, colleges, and universities have found themselves in a similar position. The concern for strains, sprains, shin splints, and fractures grew, however, as investigations revealed that thousands of injuries occurred, especially in football, and parents held the schools responsible for them.

Now sports medicine is a booming business. In 1965 only one sports medicine center existed; today there are more than 100. Today many colleges are offering degrees in athletic training on both the undergraduate and graduate levels. And for those who have been unofficial or uncertified trainers for many years, refresher courses and workshops in sports injuries are commonly available.

Unfortunately, many high schools and some colleges have a long way to go in upgrading their programs for treating and preventing sports injuries. One dismal report from northern Illinois indicated that fewer than one in twenty-five of the high schools in a six-county area had certified athletic trainers and that just under half the schools had any trainers. In the Chicago public schools, which serve over a half million students, no certified trainers were to be found. Some action has been taken in Illinois and in other states to convince the legislatures to require schools to have certified trainers.[2]

Certification requires passing a test given by the National Athletic Trainers Association. The test may be taken following a course that should involve, according to one trainer, 350 hours of instruction in treating injuries beyond what the average coach already has. Many coaches do know how to tape sore spots and treat other injuries, but they have many more additional responsibilities.

Some inquiries you ought to make about the athletic trainer(s) follow.

- How many trainers are available? Are they certified? Are their assistants certified or are they students in athletic training?
- How often are trainers available—at all practices, at all games?
- Are doctors at games?
- Do the trainers have a reputation for doing good tape jobs? (Ask some of the athletes on campus about this.)
- Do the trainers provide any sort of physical therapy?
- Do the trainers know enough to recommend weight-

training to work muscles back to their original strength?
- Does the campus have weight-training facilities?
- Do the trainers know how to use massage in treating pain?
- Do the trainers dispense painkillers or recommend them so that an athlete can compete even when injured? Do the trainers believe in doing anything to get an athlete in good enough shape to play? Do you agree with their philosophy? Do the trainers and the coach agree on their respective philosophies?
- Are whirlpools available?
- Are the trainers' rooms close to practice? Are they clean, orderly, organized?
- How well are the trainers prepared to rush an injured athlete to the campus medical center or to a hospital? Have there been any cases in which serious medical attention was necessary? How efficiently were those cases handled?
- Do the trainers know how to respond to questions concerning miscarriage, abortion, birth control, secondary amenorrhea (temporary cessation of menstruation), irregular menstruation, menstrual cramps, pregnancy, and other female health problems? Research shows that as many as 30 percent of female long-distance runners and women involved in other strenuous sports have irregular periods, and sometimes no periods at all. While some have urged doctors to urge women to stop their running or exercise altogether, for fear that these women will become infertile, evidence shows that a woman's cycle will become normal once the intense exercising ends. While more information is obviously needed, Dr. Dorothy Harris, director of the Research Center for Women in Sports at Penn State, said, "Everything we know about sports for women—how it affects behavior, physiology, growth, and development—is positive."
- Do the trainers advise or assist the coaches in designing practices, conditioning, exercises, and so on that will not

result in injuries? Or do the trainers fail to inform the coaches that their routines may be more harmful than helpful to the athletes?
- Do the trainers organize or at least help organize conditioning programs (even ones for athletes to follow on their summer vacations) and weight-training schedules?

What Kind of Help Is Available to the Student-Athlete Who Needs Counseling or Therapy?

The growing interest in sports in America has resulted in sizable profits for athletic clothing and equipment industries. It has also created the new field of sports medicine, as discussed above. And it might soon crack open the field of sports therapy and psychology. A lot of research has been done on the effects of sports on character and personality. Much has been researched, too, concerning the group dynamics of a team and on the needs and/or drives human beings have to compete and to win. Even back in the 1920s literature was published on such subjects as "sanity as related to athletics" and "the competitive personality."

Some universities already have team psychologists. This is not yet a common practice, but more concern for the mental health of athletes will be shown in the future. In the past an athlete took time off from sports because of a physical injury. Now you might hear about a different kind of injury, such as when Chris Evert Lloyd admitted she needed time off from tennis because she was feeling burnt out and down. You now read about athletes like skater Beth Heiden feeling pressure and dismay instead of joy and elation after winning her Olympic medals in the winter '80 games. You wonder what it was like for fourteen-year-old Andrea Jaeger to miss so much of her high school social life and education in order to enter the pro tennis circuit. And how did it feel for her to be ranked among the top ten after less than a year of playing?

Although the tension may not be as great for the ordinary players as for the stars, sports psychiatrist David Marcotte said "deviant—really weird—behavior is tolerated among star athletes, which keeps them in a state of arrested development. They can't function, yet everyone expects miracles, and the pressure wrecks the games."[3] Even on the collegiate level, Marcotte insists, there are more than a few psychotics running around.

On the other hand, doctors have testified to the benefits for mental health that athletics produces. Many runners say they feel peace and can meditate effectively as they cover their distances. Others in strenuous sports speak of gaining a sense of confidence and self-esteem after becoming involved. Feelings of shyness or introversion, often dissipate when one becomes an athlete. Sports therapy may be becoming a common practice, but don't let this convince you that you're going to become a basket case because you're an athlete. Chances are you'll be more emotionally stable than your nonathletic classmates. But, of course, only you can decide whether athletics is contributing to your mental and physical well-being or detracting from it. The environment you choose for sports can be the determining factor.

The social, academic, and athletic pressures of college life should not be underestimated. Most campuses have responded to the mental health needs of their students by providing counseling and therapy at very little or no cost to the student. One coach says she is even trying to obtain funds to sponsor a weekend retreat with some workshops on psychocybernetics and psychological adjustment to sports. So, when you look into a college, even if you decide not to become a collegiate athlete, you should find out the details on the following points.

• What types of counseling are available: group, individual, family? If you're close to home or if you commute, consider whether you might benefit from family counseling. How much of the health insurance you have through the college would cover your entire family's counseling? Or would they just refer your family to another therapist?

• If individual counseling is available, how often can you schedule appointments—weekly, monthly? Are you limited to a total of three or six months of counseling? Note that some schools will provide only initial therapy and then refer you to a social worker, psychologist, or psychiatrist in town or at a nearby hospital—usually paid for by you or by your parents' health insurance.

● Are the counselors and therapists qualified? Are they social workers with masters' degrees or psychologists with doctorates or psychiatrists who are M.D.s? Are they all young and inexperienced? Are they grad students? Are they peer counselors? Can you choose the sex of your counselor?

● Do you have any choice or are counselors assigned?

● Can appointments be made at your convenience so you don't have to miss classes or practices?

● Are counseling facilities on campus or far from it? If you must go at night, will you be safe on your way to and from?

Of course, there are many more inquiries that could be made. But the primary things to find out are how available the services are and how competent the staff is.

What Is the Coach Like?

This is perhaps the most important question for you to ask when you consider a college athletic program. Because of its immense importance, the entire following chapter is devoted to a discussion of coaching philosophies, techniques, personalities, and practices. Read on.

CHAPTER 8

HOW TO FIND A COACH YOU WILL GET ALONG WELL WITH

"A great many coaches of women's sports shouldn't be coaching tiddlywinks. They stink. And I'm talking about both male and female coaches. I've seen some individuals ruin teams and potential athletes. There are lots of real idiots coaching in colleges and high schools, but especially in colleges." Well, you could take these harsh, supposedly objective words of a Chicago suburban sportswriter seriously or you can pass her views off as bitter, biased, or uninformed. In any case, you ought to know that coaches either make or break their teams. You can have all the talent west of the Mississippi on a team and still not have a winner unless the coach knows how to use that talent.

You know from your high school experiences that you won't have the same feelings for every coach. You love some; you hate others. Some don't evoke any strong emotions. You're willing to work and sweat wads off for some; you feel you get no support or encouragement from others. Some might play you; others might bench you. Some live and breathe their sports; others couldn't care less or would prefer to be coaching some other sports. Some win and some don't—and unfortunately it is often by that standard alone that we judge a coach's ability. After all, who are the coaches history recalls? The Knute Rocknes, the Vince Lombardis, and Ara Parseghians, and Johnny Woodens. What do they all have in common? They all coached champions. They all coached male football and basketball teams. Each had his own unique style, a personality that pervaded the stadium or gym where he would be—a presence to be feared, emulated, occasionally loved.

Perhaps in the not-too-distant future we will also hear about great coaches of women athletes. Perhaps some of these coaches will even be women. Whereas most coaches of college women are women, in the women's pro basketball league there have been only two female coaches. Some observers have questioned whether there have been enough good women coaches to coach the pros. Rita Easterling, Chicago Hustle star and the league's most valuable player in 1979, said there have been some very good women coaches but they're "not coaching the pros yet because they don't want to give up what they have on the college level. They're just in the midst of building college programs. Why give that up for something (the pros) that might fall through?"

Despite the fact that coaching women still has a way to go, there is excellent college coaching in all three divisions, in all sports, in all conferences; the trick is to find it. Many an athlete will relate how a coach caused her to quit the team or to lose her motivation or even to transfer schools. That's pretty serious. That's why checking out a coach is a task that shouldn't be taken lightly. You can often drop out of a class if you don't like the professor or the work. But you can't always quit a team—especially if you're on a scholarship—if you can't tolerate the coach.

You should try to observe a coach in as many of the following situations as possible.

- At an interview
- At practice with the team
- At an athletic event with the team
- At an audition
- On the telephone and in correspondence

You can also learn much more with some behind-the-scenes investigation. In other words, talk to the athletes.

Your interview with the coach may determine whether or not the coach will want you on the team. It should also help determine how anxious *you* will be to play for the coach. Job counselors will tell you that when you are being interviewed for a job, *you* should also be interviewing your prospective employer. The same is true here.

While the coach is trying to find out about your personality, performance, and goals, you should be trying to find out the very same things about the coach. First of all, come prepared. Just as the coach probably has some letter of yours or some data concerning your background on file, you also have to do your homework. College brochures, if available, usually contain some biographical information about their coaching staffs. If you can obtain the data, familiarize yourself with it. Don't ask questions if you already know the answers. And, of course, don't flaunt your knowledge of the coach's accomplishments.

Here are many things you will want to know about a coach. Even if you can take good mental notes, bring a paper and pen along to the interview. A lot will be said and you will need to remember most of it. You can ask many of these questions at an interview, but the rest will have to be answered while observing the coach at practices and games and while talking to the coach's team.

Background

How long has the coach been at the school?
Where else has the coach been? For how long?

How many sports does the individual coach? Some coaches are still overburdened with several sports. In the good old days, as in 1975, a small Colorado college hired Laura Golden, then a PE professor at a Georgia school, to start a women's sports program. During her first year, she said, "I coached six sports, to see where the interest would be—what would go and what wouldn't. We finally ended up with eight intercollegiate team sports and two club sports." And, it might be added, many more coaches were added as Golden was promoted to codirector of athletics.

Does the coach get involved in off-season sports, clinics, camps, the Olympic teams, intramurals, park district teams? Would the coach want you also to be involved in any of these outside areas?

Does the coach participate on any teams? Or, at least, does the coach keep in shape by swimming, cycling, running?

Does the coach teach as well as coach?

Are there assistant coaches? Does the coach feel that they provide enough support? What do the assistants do? How much will you be in contact with the assistant(s)? Do team members ever take over drills or other responsibilities? What will be expected of you?

Does the coach have good secretarial support services to allow more time for actual coaching?

Does the coach intend to stay at the school or take off for the next better position offered? Wait a minute! You really can't come out and ask this question. Or, at least, you really shouldn't. But if you're perceptive, you can tell how much in love with the team and the campus the coach is. The coach can exude a feeling of pride and belonging at a school. Or the coach can act as if she/he is doing the world a favor by breathing. Check this out. If a coach is itching to leave, you might end up catching the same disease.

Expectations

Obviously, some questions about what the coach expects

of players are in order. The following should be asked of either the coach or the players. Many of these questions can be answered fairly only by the athletes themselves. By observing practices and competitions, you will learn the answers to many of them.

What kinds of off-season activities related to your sport does the coach expect of you?

What kinds of clinics, workshops, camps, and off-season tourneys will you be urged, prodded, or required to attend? Will they keep you from your studies or job too often?

What does the coach do to help an athlete improve? Are drills and practices generalized or personalized? Will you be expected to learn, or taught to learn, new strokes, positions, and techniques, or will you just be kept at second base or center fullback? How much say will you have in the events that you'll swim or ski, the races that you'll run? Does the coach accept team members' opinions?

Will the coach give you any idea of how good your chances are of starting or competing as a frosh? How does a coach pick who competes and who doesn't? How often do the lineups change—or are positions and events set for the season right from the start? If you improve by mid-season or even by the end, would there still be a chance for you to compete?

What happens if you're injured? Will you ruin your chances for the following year or be asked to give up your athletic scholarship (if you have one)?

What kind of behavior, dress code, and diet does the coach require—not only on road trips where the team is highly visible but also at home? One coach doesn't allow his players to wear jeans, painter's pants, or overalls on road trips. Another is so concerned about diet that she makes her crew eat consistently at health food restaurants and, as one of her athletes complained, "All she did was to watch to see if I was salting my food too much. And she told my friend on the team a couple of times to tell her if she saw me using too much salt."

Another concern is your personal habits. Does the coach

prohibit drinking, smoking, or spending the night away from the hotel on road trips? Probably so. This is expected behavior since you represent your school. If you do not conform to such rules and expectations, you may be penalized or even booted off the team. Curfews are common. But when you have to play in a tournament the next day, you don't usually question that sort of detail.

If your grades start to decline, does the coach urge or demand that you obtain a tutor? Does the coach care? Does the coach punish players for not keeping up their grades, even if they're passing?

If you need to miss a practice or event because of school obligations, will the coach allow it? Most coaches prefer academics to come first.

Does the coach expect you to give 90, 95, or 100 percent of your time and energy to athletics? In other words, will you be an outcast if you spend a lot of time studying, socializing, or working? Must you be *fully* dedicated? How fully? Do the expectations coincide with your own?

Does the coach expect you to perform stunts you can't perform, improve where you know realistically that you can't (although no athlete likes to admit this)? Does the coach have unrealistic expectations?

If an athlete cannot or does not present a peak performance, is she ridiculed, shouted at, criticized? Does the coach ever embarrass the team or individuals on it? Does the coach compare teammates to each other in such a way that the comparison creates jealousy or division on the team?

Does the coach have sufficiently high expectations to motivate the players? Or is the coach too easygoing, too seldom a pusher?

Is the coach concerned about the physical well-being of the athletes? Are long practices in the hot sun avoided? Does the coach warn the team in advance of how long and how tough practices will be so they can be prepared psychologically as well as physically? Are there extra tough workouts following losses—to punish the players? Is care taken to aid an injured player or is that athlete pushed to play until she keels over or drowns?

Coach's Personality and Behavior Toward Athletes

Is the coach concerned with the mental health of the athletes? Is the coach aware of the pressures of finals, tournament play, competitiveness among teammates, personal traumas, personality clashes between teammates, the effects of the coach's personality on the team? Does the coach strive for group cohesion or actually function as a divisive force? Does the coach perceive fear or anxiety in the athletes? What does the coach do to relieve the troubled athlete?

Does the coach ever admit to making errors? Does he or she expect to be infallible or expect you to believe he or she is infallible?

Is the coach friendly toward the athletes? Does the coach seem genuine and sincere? Is the coach too much like a friend and too little like an authority figure? Does the coach become involved in the athletes' lives? Too involved? Does the coach command respect without being intimidating?

Does the coach relate sexually to members of the team? Or does the coach invite the opportunity to engage in sexual activity with team members? Problems have erupted on numerous teams because a coach has carried on sexually with one or more athletes. In some cases, the results have been lawsuits, firings or quiet dismissals. While some athletes do not mind the sexual invitations or flirtations of their coaches, others view the overtures as distasteful and unprofessional, and as sexual harassment. Although these cases are rare, sexual involvement between coaches and athletes does occur. Both parties have a lot at stake, however, and would do well to be concerned about how it will affect the rest of the team if their relationship is made public, which does seem to be the usual case. Or even if they are not discovered, how will their intimacy affect the team?

In one such case, a track and field coach was asked to

resign amid charges that he had come on sexually to women on the team. Janice Kaplan discussed this case in her book *Women and Sports:*

> . . . But Debus was able to resolve the women's conflicts about being jocks, making them feel that their desirability increased with their athletic prowess. "We shouldn't have been competing just to get an attractive man's approval," says one woman, "but Chuck paid a lot more attention to you if you were doing well. You spend your whole life hearing that you must be a lesbian because you're a jock, and then a Chuck Debus comes along and understands that it doesn't work that way at all."
> . . . "He could make you feel like the neatest, sexiest broad ever. When he said, 'Hey, baby,' you listened."[1]

One athlete on a predominantly lesbian rugby team in Ohio said male officials and coaches made sexual advances quite frequently "because it was a challenge to them if you were a lesbian. And if you were straight, you'd be pressured to prove you weren't gay."

Women coaches have also been dismissed in a couple of cases because of their sexual involvement with their athletes or with fellow coaches.

Since sexuality may become an issue on a team, it would be wise to find out what sort of conflicts exist. "It usually never bothered me and I never thought there were many gay players on my team," said a volleyball and softball player, who also coaches high school sports, "but what bugs me is when someone is trying to figure out if I'm a lesbian or not. Why don't they just come out and ask me?"

One tennis player said, "It's a definite issue that can't be overlooked. My coach harassed me and my lover and didn't want us rooming together on road trips. She even called my parents about it and tried to get them to break us up. And the thing about it was that she was gay herself! We all knew it but nobody bothered *her* about it."

What kinds of pressures do these sexual issues create on a team? Is there too much pressure to be straight, to be gay, or to hide your sexuality? It might be wise to ask a couple of questions about this, even though it's a difficult issue to bring up and often embarrassing. It should not be a big deal, but often it is, so you might be careful about whom you ask or how you ask about the issue.

It would be wise to judge coaches not only on the above suggestions, but also on the AIAW Code of Ethics.

Ethical considerations for the coach:

1. Respect each player as a special individual with unique needs, experience, and characteristics and develop this understanding and respect among the players.

2. Have pride in being a good example of a coach in appearance, conduct, language, and sportsmanship, and teach the players the importance of these standards.

3. Demonstrate and instill in players a respect for and courtesy toward opposing players, coaches and officials.

4. Express appreciation to the officials for their contribution and appropriately address officials regarding rule interpretations of officiating techniques. Respect their integrity and judgment.

5. Exhibit and develop in one's players the ability to accept defeat or victory gracefully without undue emotionalism.

6. Teach players to play within the spirit of the game and the letter of the rules.

7. Develop understanding among players, stressing a spirit of team play. Encourage qualities of self-discipline, cooperation, self-confidence, leadership, courtesy, honesty, initiative and fair play.

8. Provide for the welfare of the players by:
    a. Scheduling appropriate practice periods.
    b. Providing safe transportation.
    c. Scheduling appropriate number of practice and league games.
    d. Providing safe playing areas.

    e. Using good judgment before playing injured, fatigued, or emotionally upset players.

    f. Providing proper medical care and treatment.

9. Use consistent and fair criteria in judging players and establishing standards for them.

10. Treat players with respect, equality, and courtesy.

11. Direct constructive criticism toward players in a positive, objective manner.

12. Compliment players honestly and avoid exploiting them for self-glory.

13. Emphasize the ideals of sportsmanship and fair play in all competitive situations.

14. Maintain an uncompromising adherence to standards, rules, eligibility, conduct, etiquette, and attendance requirements. Teach players to understand these principles and adhere to them also.

15. Be knowledgeable in aspects of the sport to provide an appropriate level of achievement for her players. Have a goal of quality play and excellence. Know proper fundamentals, strategy, safety factors, training and conditioning principles, and an understanding of rules and officiating.

16. Attend workshops, clinics, classes, and institutes to keep abreast and informed of current trends and techniques of the sport.

17. Obtain membership and be of service in organizations and agencies which promote the sport and conduct competitive opportunities.

18. Use common sense and composure in meeting stressful situations and in establishing practice and game schedules which are appropriate and realistic in terms of demands on player's time and physical condition.

19. Conduct practice opportunities which provide appropriate preparation to allow the players to meet the competitive situation with confidence.

20. Require medical examinations for all players prior to the sports season and follow the medical recommendations for those players who have a history of medical problems or who have sustained an injury during the season.

21. Cooperate with administrative personnel in establishing and conducting a quality athletic program.
22. Accept opportunities to host events and conduct quality competition.
23. Contribute constructive suggestions to the governing association for promoting and organizing competitive experiences.
24. Show respect and appreciation for tournament personnel and offer assistance where appropriate.
25. Be present at all practices and competitions. Avoid letting other appointments interfere with the scheduled team time. Provide time to meet the needs of the individual players.
26. Encourage spectators to display conduct of respect and hospitality toward opponents and officials and to recognize good play and sportsmanship. When inappropriate crowd action occurs, the coach should assist in curtailing the crowd reactions.

Coaching Philosophy

Much of what you may have already observed about the coach's personality and concern for the players indicates an underlying philosophy of sport. Some questions concerning this philosophy might be as follows:

- How important is winning? Is winning everything and the only thing, as Vince Lombardi once said?
- Is winning of so little importance that athletes feel unappreciated and indifferent?
- Does the coach see the athletic experience as contributing to the athlete's overall education and socialization?
- Does the coach try to instill a sense of fair play and healthy competition among the athletes and a noncombative attitude toward the opposing teams?
- Does the coach see the athletic experience as a character builder? What does the coach do to contribute to this process?
- Does the coach devote her/his whole life to winning and therefore expect the team to do the same?

Male Vs. Female Coaching of College Women

Opinions vary greatly on whether men or women coach women more competently. Men used to be considered superior coaches because of their greater participation and longer affiliation with the sports world. Now that women's college teams have been around for a while, more and more women have the playing experience necessary to do justice to high school and college coaching.

One softball coach from suburban Chicago said she couldn't stand seeing the basketball games at her high school because of the way the male coaches treated the girls, not allowing them to think for themselves:

> Go to a basketball game where there are two male coaches and two male officials. And before you go, define what you think a person's goals should be in interscholastic sports. If our goals are social development, ability to compete and if we hope interscholastic competition leads to habits that will help the girls throughout life, then I invite you to a girls' basketball game. The girls under male coaches, as far as I've seen, are not playing but working physics problems. You have X, Y, Z, and all this stuff and you plug them into the formula and that seems to me that's all they teach them. The men coaches talk to the players the entire game. Almost every move. The coach ought to be quiet and motivate them to think for themselves. They make the girls feel they're incapable of thinking for themselves. I'm appalled that these coaches lack so much confidence in their kids.

Perhaps women don't dislike their male coaches because they like to be controlled by men, as marathon runner Frank Shorter suggests: "Men like coaching women because they can control them. . . .The women don't have much sports background, and they're ripe to have someone come in and dominate them. That's great for a coach's ego. He can tell them to do anything and they never stop and say, 'What is this bullshit? I know what I should do.' "[2]

One male coach said he does not feel an ego boost in controlling high school girls, but he finds them easier to work with than boys. "We know they don't have the skills. But they're more willing to improve themselves. They have a better, fresher attitude."

A softball, basketball, and volleyball player in college who has also coached high school said, "The sex of the coach should not matter to the athlete. You can't say who's better at coaching women or who *should* be coaching women. I've seen some very good and some very lousy men and women alike coaching."

Coaches can be as diverse in personality and philosophy as the athletes they work with. Lloyd Percival of Canada once did a survey of athletes' perceptions of their coaches. His survey, as discussed in a sports psychology text, led to the following descriptions of negative types of coaches.

Insulter—by far the most disliked type of coach.

Shouter—feels that coaching success depends upon decibel rating.

Avenger—leads athletes to feel that their failures were threatening to his job and thus takes a vengeful view of their less adequate efforts.

Choker—is fine at practice but goes into shock when the game approaches; closely related to shaky.

Shaky—loses his cool in competition; smokes two cigarettes at once.

General Custer—his strategies never change, thus leading to his demise in competition, just like the original general.

Hero—rushes constantly up to congratulate his winners so everyone will know *he* is the coach.

Scientist—scientifically psyches himself and his athletes out by his overly complex battle plans, strategies, and preparations.[3]

Some of Percival's other negative types included the Hitler, Fast Mouth, Black Catter (superstitious), Blister (shows up when all work is done), Rapper (constant leveler of fines), Rockney (believes giving pep talks is the total answer), and Superfriend.

However, there were also positive images of coaches in Percival's survey:

Supporter—was on the athletes' side, offered emotional support when the action was tough, admonished them for mistakes, but offered encouragement for better future performances.

Mr. Cool—was not likely to become ruffled in tense situations, was able to make sound decisions under stress, portrayed a positive model of self-control for his athletes, criticized in private, and could settle his athletes down when they became excited.

Shrink—could psyche athletes up to optimum levels prior to contests and could deal with defeat equally well; could turn fear into tactical advantages and understood the athletes' emotional feelings prior to and during a competition.

Tourist—related to *all* team members—the stars as well as the substitutes—talked and worked with athletes who were having problems; spread himself around, giving everyone some attention.[4]

Percival identified these additional positive types: Counselor, Doctor (takes care of them physically and emotionally), Salesman (the motivator, trying to sell them on the idea of working hard).

As you grow older and life becomes more complex, you will become aware of how important it is to be comfortable with a coach and a coaching style. So, if you plan to become a college athlete, don't neglect to check out the coaching staff as thoroughly as you possibly can.

CHAPTER 9

IS THERE A SUMMER SPORTS CAMP FOR YOU?

It's never too early to start inquiring about summer sports camps. Hundreds of camps cover a wide range of sizes, locations, costs, and reputations. It's up to you to send for the brochures and to check out a camp. Here are some questions you should attempt to answer.

What levels of ability and what ages does the camp accommodate?

Some camps are only for junior high students. Others try to cover all levels and all ages. Some even invite entire families. Many are coed. Try to match your needs with the camp that looks like it will serve you best.

Usually, the best way to check this out is to visit the camp, which is not practical for most athletes, or to talk to someone who has already attended the camp. Ask this person how demanding the routines and/or drills, the coaches, and the competition were. However, some camps—particularly for

159

sports like skiing and gymnastics—will not be so competitive, as the emphasis will be on improving individual skills in individual events. For team sports, you will find the competitive atmosphere is more prevalent, as there will be many games set for the camp teams.

Often your high school coach or seniors can advise you about camps with which they are familiar.

What is the total cost of the camp?

You need to check at least several things. First, what is the cost of the camp session, as advertised? Does the price include all meals? How much will transportation cost? Consider airplane, train or bus fare. Would transportation involve a day-long ride in a gas-guzzling family sedan? If you take a plane, what kind of transportation is available from the airport to the camp—shuttle service, cab, bus? Would it be possible to carpool with several others from your area?

You also have to consider hidden costs. For instance, will you be paying for entertainment (perhaps movies) every night or does the camp provide things to do? If the camp has horseback riding, must you pay an extra fee for it? Will you need to buy special equipment at camp or at home before you go? Will you be likely to buy souvenirs, T-shirts, and so on, that are on sale at the camp? Do you have to pay extra for additional coaching or special optional sessions?

Since the costs may run quite high, can you afford it? If not, look into getting a sponsor from your high school—perhaps the Boosters or the girls' sports organization would be willing to fund you in part. There's no harm in suggesting that they do. You can also inquire at local businesses; they are often willing to sponsor students' attendance at leadership and sports camps.

If all of the above attempts fail, and you can't afford the camp, apply for a camp scholarship through the Women's Sports Foundation. Forms have to be filed by May 1 preceding the summer you plan to attend. Applications include recommendations, medical releases, and other forms. These take time to fill out, so apply early. For more information, write: Women's Sports Foundation, 195 Moulton St., San Francisco, CA 94123.

Also check out the camp guide published by *Women's Sports* magazine every year in their April issues. The guide is reprinted in this chapter for your convenience.

What kinds of athletes attend the camp?

Will you be in a group that you will find comfortable? Will there be too many or too few participants? Are the athletes generally too experienced? Are there too many or too few from a certain geographic area?

Some camps invite athletes to attend. If you are good enough to be invited, it might be difficult to turn down the offer. But first give yourself a fair chance to check out the camp. Sure, it's flattering to be known as a star and to have the opportunity to practice with others as superb as yourself.

But before you invest any money in a camp, be sure the returns will be worth it.

How rigorous is the camp?

Check the camp schedule. One is undoubtedly included in every camp brochure. Determine whether or not you will be given a strong enough workout at the camp. Some athletes like more free time than is allowed. Others think the camps have too much free time and they get bored.

How good are the camp's instructors?

You can't always tell how good a coach or instructor will be by the individual's age or experience or the school the coach represents. Sometimes, however, these are noteworthy factors in choosing a camp. Your best bet, though, is to talk to athletes who know the instructors. If this is not possible, perhaps you can telephone the camp and ask the management about the coaches.

How much individual help will you get?

Study the schedule. See if time is set aside for individual skills improvement. Also figure out the number of campers relative to the number of coaches. Are there twelve athletes or thirty-five per instructor? If the brochure advertises seven different coaches and three different sessions, which and how many of those coaches will be at each session? If a well-known coach or pro is advertised as a camp instructor, does that mean that person will be there for the entire session or just for one afternoon? Don't be misled. Read the information thoroughly and, if a long-distance phone call is necessary, don't hesitate.

What are the facilities and equipment like?

How new is the camp? It is well kept? Is the equipment up to date and safe? Is the equipment similar to the kind you use at school? Are the sleeping quarters clean and adequate?

And, of course, is the food good and the cafeteria well kept and clean?

Does the camp offer you the opportunity to use university or college faclities?

Very often you will find that a college that interests you offers sports camps. Well, aren't you lucky? This could be the best way to visit a campus and meet the coach. Give serious thought to this possibility. If you attend a school's camp, that's at least one step in letting them know you exist and that you might be interested in going to that school someday.

You could probably think of dozens more questions to ask. Don't be afraid to talk to friends and coaches or to make a couple of phone calls regarding a camp.

A good way to start looking for a camp is to check the listing compiled by *Women's Sports* magazine. Act now and send for information. Attending a sports camp will not only help you perform better, it will also help you determine, in some cases, whether or not you will want to compete on the college level.

CHAPTER 10
TAKING THOSE FINAL STEPS

Once you have entered the last semester of your senior year in high school, you probably fit into one of these categories:

Case I: You've chosen a school that's offering you a scholarship.

Case II: You've chosen a school that's not offering you a scholarship.

Case III: You're still undecided.

Case I

If you fall into this category, you will have to deal with the AIAW procedure of signing a *letter of intent*. A sample letter and the AIAW explanation of the letter are in this chapter.

Any recruiting college or university will mail you a letter of intent no earlier than the first Monday of March preceding the fall in which you intend to enroll. Carefully read all the AIAW regulations concerning the letter of intent. Note that you can sign only one letter of intent, but that if you change your mind later you may petition to be released from the letter of intent. It is extremely important to realize that if you are not academically eligible under a school's admissions policies, the letter of intent is automatically void.

The letter of intent is always sent to you along with an offer of financial aid based on your athletic ability. The letter of intent must be returned within fourteen days. If it isn't, the school may send you another one. However, the accompanying financial aid offer need not be returned within fourteen days, according to AIAW rules. Some schools do, however, establish their own deadline for the return of the aid agreement.

Now, if a school wants you on its team but you have already accepted an academic scholarship, you will not be required to sign a letter of intent. Instructions for filing a letter of intent and a sample copy are on the next two pages.

Case II

If you are a senior athlete who is not expecting to get a scholarship from your chosen school, will need to apply for admission early enough to meet all deadlines and you will have to meet all academic qualifications.

If you've already applied and have been accepted at the institution of your choice, you're all set. All you need to do is apply for housing (unless you'll be commuting) and preregister for classes. If you haven't been offered an athletic scholarship, that doesn't mean you can't try out for the team. In fact, many coaches will tell interested athletes that they have used up all their scholarships but would love to see them try out. If you really prove yourself on the team, assuming you are selected at tryouts, you might qualify for an athletic scholarship for the next season.

AIAW LETTER OF INTENT

Instructions

An AIAW Letter of Intent is a formal statement by a prospective student-athlete that she intends to enroll in a named AIAW member institution and that financial aid based on her athletic ability has been offered. It is a statement which other AIAW member institutions and their representatives are obligated to respect. Once a prospective student-athlete signs an AIAW Letter of Intent, all recruiting activities on behalf of other AIAW member institutions must cease. AIAW member institutions are obligated to honor only the AIAW Letter of Intent. A prospective student-athlete is obligated to inform representatives of member institutions that she has already signed an AIAW Letter of Intent if she is contacted after signing.

An AIAW Letter of Intent may be used whenever financial aid based on athletic ability is awarded a prospective student-athlete who is entering a collegiate institution.

The signing of an AIAW Letter of Intent signifies that the prospective student-athlete has made a decision to attend the named AIAW member institution, and that financial aid based on athletic ability has been offered. While the athlete who signs this Letter of Intent is free to attend any other collegiate institutions, she may not receive an athletic scholarship until she has completed one year of normal progress at the collegiate institution she attends.

No AIAW Letter of Intent may be issued:
1. Prior to the first Monday in March preceding the year of enrollment;
2. If no financial aid based on athletic ability is to be awarded the propsective student-athlete;
3. If a prospective student-athlete has not yet commenced her senior year in high school;
4. If a prospective student-athlete has already signed another AIAW Letter of Intent for the same academic year (September-August).

Directions for using the AIAW Letter of Intent:
1. The terms and conditions of the financial aid based upon athletic ability (including amount and duration) must accompany (or precede) the issuance of the AIAW Letter of Intent to a prospective student-athlete. NOTE: Award of such financial aid based on athletic ability may be conditioned upon admission to the institution but may not be conditioned upon future athletic achievement (e.g., making the varsity squad or team).
2. The AIAW Letter of Intent expires 14 days after the date of issuance unless signed by the prospective student-athlete.
3. The signed AIAW Letter of Intent must be returned to the institution which issued it. In turn, the institution shall mail the original copy of the signed Letter of Intent to the AIAW national office within 14 days of its being signed by the prospective student-athlete.

Release from signed AIAW Letter of Intent:
If an AIAW Letter of Intent has been signed by a prospective student-athlete and she believes that extraordinary circumstances warrant her release from such Letter, a request for release may be filed with the AIAW Ethics and Eligibility Committee.

A prospective student-athlete who has signed a Letter of Intent may not initiate recruitment contacts with other institutions whether or not she is seeking financial aid based on athletic ability at the other institution until she has been issued a "Release Pending" notification by the national office. (Upon receipt of a request for release from the Letter of Intent, the national office will issue a "Release Pending" notification which explains what further action, if any, is necessary.) The student's request should be sent to the AIAW Ethics and Eligibility Chairperson, AIAW National Office, 1201 16th Street, NW, Washington, DC 20036.

Caution: Release from a signed AIAW Letter of Intent does not affect any contractual obligations between the prospective student-athlete and the institution.

Your next step is to wait for tryouts and to practice in the meantime so that you can give it your best shot. Stay in condition for your sport(s) and don't lose sight of your academic work, even though you may be nervous about the upcoming athletic season. Remember, not everyone on the team can possibly be awarded an athletic scholarship. Many

Association for Intercollegiate Athletics for Women
1201 Sixteenth Street, N.W., Washington, D.C. 20036· (202) 833-5485

LETTER OF INTENT

Name of prospective student-athlete_____

(print or type full legal name)

This is to certify my decision to enroll at _____

(name of institution)

at _____ in the academic year_____

(location of institution)

In signing this AIAW Letter of Intent, I state that I have read the instructions accompanying this form, that I have received the AIAW regulations for the awarding of financial aid based on athletic ability, and further understand that:

(1) Receipt of a Letter of Intent does not bind me in any way until I have signed it and if I allow an unsigned Letter to expire by passage of fourteen (14) days, I shall remain eligible to sign another AIAW Letter of Intent issued by the same or any other institution.

(2) THIS IS NOT AN AWARD OF FINANCIAL AID. (Do not sign this Letter of Intent unless you have received a written statement of the amount, duration, conditions and terms of financial aid based on athletic ability which the institution has promised.)

(3) If I decide to enroll in a collegiate institution other than the one for which this Letter of Intent was signed, I understand that I will not be eligible for financial aid based upon athletic ability until I have completed one year of normal progress at a collegiate institution. I further understand that I may receive other forms of financial aid available to all students at that institution.

(4) If extraordinary circumstances occur, I understand that I may file a request for release from the Letter of Intent from the AIAW Ethics and Eligibility Committee. Details for obtaining a release are found on the reverse side under Instructions.

(5) I may sign only one Letter of Intent unless a "Release from Letter of Intent" is granted, in writing, by the AIAW Ethics and Eligibility Committee.

(6) If I am under eighteen (18) years of age and my parent or legal guardian fails to co-sign this AIAW Letter of Intent, it will be rendered null and void; however, I will be prohibited from signing another AIAW Letter of Intent just as if the first Letter had been validly signed.

Realizing that all AIAW member institutions are obligated to respect my decision to enroll at the above named institution and to cease recruiting activities once I have signed an AIAW Letter of Intent, I understand it is my obligation to inform any coach or representative of an institution that I have signed a Letter of Intent if I am contacted after the date of signing. I understand that failure to fulfill this responsibility may render me ineligible to participate in intercollegiate athletics.

Signed: _____   _____

(signature of student)   (date of signature)

Address: _____   _____

(street number)   (city, state, zip code)

Signed: _____   _____

(signature of parent or legal guardian   (date of signature)
if under 18 years old)

Submission of this Letter is authorized by:

Signed: _____   _____

(Athletic Director*)   (date of signature)

_____   _____

(institution)   (sport)

*AIAW Letter of Intent must be signed by the Athletic Director before submission to the prospective student-athlete and her parent or guardian for signature.

COPY FOR INSTITUTION

will be on academic scholarships and others will receive no aid at all. Just shape up and try out.

Case III

It's graduation day and you still haven't made a choice. Should you work for a semester or a year? Should you attend a junior college or enroll as a part-time student at a nearby commuter college? Or should you keep looking?

If you do decide to postpone college for a year or two, you will still be able to go out for sports when you do matriculate, even though you'll be older than the other students. Jamie Fahey Risberg, originally of New Jersey, graduated from high school in 1973 but didn't go to college until 1979 when she was already married and had a baby daughter. Although she holds a part-time job and helps her husband care for their daughter, Jamie still has time to compete on the basketball team at Colorado College.

Other students have followed the same course. Some have decided to lighten the financial burden of higher education by working and saving for college. Others have found they can still go to school and save by attending a junior college or a commuter school. You do not lose eligibility when you transfer schools. But do read AIAW regulations carefully concerning transferring, especially if you will be leaving a four-year institution for another four-year institution.

APPENDIX 1:
WOMEN'S SPORTS FOUNDATION SCHOLARSHIP GUIDE

Women's Sports Foundation 1981 College Scholarship Guide sponsored by Maybelline. Reprinted with permission of *Women's Sports* magazine and Maybelline. © 1981 *Women's Sports* magazine.

KEY TO ABBREVIATIONS

Arch	Archery
Bad	Badminton
BB	Basketball
B	Bowling
CC	Cross Country
Fenc	Fencing
FH	Field Hockey
G	Golf
Gym	Gymnastics
IH	Ice Hockey
Lax	Lacrosse
Rifl	Riflery
Sail	Sailing
Ski	Skiing
SB	Softball
Swim	Swimming
S&D	Swimming & Diving
Sync	Synchronized Swimming
Ten	Tennis
T&F	Track & Field
VB	Volleyball

ALABAMA

Alabama Christian College
Barbara Main, Coach
5345 Atlanta Hwy.
Montgomery, AL 36109
Ten. 6 scholarships. Tuition, room &
board.

Alabama State University
Brenda C. Johnson, Athletic Director
915 S. Jackson
Montgomery, AL 36195
BB (12), Ten (7), VB (10), T&F (20).
Values vary.

Auburn University
Dr. Joanna Davenport, Women's Athletic
Director
Auburn, AL 36830
BB, G, Gym, S&D, Ten, T&F, VB.
Number and values vary.

Birmingham-Southern College
Donald Green, Athletic Director
800 8th Ave. W.
Birmingham, AL 35204
Ten, VB, Tuition scholarships.

Brewer State Junior College
Dick Anderson, Athletic Director
U.S. Hwy. 43
Fayette, AL 35555
Ten. 5 scholarships. Tuition and books.

Calhoun Community College
Mary McCoy, Women's Tennis Coach
Decatur, AL 35601
BB, Ten. 18 scholarships. Values from
$250 to $300.

**Chattahoochee Valley Community
College**
Doug Key, Athletic Director
2602 Savage Dr.
Phenix City, AL 36867
BB, Ten. 18 scholarships. Tuition, books
& fees.

Enterprise State Junior College
Ken Deavers, Athletic Director
Enterprise, AL 36330
BB, Ten. 20 scholarships. Tuition-$70 to
$100 per quarter.

Gadsden State Junior College
Robert Dobbs, Athletic Director
Gadsden, AL 35901
BB. 12 scholarships. Values vary.

**George C. Wallace State Community
College**
Johnny Oppert, Athletic Director
Dothan, AL 36301
Ten. 6 scholarships. Tuition, books &
fees.

Jacksonville State University
Ronnie Harris, Women's Athletic
Director
Jacksonville, AL 36265
BB, Gym, Ten, T&F, VB. 41
scholarships. Values from $100 to $1600.

Jefferson Davis State Junior College
Karen Reynolds, Women's Athletic
Director
Alco Dr.
Brewton, AL 36426
Gym, SB, Ten. 27 scholarships. Tuition
& books.

Jefferson State Junior College
Marcha Morre, Women's Athletic
Director
2601 Carson Rd.
Birmingham, AL 35215
BB, Gym, Ten. 26 scholarships. Tuition,
books & fees.

Livingston University
Ed Murphy, Athletic Director
Washington St.
Livingston, AL 35470
BB, VB. 16 scholarships. Half tuition.

Northeast State Junior College
Harold Bookshire, Athletic Director
Box 159
Rainsville, AL 35989
BB. 12 scholarships. From $250 to $500

Snead State Junior College
Luke Worthy, Athletic Director
Boaz, AL 35957
BB. Tuition, books & fees.

Southern Benedictine College
Linda Foust, Coach and Instructor
St. Bernard, AL 35138
Ten, VB. Number and values vary.

Southern Union State Junior College
Frank Gourdouze, Athletic Director
Wadley, AL 36276
12 scholarships. Tuition, books & fees.

Spring Hill College
Jeannie Milling, Women's Athletic
Coordinator
Old Shell Rd.
Mobile, AL 46608
BB, Ten, VB. Tuition, room & board.

Talladega College
James W. Adams, Athletic Director
Talladega, AL 35160
BB. 8 scholarships. From tuition to full
ride.

Troy State University
Joyce Sorrell, Athletic Director
Troy, AL 36081
BB, G, Ten, T&F, VB. 26 scholarships.
From tuition to full ride.

Tuskegee Institute
Tiny Laster, Coordinator of Women's
Athletics
Physical Education Dept.
Tuskegee, AL 36088
BB, Ten, T&F, VB. 20 scholarships.
Value: $3700.

University of Alabama
Ann Marie Lawler, Women's Athletic
Director
Box 6449
University, AL 35486
BB, CC, G, Gym, S&D, Ten, T&F, VB.
72 scholarships. Values from $300 to full
ride.

University of Alabama (Huntsville)
Bonnie Pike, Athletic Director
P.O. Box 1247
Huntsville, AL 35807
BB, Ten. 18 scholarships. Values from
$624 to $2500.

University of Montevallo
Beverly Warren, Athletic Director
Station 181, Division of Women's
Athletics
Montevallo, AL 35115
BB, Ten, VB. 16 scholarships. Partial to
full ride.

University of North Alabama
Bill Jones, Associate Athletic Director
Box 5167
Florence, AL 35630
BB, Ten, VB. 13 scholarships. Full and
partial.

University of South Alabama
Martha Signa, Women's Coordinator of
Athletics
307 University Blvd.
Mobile, AL 36688
BB, Ten, VB. Number varies. Values
from $200 to $755 per quarter.

ALASKA

University of Alaska (Anchorage)
Dr. Gene Templeton, Athletic Director
2651 Providence Dr.
Anchorage, AK 99504
BB, Rifl, Ski, Swim, VB. 18 scholarships.
From tuition & fees to $4200.

University of Alaska (Fairbanks)
Dr. John C. Gilmore, Director of
Athletics and Physical Education
Fairbanks, AK 99701
BB, Cross Country Skiing, Rifl, VB. 18
scholarships. Values vary up to full rides.

ARIZONA

Arizona State University
Mona Plummer, Associate Athletic
Director
Tempe, AZ 85281
Arch, Bad, BB, CC, G, Gym, SB, S&D,
Ten, T&F, VB. 93 scholarships. Values
from $100 to $4095.

Central Arizona College
Lin L. Laursen, Athletic Director
Coolidge, AZ 85228
BB, CC, SB, Ten, VB. 36 scholarships.
Values from $200 to $1600.

Cochise College
Paula Shelton, Athletic Director
Hwy. 80 W.
Douglas, AZ 85604
Ten. 16 scholarships. Books & fees to full
tuition.

Glendale Community College
Nelda R. Knoppe, Women's Athletic
Director
6000 W. Olive
Glendale, AZ 85301
Arch, BB, CC, G, Gym, SB, Ten, T&F,
VB. Number and values vary.

Mesa Community College
Kaye McDonald, Athletic Director
1833 W. Southern Ave.
Mesa, AZ 85202
BB, CC, G, SB, Ten, T&F, VB. 64
scholarships. Fees & books.

Northern Arizona University
T.H. Anderson, Athletic Director
Flagstaff, AZ 86011
BB, SB, Ten, VB. 40 scholarships. Values
from $500 to $1860.

Phoenix College
Dorothy J. Naples, Women's Athletic
Director
1202 W. Thomas Rd.
Phoenix, AZ 85013
Arch, BB, CC, G, Gym, SB, Ten, T&F,
VB. 70 scholarships. Values from $45 to
$90.

Pima Community College
Maureen Murphy, Asst. Athletic Director
2202 W. Anklam Rd.
Tucson, AZ 85709
Arch, BB, CC, SB, Ten, T&F, VB. 61
scholarships. Value of $120 each.

Scottsdale Community College
Kathy Gillett, Athletic Director
9000 E. Chaparral Rd.
Scottsdale, AZ 85258
Arch, BB, CC, G, Gym, SB, Ten, VB.
Values from $45 to $90.

The University of Arizona
Dr. Mary Roby, Women's Athletic
Director
Physical Education Bldg.
Tucson, AZ 85721

BB, C, FH, G, Gym, SB, S&D, Sync, Ten, T&F, VB. 124 scholarships. Values from $600 to $4787.

Yanapai Community College
David Brown, Athletic Director
1100 E. Sheldon
Prescott, AZ 86301
BB, SB, VB. 37 scholarships. Values from $300 to $1700.

ARKANSAS

Arkansas State University
Kay Woodiel, Athletic Director
Athletic Dept., Drawer 1000
State University, AR 72467
BB, Ten, VB. 15 full scholarships.

Arkansas State University (Beebe)
Gene Adams, Women's Basketball Coach
Beebe, AR 72012
10 scholarships. From tuition to full ride.

Henderson State University
Bettye Wallace, Women's Athletic Director
Box H1060
Arkadelphia, AR 71923
BB, S&D, Ten, VB. 22 scholarships. Values from $460.

Hendrix College
Earlene Hannah, Athletic Director
Conway, AR 72032
S&D, Ten, VB. 15 scholarships.

Mississippi County Community College
Cecil H. Holifield, Assistant to President
Box 1109
Blytheville, AR 72315
10 scholarships. Tuition.

North Arkansas Community College
Dr. Sue McDonald, Women's Volleyball Coach
Jim Stockton, Women's Basketball Coach
Pioneer Ridge
Harrison, AR 72601

BB, VB. 17 scholarships. Values from $300 to $800.

Phillips County Community College
Earl Wilson, Jr., Athletic Director
P.O. Box 785
Helena, AR 72342
BB. 12 scholarships. Partial to full.

University of Arkansas (Fayetteville)
Ruth Cohoon, Director of Women's Athletics
Barnhill Arena
Fayetteville, AR 72701
BB, CC, S&D, Ten, T&F. 55 scholarships. Partial to full.

University of Arkansas (Little Rock)
Betty Jo Stephens, Women's Athletic Director
33rd and University
Little Rock, AR 72204
BB, S&D, Ten, VB. 12 scholarships. Values from $200 to $1800.

University of Arkansas (Monticello)
Alvy Early, Women's Basketball Coach
P.O. Box 2555—UAM
Monticello, AR 71655
AIAW Div. II.
6 BB scholarships. Also work study jobs available.

University of Arkansas (Pine Bluff)
Alma F. Murphy, Athletic Director
P.O. Box 4096, UAPB, Hwy. 79N
Pine Bluff, AR 71601
BB, VB. 12 scholarships. Values from $649 to $2329.

CALIFORNIA

Azusa Pacific College
Dr. Cliff Hamlon, Athletic Director
Azusa, CA 92701
BB, VB, T&F. Values from $100 to $2300.

Biola College
Betty Norman, Women's Athletic Director

LaMirada, CA 90639
BB, Ten, VB. Values from $500 to full tuition.

California Lutheran College
Dr. Robert Doering, Director Physical Education Athletics
60 Olsen Rd.
Thousand Oaks, CA 91360
BB, CC, SB, Ten, T&F, VB. Values from $100 to $1000.

California State Polytechnic University (Pomona)
Darlene May
3801 W. Temple
Pomona, CA 91768
BB, Gym, Ten, SB, T&F, VB. Number and values vary.

California State Polytechnic University (San Luis Obispo)
Evelyn I. Pellaton, Associate Athletic Director, Women
San Luis Obispo, CA 93407
BB, CC, Gym, SB, S&D, Ten, T&F, VB. Values from $210 to $2100.

California State University (Bakersfield)
Gloria Ann Friedman, Asst. Athletic Director and Women's Tennis Coach
9001 Stockdale Hwy.
Bakersfield, CA 93309
CC, Ten, T&F, VB. Tuition to full ride.

California State University (Dominguez Hills)
Sue Carberry, Athletic Director
1000 E. Victoria St.
Dominguez Hills, CA 90747
BB, CC, SB, Ten, VB. 15 scholarships. Values to $400.

California State University (Fresno)
Joanne Schroll, Administrator of Women's Athletics
Fresno, CA 93740
Bad, BB, Gym, SB, S&D, Ten, VB. Number varies. Values from $238 to $2230.

California State University (Fullerton)
Leanne Grotke, Athletic Director
800 N. College
Fullerton, CA 92361
BB, CC, Fenc, G, Gym, SB, Ten, VB. Number and values vary.

California State University (Long Beach)
Perry C. Moore, Athletic Director
1250 Bellflower Blvd.
Long Beach, CA 90840
BB, CC, FH, G, Gym, S&D, Ten, T&F, VB. Tuition & fees to full scholarships.

California State University (Los Angeles)
Marge Callahan, Women's and Coed Athletic Director
5151 State University Dr.
Los Angeles, CA 90032
Arch, Bad, BB, B, CC, Fenc, Gym, S&D, Ten, T&F, VB. 106 scholarships. Values from $100 to $2824.

California State University (Northridge)
Dr. Judith M. Brame, Athletic Director for Women
18111 Nordhoff
Northridge, CA 91330
BB, CC, Fenc, Gym, SB, Swim, Ten, T&F, VB. Number and values vary.

California State University (San Jose)
Joyce Malone, Women's Athletic Director
125 S. 7th St.
San Jose, CA 95114
BB, Fenc, FH, G, Gym, S&D, Ten, VB. Numbers vary. Partial to full scholarship.

Chaffey College
Mary Gonzales, Athletic Director
5885 Haven Ave.
Alta Loma, CA 91701
BB, CC, S&D, Ten, T&F, VB. Job assistance.

Chapman College
Walt Bowman, Athletic Director
333 N. Glassell
Orange, CA 92666

BB, SB, VB. Number varies. Values from
$1000 to $4000.

Loyola Marymount University
Robert Arias, Athletic Director
7101 W. 80th St.
Los Angeles, CA 90045
BB, CC, Ten, VB. 9 scholarships. $100 to
full.

Occidental College
Ruth M. Berkey, Director of Athletics
1600 Campus Rd.
Los Angeles, CA 90041
Bad, BB, S&D, Ten, T&F, VB.
Scholarships based on need.

Pepperdine University
Laurie Billes, Asst. Athletic Director
24255 Pacific Coast Hwy.
Malibu, CA 90265
BB, Ten, VB. 17 scholarships. Values to
$6000.

Point Loma College
Dr. Carroll Land, Athletic Director
3900 Lomaland Dr.
San Diego, CA 92106
BB, C, SB, Ten, T&F, VB. Number
varies. Values to $2800.

Pomona College
Les Nagler, Athletic Director
Claremont, CA 91711
BB, CC, S&D, Ten, T&F, VB. All
financial aid based on need.

San Diego State University
Mary A. Hill, Associate Director of
Athletics
San Diego, CA 92182
BB, CC, G, Gym, SB, S&D, Ten, T&F,
VB. Scholarship values from partial to
full.

Stanford University
Andy Geiger, Director of Athletics
Dept. of Athletics
Stanford, CA 94305
BB, CC, FH, G, Gym, S&D, Ten, T&F,
VB. 70 scholarships. Values to $9100.

United States International University
Nancy Hagman
10455 Pomerado Rd.
San Diego, CA 92131
BB, CC, G, SB, Ten, T&F, VB. 47
scholarships. Values to $6180.

University of California (Berkeley)
Dr. Luella J. Lilly, Director of Women's
Athletics
100 Hearst Gym
Berkeley, CA 94720
BB, CC, FH, Gym, SB, S&D, Ten, T&F,
VB. 110 scholarships. Values from $450
to $5500.

University of California (Irvine)
Linda B. Dempsay, Director of Athletics
Crawford Hall
Irvine, CA 92717
BB, S&D, Ten, T&F, VB. Number and
values vary.

University of California (Los Angeles)
Judith R. Holland, Athletic Director
405 Hilgard Ave.
Los Angeles, CA 90024
Bad, BB, CC, G, Gym, SB, S&D, Ten,
T&F, VB. Values to $4942.

University of California (Riverside)
Sue Gozansky, Assistant Athletic Director
Physical Education Dept.
Riverside, CA 92521
BB, Gym, VB. 19 scholarships. Values to
$2700.

University of California (San Diego)
Judith M. Sweet, Athletic Director
Physical Education Dept. C-017
San Diego, CA 92093
Scholarships based on need.

University of California (Santa Barbara)
Alice Henry, Coordinator of Women's
Athletics
Dept. of Athletics and Leisure Services
Santa Barbara, CA 93106
BB, CC, Gym, SB, S&D, Ten, T&F, VB.
Number and values vary.

University of San Diego
Patrick Cahill, Athletic Director
Alcala Park
San Diego, CA 92110
BB, S&D, Ten, VB. 32 scholarships.
Values from $500 to $6000.

University of San Francisco
Dr. Sandee L. Hill, Women's Athletic
Director
Memorial Gym
San Francisco, CA 94117
BB, SB, Ten, VB. 24 scholarships. Values
from $500 to $6100.

University of Santa Clara
Marygrace Colby, Director of Women's
Athletics
Santa Clara, CA 95053
BB, Ten, VB. Number varies. Values
from $1000 to $6165.

University of Southern California
Barbara Hedges, Associate Athletic
Director
Heritage Hall, University Park
Los Angeles, CA 90007
BB, G, Gym, S&D, Ten, T&F, VB. 72
scholarships. Values from $1000 to $7500.

University of the Pacific
Cynthia C. Spiro, Coordinator of
Women's Athletics
3601 Pacific Ave.
Stockton, CA 95211
BB, FH, SB, S&D, Ten, VB. 45 tuition
scholarships. Values from $200 to $5682.

COLORADO

Adams State College
Charleen J. Kahre, Women's Athletic
Director
Alamsa, CO 81102
BB, CC, Gym, SB, T&F, VB. 28
scholarships. Values from $406 to $1612.

**Colorado Northwestern Community
College**
Elaine Fox, Director Women's Athletics
Rangely, CO 81648

Arch, BB, SB. Number varies. Values
from $200 to $2200.

Colorado School of Mines
R. Bruce Allison, Athletic Director
Golden, CO 80401
BB, VB. Values from $100 to $3672.

Colorado State University
Dr. Nancy J. O'Connor, Athletic Director
Fort Collins, CO 80523
BB, Gym, S&D, T&F, VB. 69
scholarships. Partial to full ride.

Colorado Women's College
Carmen Kehtel, Athletic Director
Montview Blvd. and Quebec St.
Denver, CO 80220
BB, Ski, SB, Ten, VB. 30 scholarships.
Values to $5615.

Lamar Community College
Steve Carel, BB, Theresa Emick, VB
Lamar, CO 81052
12 scholarships. $500. Instate only.

Mesa College
Doug Schakel, Athletic Director
Grand Junction, CO 81501
BB, SB, VB. 23 scholarships. Tuition &
fees.

Metropolitan State College
Jane Kober, Women's Athletic Director
Box 25, 1006 11th St.
Denver, CO 80204
BB, SB, Ten, VB, Soccer. 21 scholarships.
Values from $204 to $408.

Northeastern Junior College
Sheila R. Worley, Director of Athletics
Sterling, CO 80751
BB, SB, T&F, VB. 41 scholarships. Values
from $90 to $1500.

Regis College
Margie Haller, Athletic Director
W. 50th and Lowell Blvd.
Denver, CO 80221
BB, S&D, Ten, VB. 36 scholarships.
Values from $300 to $4200.

Trinidad State Junior College
Marvin Wetzel, Women's Basketball
Coach
Trinidad, CO 81082
14 scholarships. Values vary.

University of Colorado (Boulder)
Bill Crowder, Coordinator of Women's
Athletics
Campus Box 378
Boulder, CO 80309
BB, CC, Gym, Ski, S&D, Ten, T&F.
Values from $100 to full ride.

University of Denver
Diane T. Wendt, Director of Women's
Athletics
Denver, CO 80208
BB, FH, Gym, Ski, Ten. 12 scholarships.
Values to $6100.

University of Northern Colorado
Rosemary Fri, Women's Athletic Director
Greeley, CO 80639
BB, CC, Gym, SB, S&D, Ten, T&F, VB.
Number varies. Tuition to full ride.

University of Southern Colorado
Jessie F. Banks, Coordinator of Women's
Athletics
2200 Bonforte
Pueblo, CO 81001
BB, Ten, T&F. 4 scholarships. Values
from $308 to $618.

CONNECTICUT

Eastern Connecticut State College
Bill Holoway, Director of Athletics
Willimantic, CT 06266
BB, SB, VB. Scholarships based on need.

Fairfield University
C. Donald Cook, Director of Athletics
Fairfield, CT 06430
BB, FH, Ten. Number and values vary.

Mitchell College
Douglas Yarnall, Athletic Director
437 Pequot Ave.
New London, CT 06320
BB, FH, SB, Ten. Scholarships based on
need.

Sacred Heart University
Dave Bike, Athletic Director
Park Ave.
Bridgeport, CT 06604
BB, SB, VB. Partial to full tuition.

University of Bridgeport
Ann Fariss, Athletic Director
120 Waldemere Ave.
Bridgeport, CT 06602
BB, FH, Gym, SB, Ten, VB. Numbers
and values vary.

University of Connecticut
Rita L. Custeau, Coordinator of
Women's Athletics
U-78
Storrs, CT 06268
BB, CC, FH, Gym, SB, S&D, Soccer, Ten,
T&F, VB. Number and values vary.

University of Hartford
Gordon McCullogh, Director of Women's
Programs
200 Bloomfield Ave.
West Hartford, CT 06117
BB, SB, Ten, VB. Number and values
vary.

University of New Haven
Deborah Chin, Associate Athletic
Director
300 Orange Ave.
West Haven, CT 06516
BB, SB, Ten, VB. Number and values
vary.

Yale University
Dr. Frank Ryan, Athletic Director
402A Yale Station
New Haven, CT 06520
Scholarships based on need.

DELAWARE

University of Delaware
Mary Ann Campbell, Coordinator of
Women's Athletics
Delaware Field House
Newark, DE 19711
BB, FH. Number varies. Values up to
full tuition, room, board, and fees.

DISTRICT OF COLUMBIA

George Washington University
Lynn George, Women's Athletic Director
Smith Center 204
Washington, DC 20052
Bad, BB, Crew, Gym, Squash, S&D,
Soccer, Ten, VB. 50 scholarships. Values
from $600 to $5600.

Georgetown University
Coach (of specific sport)
McDonough Gym
Washington, DC 20007
BB, Crew, CC, Lax, Ten, T&F, Swim,
VB. Number and values vary.

Howard University
Leo F. Miles, Athletic Director
Dept. of Intercollegiate Athletics
6th and Girard Streets, N.W.
Washington, DC 20059
BB, S&D, T&F, VB.

The American University
Robert H. Frailey, Athletic Director
Washington, DC 20016
BB, FH, S&D, Ten, VB. Values vary.

University of the District of Columbia
Orby Moss, Athletic Director
1529 16th St. N.W.
Washington, DC 20036
BB, CC, T&F, VB. 44 scholarships.
Values from $256 to $3500.

FLORIDA

Brenau College
Dr. Polly Cage Roberts, Director of
Intercollegiate Athletics
Gainesville, FL 30501
S&D, Ten. Number and values vary.

Brevard Community College
Robert A. Anderson, Dean of
Collegewide Student Services
1519 Clearlake Rd.
Cocoa, FL 32922
BB, CC, SB, S&D, Ten, T&F, VB. 57

scholarships. Tuition & fees.

Broward Community College
Rex Brumley, Director of Athletics
225 E. Las Olas Blvd.
Ft. Lauderdale, FL 33301
North Campus: Ten—6, SB—12, VB—12;
South Campus: Ten—3; Central Campus:
BB—12, G—6, SB—12, S&D—10, Ten—6,
VB—12. Values from $213 to $493.

Broward Community College (North)
Andy Andrews, Athletic Director
1000 Coconut Creek Blvd.
Pompano Beach, FL 33066
SB, Ten, VB. 30 scholarships. Tuition &
books.

Central Florida Community College
Mel Carpenter, Athletic Director
Box 1388
Ocala, FL 32670
BB, Ten. 18 scholarships. Values from
$250 to $2000.

Daytona Beach Community College
Bud Farmer, Athletic Director
P.O. Box 1111
Daytona Beach, FL 32015
S&D, Ten, VB. 36 scholarships. Values
from $1000 to $3000.

Eckerd College
Mary Ann J. Giacchino, Women's
Athletic Director
P.O. Box 12560
St. Petersburg, FL 33733
BB, SB, Ten, VB. Values vary.

Edison Community College
Bill Szalay, Athletic Director
College Pkwy.
Ft. Myers, FL 33901
G—6; SB (slow)—12; Ten—6; VB—6.
Tuition & books.

Edward Waters College
John Lee, Jr., Athletic Director
1658 Kings Rd.
Jacksonville, FL 32209
BB, T&F. 28 scholarships. Grant & aid.

Florida Agricultural and Mechanical University
Sarah E. Hill, Coordinator of Women's Athletics
South Boulevard St.
Tallahassee, FL 32307
BB, CC, G, SB, Swim, Ten, T&F. 85 scholarships. Partial to full.

Florida Atlantic University
Jack Mehl, Director of Sports and Recreation
500 N.W. 20th St., Fieldhouse
Boca Raton, FL 33431
G, Ten. 20 scholarships. $200 per quarter.

Florida International University
Nancy Olson, Athletic Director
Tamiami Trail
Miami, FL 33199
BB, G, SB, Ten. 40 scholarships. Values from $300 to $3000.

Florida Southern College
Hal Smeltzly, Athletic Director
Lakeland, FL 33802
BB, Ten, VB. 8 scholarships. Partial to full.

Florida State University
Barbara Palmer
204 Tully Gym
Tallahassee, FL 32306
BB, CC, G, SB, S&D, Ten, T&F, VB. Values to $3000.

Florida Technological University
Jack O'Leary, Athletic Director
Box 25000
Orlando, FL 32816
BB, SB, Ten, VB. 33 scholarships. Tuition to full ride.

Gulf Coast Community College
Bill Frazier, Athletic Director
5230 West Highway 98
Panama City, FL 32401
12 Women's BB. Approx. $1600 per year.

Hillsborough Community College
Sam P. Rodriguez, Athletic Director
P.O. Box 22127
Tampa, FL 33622
B, CC, Ten, T&F, VB. 34 scholarships. $360 per year.

Indian River Community College
Bob Bottger, Director of Athletics
3209 Virginia Ave.
Ft. Pierre, FL 33450
BB, S&D, Ten, VB. 38 scholarships. Values from $400 to $2000.

Jacksonville University
Dr. Judson B. Harris, Jr., Director of Athletics and Physical Education
Jacksonville, FL 32211
Crew, SB, Ten, VB. Number and values vary.

Lake City Community College
Jean Williams, Coordinator of Women's Athletics
Lake City, FL 32055
SB, VB. Values from $900 to $1900.

Manatee Junior College
Sandra J. Holliman, Women's Athletics
5840 26th St., W.
Bradenton, FL 33507
BB, SB, VB. 36 scholarships. Values from $500 to $1200.

Miami Dade Community College (New World Center)
Fran Bishop, Women's Coordinator
300 N.E. Second Ave.
Miami, FL 33132
BB, SB, Ten, VB. 42 scholarships. $450 per year.

Miami Dade Community College (North)
Mary Dagraedt, Athletic Director
11380 N.W. 27th Ave.
Miami, FL 33167
BB, G, SB, VB. 42 scholarships. Values from $450 to $1400. Additional aid based on need.

Miami Dade Community College (South)
Roberta Stokes, Women's Athletic
Director
11011 S.W. 104th St.
Miami, FL 33176
BB, SB, Ten, VB. 42 scholarships.
Tuition.

North Florida Junior College
Joseph M. Patton, Athletic Director
201 E. Livingston St.
Madison, FL 32340
BB, SB, VB, Cheerleading. 36
scholarships. Tuition, books & partial
board.

Palm Beach Junior College
Thomas D. Mullins, Director of Athletics
4200 Congress Ave.
Lake Worth, FL 33461
G, SB, Ten. 24 scholarships. $448 each.

Pensacola Junior College
Dr. Donn Peery, Athletic Director
1000 College Blvd.
Pensacola, FL 32504
BB, VB. 26 scholarships. Values from
$195 to $2400.

Rollins College
Joseph Justice, Athletic Director
Winter Park, FL 32789
G, Ten. 7 scholarships. Values to $5000.

Seminole Community College
Joe Sterling, Athletic Director
Hwy. 17–92
Sanford, FL 32771
BB, SB, Ten, VB. 34 tuition scholarships.

St. Petersburg Junior College
Dr. T.B. Rawls, Athletic Director
P.O. Box 13489
St. Petersburg, FL 33733
SB, Ten, VB. 22 tuition scholarships.

Stetson University
Athletic Director
Box 1359
DeLand, FL 32720
BB, SB, Ten, VB. 13 scholarships. Values
from $400 to full.

University of Florida
Dr. Ruth H. Alexander, Athletic Director
Gainesville, FL 32601
BB, CC, G, Gym, S&D, Ten, T&F. 94
scholarships. Tuition $3800 in-state.

University of Miami
Lin Dunn, Director of Women's Athletics
Hecht Athletic Center, University of
Miami
Coral Gables, FL 33124
G—8, Ten—8, BB—10, SB—10, S&D—15,
VB—10. Value $6500 each.

University of South Florida
Dr. Connie Wamboldt, Athletic Director
4202 E. Fowler Ave.
Tampa, FL 33620
BB, G, S&D, Ten, VB. Tuition to full
ride.

University of Tampa
Robert Birrenkott, Athletic Director
401 W. Kennedy
Tampa, FL 33606
BB, VB. 22 scholarships. Values from
$500 to $3000.

Valencia Community College
Phyllis Shemelya, Women's Athletic
Coordinator
P.O. Box 3028
Orlando, FL 32802
BB, G, SB, Ten, VB. 47 scholarships.
$596 per year.

GEORGIA

Armstrong State College
Dr. Roy J. Sims, Athletic Director
11935 Abercorn St.
Savannah, GA 31406
BB, SB, Ten. 22 scholarships. In-state
tuition & fees.

Augusta College
Marvin Vanover, Athletic Director
2500 Walton
Augusta, GA 30904
BB, S&D, Ten, VB. Tuition.

Columbus College
Mary V. Blackmon, Athletic Coordinator
Alonquin Dr.
Columbus, GA 31907
SB, Ten, VB. 12 scholarships. Values
from $100 to full ride.

Dekalb Community College (South)
Dr. Tom Bigelow, Athletic Director
495 N. Indian Creek Dr.
Clarkston, GA 30021
BB, Ten. 6 scholarships. $465 each.

Fort Valley State College
J.E. Hawkins, Athletic Director
State College Dr.
Fort Valley, GA 31030
BB, T&F. 16 scholarships. Values vary.

Gainesville Junior College
Wendell W. Whiteside, Athletic Director
Gainesville, GA 30501
BB, Ten. 10 scholarships. Values from
$150 to $1000.

Georgia Southern College
Coach (of specific sport)
Statesboro, GA 30458
BB, SB, S&D, Ten. Number and values
vary.

Georgia State University
Libby L. Roquemore, Asst. Athletic
Director
Atlanta, GA 30303
BB, Ten, VB. 6 scholarships. Values from
$190 to $570.

Gordon Junior College
Paula Edney, Coach
Barnesville, GA 30204
BB. Number varies. Values from $405 to
full scholarship.

Mercer University
Women's Basketball Coach
1400 Coleman Ave.
Macon, GA 31207
BB. Number and values vary.

Morris Brown College
Charles Hardnett, Athletic Director
643 Martin L. King Dr. S.W.
Atlanta, GA 30314

BB. 10 scholarships. Values vary.

North Georgia College
Barbara Brown, Athletic Director
Dahlonega, GA 30533
BB. Values vary.

University of Georgia
Elizabeth Murphey, Women's Athletic
Director
Athletic Dept., Box 1472
Athens, GA 30613
BB, G, Gym, S&D, Ten, T&F, VB. 70
scholarships. Values from $302.50 to
$4189.50.

Truett-McConnell Junior College
Colby Tilley, Physical Education
Instructor
Cleveland, GA 30528
BB, Ten. 7 scholarships. Values vary.

West Georgia College
Dorothy McNabb, Director of
Intercollegiate Athletics for Women
Carrolton, GA 30117
BB, SB, VB. 10 scholarships each. Values
from $200 to $1000.

HAWAII

University of Hawaii
Dr. Donnis Thompson, Women's
Athletic Director
1337 Lower Campus Rd.
Honolulu, HI 96822
BB, CC, G, S&D, Ten, T&F, VB. 75
scholarships. Tuition to full ride.

University of Hawaii at Hilo
Ramon Goya, Athletic Director
P.O. Box 1357
Hilo, HI 96720
Ten, VB. 10 scholarships. Tuition, room
& board.

IDAHO

Boise State University
Carol Ladwig, Asst. Athletic Director for
Women
Boise, ID 83725
BB, FH, Gym, Ten, T&F, VB. Number‐

varies. Values from $100 to $3000.

Idaho State University
Kathleen Hildreth, Women's Athletic
Director
Box 8173
Pocatello, ID 83209
BB, CC, SB, Ten, T&F, VB. 67
scholarships. Values from $1760 to $3290.

Lewis-Clark State College
Richard R. Hannan, Athletic Director
Lewiston, ID 83501
BB, Ten, VB. 20 scholarships. Values
vary.

North Idaho College
Daralyn Atwood, Coordinator of
Women's Athletics
1000 W. Garden Ave.
Coeur d'Alene, ID 83814
BB, CC, Ten, T&F, VB. 36 scholarships.
Values from $100 to $519.

Ricks College
Charles Grant, Athletic Director
Rexburg, ID 83440
BB, Gym, VB. 26 scholarships. Values to
$200.

University of Idaho
Kathy Clark, Athletic Director
Moscow, ID 83843
BB, CC, FH, Gym, S&D, Ten, T&F, VB.
94 scholarships. Values from $245 to
$3634.

ILLINOIS

Bradley University
Annelle Griffin, Women's Athletic Dept.
1501 W. Bradley Ave.
Peoria, IL 61625
BB, SB, Ten, T&F, SB. 30 scholarships.
Values from $1700 to $3400.

Chicago State University
Gerald Bulter, Athletic Director
95th and King Dr.
Chicago, IL 60628

BB, SB, T&F, VB. 45 scholarships.

College of St. Francis
Susan Krsnich
500 Wilcox St.
Joliet, IL 60435
BB, Ten, VB. 32 scholarships.

DePaul University
Tina Brown, Asst. Athletic Director for
Women's Sports
1011 W. Belden
Chicago, IL 60614
BB, SB, Ten, VB. Number varies. Values
from $520 to $5500.

Eastern Illinois University
Joan Schmidt, Associate Athletic Director
262B Lantz
Charleston, IL 61920
Bad, BB, CC, FH, SB, S&D, Ten, T&F,
VB. Number varies. Values from $200 to
$3650.

Elmhurst College
Eileen Hackman, Director of Women's
Athletics
Elmhurst, IL 60126
BB, SB, Ten, VB. Number varies. Values
from $100 to $1000.

Illinois State University
Jill Hutchison, Acting Women's Athletic
Director
Normal, IL 61761
Bad, BB, CC, FH, G, Gym, SB, S&D,
Ten, T&F, VB. 155 scholarships. Values
from $871 to $3887.

Judson College
William Forlow, Athletic Director
1151 N. State St.
Elgin, IL 60120
BB, SB, VB. Number varies. Partial
scholarship.

Knox College
Harlan Knosher, Athletic Director
Galesburg, IL 61401
Based on need.

Lewis University
Paul Ruddy, Athletic Director
Rt. 53
Romeoville, IL 60441
BB, SB, Ten, VB. Available in all sports.
Values from $500 to full ($5200).

Moody Bible Institute
Joseph Greensbaum, Athletic Director
820 N. LaSalle St.
Chicago, IL 60610
BB, VB. Values vary.

North Central College
Hank Guenther, Athletic Director
Naperville, IL 60540
BB, CC, SB, S&D, Ten, T&F, VB. Based
on need.

Northeastern Illinois University
Betty Guzik
5500 N. St. Louis
Chicago, IL 60625
BB, Gym, SB, Ten, VB.

Northern Illinois University
Susie Jones, Women's Intercollegiate
Director
DeKalb, IL 60115
Bad, BB, CC, FH, G, Gym, SB, S&D,
Ten, T&F, VB.

Northwestern University
John Pont, Athletic Director
Evanston, IL 60201
BB, FH, SB, S&D, Ten, T&F, VB.
Number varies. Values from $1000 to
$8000.

Quincy College
Sharlene A. Peter, Athletic Director
Quincy, IL 62301
BB, SB, Ten, VB. Partial to full ride.

**Southern Illinois University
(Carbondale)**
Charlotte West, Director for Women's
Athletics
Carbondale, IL 62901
Bad, BB, CC, FH, G, Gym, SB, S&D,
Ten, T&F, VB. 125 scholarships. Tuition
to full ride.

**Southern Illinois University
(Edwardsville)**
Cindy Jones, Assistant Athletic Director
Box 129, SIUE
Edwardsville, IL 62026
BB, CC, FH, SB, Ten, T&F. Values from
$615 to $2000.

Spoon River College
Edward Georgieff, Athletic Director
Rt. 1
Canton, IL 61520
BB, G, SB, T&F, VB. 16 scholarships.
Values from $350 to $400.

St. Xavier College
Juliane Kowalczyke, Women's Athletic
Coordinator
3700 W. 103rd St.
Chicago, IL 60655
BB, SB, VB. 13 scholarships. Values from
$500 to $3000.

University of Illinois (Champaign)
Karol Kahrs, Asst. Director of Athletics
Assembly Hall, Mobile Headquarters,
N.E. Entrance
Champaign, IL 61820
BB, CC, G, Gym, S&D, Ten, T&F, VB.
85 scholarships. Values from $634 to
$3900.

University of Illinois (Chicago Circle)
Sandy Abbinanti, Associate Athletic
Director
Box 4348
Chicago, IL 60680
BB, CC, Gym, SB, S&D, Ten, T&F, VB.
Number and values vary.

Urbana College
Robert Cawley, Athletic Director
College Way
Urbana, IL 61820
BB, VB. 6 scholarships. $500.

Western Illinois University
Marion Blackinton, Women's Athletic
Director
Macomb, IL 61455
Bad, BB, FH, Gym, SB, S&D, Ten, T&F,
VB. 120 scholarships. Partial to full ride.

INDIANA

Ball State University
Eileen Keener, Women's Athletic Director
2000 University Ave.
Muncie, IN 47306
Bad, BB, CC, FH, G, Gym, Lax, SB,
S&D, Ten, T&F, VB. 134 scholarships.
Tuition/room, board.

Butler University
Dr. Xandra Hamilton, Chairperson,
Women's P.E.
4600 Sunset
Indianapolis, IN 46208
BB, SB, Ten, VB. Number and values
vary.

Franklin College
Ruth Callon, Women's Athletic Director
Franklin, IN 46131
BB, FH, SB, Ten, T&F, VB. Number
varies. Values from $1000 to $1200.

Grace College
Karen Miller, Coordinator of Women's
Athletics
Winona Lake, IN 46590
BB, SB, VB. 3 to 5 scholarships. Values
from $200 to $700.

Huntington College
Pat Zezula, Athletic Director
College Ave.
Huntington, IN 46750
BB, Ten, T&F, VB. 44 scholarships.
Values vary.

Indiana Institute of Technology
Gary S. Cole, Athletic Director
1600 E. Washington St.
Fort Wayne, IN 46803
8 VB. Values from $600 to $1600.

Indiana State University
Alpha Cleary, Athletic Director
Women's Physical Education
Terre Haute, IN 47809
Arch, Bad, BB, B, CC, FH, G, Gym, SB,
S&D, Ten, T&F, VB. 124 scholarships.
Tuition to full ride.

Indiana State University (Evansville)
Wayne Boultinghouse, Athletic Director
8600 University Blvd.
Evansville, IN 47712
BB, SB, Ten, VB. 29 full tuition
scholarships.

Indiana University
Isabella Hutchison, Athletic Director
Assembly Hall
Bloomington, IN 47401
BB, CC, FH, G, Gym, SB, S&D, Ten,
T&F, VB. Number varies. Values from
$722 to $2880.

**Indiana-Purdue University at
Indianapolis**
Dr. Robert Bunnell, Athletic Director
1010 W. 64th St.
Indianapolis, IN 46260
BB, SB, VB. 27 tuition scholarships.
Values from $156 to $990 per semester.

Oakland City College
Dr. Monica Mize, Athletic Director
Oakland City, IN 47660
BB, SB, VB. 17 tuition scholarships.

Purdue University
Rm. 15, Mackey Arena
W. Lafayette, IN 47907
BB, FH, S&D, Ten, T&F, CC, VB. 16
scholarships. Values from $100 to full
ride.

St. Francis College
Thelma Morgan, Athletic Director
2701 Spring St.
Ft. Wayne, IN 46808
BB, SB, VB. Number varies. Values from
$100 to $900.

St. Joseph's College
Richard F. Scharf, Athletic Director
Rensselaer, IN 47978
BB, Ten, T&F, VB. 44 scholarships.
Quarter tuition.

Valparaiso University
Wm. L. Steinbrecher, Athletic Director
Valparaiso, IN 46383

BB, FH, Gym, S&D, Ten, VB. 71
scholarships. Values from $500.

Vincennes University
Andrea Myers, Division Chairperson of
Physical Education
Vincennes, IN 47591
BB, B, VB. 21 scholarships. Values from
$370 to $2500.

IOWA

Buena Vista College
Harriet Henry, Athletic Director
Storm Lake, IA 50588
BB, G, SB, Ten, T&F, VB. Values from
$100 to $1000.

Drake University
Betty Werner Miles, Athletic Director
Des Moines, IA 50311
BB, SB, Ten, T&F, VB. 33 scholarships.
Values vary.

Graceland College
Barbara Hamann, Coordinator of
Women's Athletics
Lamoni, IA 50140
BB, FH, SB, Ten, T&F, VB. 30
scholarships. Based on need. Values from
$200 to $600.

Grand View College
Ann Rainey, Athletic Director
Des Moines, IA 50316
BB, SB, VB. 37 scholarships. Values from
$100 to $4040.

Iowa State University
Louis G. McCullough, Athletic Director
Ames, IA 50011
BB, CC, G, Gym, SB, S&D, Ten, T&F,
VB. Values vary.

Iowa Wesleyan College
Frederick Hodam, Athletic Director
Mt. Pleasant, IA 52641
BB, FH, G, SB, S&D, Ten, T&F, VB.
Number varies. Values from $250 to $750.

Iowa Western Community College
Walt G. Stanton, Athletic Director

Clarinda, IA 51632
BB. Values from $150 to $300.

**Iowa Western Community College
(Council Bluffs)**
Rick Mathews, Athletic Director
2700 College Rd.
Council Bluffs, IA 51501
BB. Tuition & fees.

Kirkwood Community College
Byron Lehman, Athletic Director
6301 Kirkwood Blvd. S.W.
Cedar Rapids, IA 52406
BB, SB. Tuition.

Loras College
Marcy W. Packer, Athletic Director
1450 Alta Vista
Dubuque, IA 52001
BB, SB, T&F, VB. Values from $50 to
$1000.

Marshalltown Community College
Jon Renner, Athletic Director
Marshalltown, IA 50158
BB, SB, Ten. 11 scholarships. Values
from $100 to $300.

Marycrest College
Michael Harper, Athletic Director
1607 W. 12th
Davenport, IA 52804
BB, SB, Ten, VB. Values from $500 to
full ride.

Morningside College
Roberta Boothby, Athletic Director
1501 Morningside Ave.
Sioux City, IA 51106
BB, SB, VB. Values to full ride.

Simpson College
Dr. Sharon Holmberg, Athletic Director
Indianola, IA 50125
BB, G, SB, Ten, T&F, VB. 30
scholarships. Values from $500 to $1000.

Southeastern Community College
Charles G. Spoonhour, Athletic Director
Hwy. 406 and Gear Ave.
West Burlington, IA 52655

BB, SB. 8 scholarships. Values from $100 to $200.

Southwestern Community College
Betty Gaule, Women's Athletic Director
Creston, IA 50801
BB, SB. 13 scholarships. Values from $100 to $800.

St. Ambrose College
Barbara Schuman, Women's Coordinator
518 W. Locust
Davenport, IA 52803
BB, SB, Ten, VB. Values from $150 to $1200.

University of Iowa
Christine Grant, Women's Athletic Director
Iowa City, IA 52242
BB, FH, G, Gym, SB, S&D, Ten, T&F, VB. 117 scholarships. Values from $830 to $3600.

University of Northern Iowa
Sandra C. Williamson, Associate Athletic Director
Cedar Falls, IA 50613
BB, FH, CC, G, Gym, SB, S&D, Ten, T&F, VB. 112 scholarships. Values from $100 to $2808.

Westmar College
Wanda Chittenden, Coordinator of Women's Athletics
LeMars, IA 51031
BB, SB, Ten, T&F, VB. 54 scholarships. Values from $300 to $1000.

William Penn College
Bob Spencer, Women's Athletic Director
Oskaloosa, IA 52577
BB, G, CC, Ten, T&F, SB, VB. Partial to full ride.

KANSAS

Allen County Community Junior College
Hugh L. Haire, Athletic Director
1801 N. Cottonwood
Iola, KS 66749

BB, CC, Ten, T&F, VB. 28 scholarships. Tuition & books.

Barton County Community College
Jerry Mullen, Athletic Director
Great Bend, KS 67530
BB, Ten, T&F. 20 scholarships. Values vary.

Bethel College
George Roger, Director of Athletics
North Newton, KS 67117
BB, Ten, T&F, VB. 23 scholarships. Values from $100 to $500.

Coffeyville Community College
Jack McNickle, Athletic Director
Coffeyville, KS 67337
BB, Ten, VB. 25 scholarships. Value $425.

Colby Community College
Vic Delke, Athletic Director
1255 S. Range
Colby, KS 67701
BB, T&F, VB. Values from $100 to tuition & books.

Cowley County Community College
Linda Hargrove, Women's Athletics
Arkansas City, KS 67005
BB, SB, VB. 14 scholarships. Values vary.

Dodge City Community College
Max Van Laningham, Athletic Director
U.S. 50 Bypass and 14th Ave.
Dodge City, KS 67801
BB, CC, SB, Ten, T&F, VB. 50 scholarships. Values from $450 to $550.

Emporia State University
Dr. Dorothy Martin, Coordinator of Women's Athletics
Emporia, KS 66801
BB, CC, Gym, SB, S&D, Ten, T&F, VB. 36 scholarships. Values from $100 to $600.

Friends University
Deanna M. Polly, Women's Athletic Director
2100 University Ave.
Wichita, KS 67213

BB, SB, Ten, T&F, VB. 35–55 scholarships. Values from $300 to $900.

Haskell Indian Junior College
Benny Smith, Athletic Director
Lawrence, KS 61044
BB, Ten, T&F, VB.

Hutchinson Community Junior College
Ruby Minzer, Coordinator of Women's Athletics
1300 N. Plum
Hutchinson, KS 67501
BB, Ten, T&F, VB. 12 scholarships. Values vary.

Kansas State University
Coach (of specific sport)
Inter Athletic Dept.
Manhattan, KS 66506
BB, SB, T&F, VB. 56 scholarships. Values from $200 to $3000.

Marymont College of Kansas
Salina, KS 67401
BB, SB, Ten, VB. 14 scholarships.

McPherson College
Doris Coppock, Coordinator of Women's Athletics
McPherson, KS 67460
BB, G, Ten, T&F, VB. Number varies. Values from $100 to $400.

Pittsburg State University
Joan Warrington, Women's Athletic Coordinator
Pittsburg, KS 66762
BB, SB, Ten, T&F, VB.

Pratt Community College
Charlie Divitto, Athletic Director
Highway 61
Pratt, KS 67124
BB, T&F. 30 scholarships. Tuition & books.

St. John's College
Rev. Jules Clausen, Athletic Director
7th and College
Winfield, KS 67156
BB, SB, T&F, VB. 12–15 scholarships. Values from $200 to $500.

St. Mary of the Plains College
Meri Nay, Athletic Director
Dodge City, KS 67801
BB, G, SB, Ten, VB.

Tabor College
Delmer Reimer, Athletic Director
Hillsboro, KS 67063
BB, SB, Ten, VB. Values from $100 to $600.

University of Kansas
Bob Marcum, Director of Athletics
Allen Field House
Lawrence, KS 66045
BB, G, SB, S&D, Ten, T&F, VB. 75 scholarships. Values from $200 to full ride.

Wichita State University
Natasha Fife, Associate Athletic Director
Box 114
Wichita, KS 67208
BB, CC, G, SB, Ten, T&F, VB. 83 scholarships. Values vary.

KENTUCKY

Bellarmine College
Madelene Naegele, Coordinator of Women's Athletics
Newburg Rd.
Louisville, KY 40205
BB, SB, VB. Number and values vary.

Campbellsville College
Don Bishop, Athletic Director
Hoskins Ave.
Campbellsville, KY 42718
BB, Ten. Partial to full ride.

Eastern Kentucky University
Martha Mullins, Asst. Athletic Director
Richmond, KY 40475
BB, CC, FH, Gym, Rifl, S&D, T&F, Ten, VB. 60 scholarships. Values from $1200 to $3100.

Georgetown College
Susan M. Johnson, Coordinator of
Women's Athletics
Georgetown, KY 40324
BB, Ten, VB. 12 scholarships. Values
from $500 to $2000.

Kentucky State University
Cornieth York Russell, Coordinator of
Athletics for Women
E. Main St.
Frankfort, KY 40601
BB, VB. 12 scholarships. Values from
$500 to $1000.

Morehead State University
Laradean Brown, Coordinator of
Women's Athletics
Morehead, KY 40351
BB, SB, T&F, Ten, VB. 50 scholarships.
Partial to full.

Murray State University
Johnny Reagan, Athletic Director
University Station
Murray, KY 42071
BB, CC, Ten, T&F. 38 scholarships.
Values from $500 to $2500.

Northern Kentucky University
Dr. Lonnie Davis, Director of Physical
Education and Athletics
Highland Heights, KY 41076
BB, SB, Ten, VB. Number varies. Values
from $220 to $2600.

Transylvania University
Pat Deacon, Athletic Director
300 N. Broadway
Lexington, KY 40508
BB, Ten. 20 partial scholarships.

University of Kentucky
Susan Feamster, Asst. Athletic
Director/Women
Memorial Coliseum
Lexington, KY 40506
BB, CC, G, Gym, Ten, T&F, VB. 74
scholarships. Values from $562 to $4300.

University of Louisville
Rebecca Hudson, Asst. Athletic Director
Louisville, KY 40292
BB, Gym, FH, SB, Ten, T&F, VB. 60
scholarships. Values vary.

Western Kentucky University
Dr. Shirley Laney, Coordinator of
Women's Athletics
Bowling Green, KY 42101
BB, G, Gym, Ten, T&F. 36 scholarships.
Values from $150 to $2600.

LOUISIANA

Centenary College
Floyd Horgen, Athletic Director
Box 4188
Shreveport, LA 71104
10 scholarships. Partial to full.

Louisiana State University
Pat Newman, LSU Athletic Dept.
Baton Rouge, LA 70893
BB, CC, G, Gym, S&D, SB, Ten, T&F,
VB. 90 scholarships. Values from $554 to
$4430.

McNeese State University
Margie Hinton, Women's Athletic
Director
Lake Charles, LA 70601
BB, SB, Ten. 9 scholarships.
Values from $1400 to $1930.

Nicholls State University
Marion S. Russell, Asst. Athletic
Director/Women's Sports
Box 2032, NSU
Thibodaus, LA 70301
BB, SB, Ten, VB. Values from $250 to
full ride. Out-of-state waiver possible.

Northeast Louisiana University
Betty Faught, Director of Women's
Athletics
Monroe, LA 71209

BB, Ten, VB. 21 scholarships. Values to full ride.

Northwestern State University
Patricia N. Pierson, Coach and
Coordinator of Women's Athletics
Natchitoches, LA 71457
BB, Ten, SB. 20 scholarships.

Southeastern Louisiana University
Linda Puckett, Athletic Director
P.O. Box 272 SLU
Hammond, LA 70402
BB, Ten, VB. 16 scholarships. Values
from $239 to $1816.

Newcomb College, Tulane University
Elizabeth B. Delery, Director of Women's
Athletics
1229 Broadway
New Orleans, LA 70118
BB, S&D, Ten, VB. Values vary.

University of New Orleans
Ron Maestri, Athletic Director
Athletic Dept., Lakefront
New Orleans, LA 70122
BB, SB, Ten, VB. 26 scholarships. Values
from $526 to $4250.

University of Southwestern Louisiana
Sherry LeBas, Coordinator of Women's
Athletics
Box 4-2455
LaFayette, LA 70504
BB, Ten, VB. Partial to full.

Xavier University of Louisiana
Denny Alexander, Athletic Director
7325 Palmetto St.
New Orleans, LA 70125
BB. 12 scholarships. $3500.

MAINE

Husson College
Pam Hennessey, Women's Basketball
Coach
Bangor, ME 04401

BB. 10 to 12 scholarships. Values from
$100 to $800.

University of Maine (Orono)
MaryJo Walkup, Asst. Director, Physical
Education and Women's Athletics
Lengyel Hall
Orono, ME 04473
BB, FH, Gym, Ski, S&D, Ten, T&F, VB.
Number varies. Values from $200 to
$2000.

MARYLAND

Garrett Community College
George Dailey, Athletic Director
Mosser Rd.
McHenry, MD 21541
BB, VB. Scholarships. Values from $400
to $500.

Loyola College
Anne McCloskey, Asst. Athletic Director
4501 N. Charles St.
Baltimore, MD 21210
BB, FH, Lax, VB. Number varies. Partial
to full tuition.

Mount St. Mary's College
James J. Phelan, Athletic Director
Emmitsburg, MD 21727
BB, Ten, T&F. 10 scholarships. Values
from $500 to $4800.

University of Maryland
Richard Michael Dull, Asst. Athletic
Director for Non-Revenue Sports
College Park, MD 20740
BB, FH, Gym, Lax, S&D, Ten, T&F, VB.
65 scholarships. Values from $100 to
$4400.

Towson State University
Joseph H. McMullen, Director of
Athletics
Baltimore, MD 21204
BB, FH, Gym, Lax, SB, S&D, T&F, Ten,
VB. Number varies. Partial to full
tuition.

MASSACHUSETTS

American International College
Milton J. Piepul
170 Wilbraham Rd.
Springfield, MA 01109
BB, SB, VB. Scholarships based on need.

Assumption College
Rita Castagna, Women's Athletic
Coordinator
500 Salisbury St.
Worcester, MA 01609
BB. 6 scholarships. Values from $1000 to
$2500.

Bentley College
Al Shields, Director of Athletics
450 Beaver St.
Waltham, MA 02154
BB. Number and values vary.

Boston College
Mary Miller Carson, Asst. Athletic
Director
Roberts Center
Chestnut Hill, MA 02167
BB, FH, S&D, Ten, T&F. Number and
values vary.

Boston University
Ms. Averill Haines, Women's Athletic
Director
285 Babcock St.
Boston, MA 02215
BB, Crew, CC, FH, Lax, Sail, S&D, Ten,
T&F. Values from partial to full
scholarships.

Merrimack College
Marcia Hochman, Athletic Director
Turnpike St.
N. Andover, MA 01845
BB. 2 scholarships.

Northeastern University
Jeanne Rowlands, Women's Athletic
Director
360 Huntington Ave.
Boston, MA 02115
Crew, FH, Gym, IH, Lax, S&D, Ten, VB.
40 scholarships. Values from $500 to
$6000.

University of Lowell
Denise Legault, Coordinator of Women's
Athletics
South Campus
Lowell, MA 01854
BB, FH, SB, Ten, VB. Numbers vary.
Values to full ride.

University of Massachusetts
Frank McInerny, Head, Dept. of
Athletics/Intramurals
Amherst, MA 01003
BB, Gym. Chancellor's Talent Award for
in-state students for all varsity sports
except BB and Gym. Number and values
vary.

Western New England College
Beverly Holtsberg, Coordinator of
Women's Athletics
1215 Wilbraham Rd.
Springfield, MA 01119
Financial aid based on need.

MICHIGAN

Aquinas College
Terry Bocian
1607 Robinson Rd., S.E.
Grand Rapids, MI 49506
BB, SB, Ten, T&F, VB. Scholarship
based on need.

Central Michigan University
Fran Koenig, Women's Athletic Director
Mt. Pleasant, MI 48859
BB, CC, FH, G, Gym, SB, S&D, Ten,
T&F, VB. 109 scholarships. Values from
tuition & fees to full grants.

Eastern Michigan University
Lucy N. Parker, Asst. Athletic Director
Bowen Field House
Ypsilanti, MI 48197
BB, CC, FH, Gym, SB, S&D, Ten, T&F,
VB. 51 full scholarships. Values to $2600.

Ferris State College
Patricia Dolan, Women's Coordinator
Big Rapids, MI 49307
BB, CC, G, SB, Ten, T&F, VB. 49
scholarships. Tuition.

Glen Oaks Community College
Don Spoerner, Athletic Director
Centreville, MI 49032
BB, VB. 24 scholarships. Tuition.

Grand Rapids Baptist College
Roger E. Haun
1001 E. Beltine N.E.
Grand Rapids, MI 49505
BB, SB, VB. 6 scholarships. Values from
$100 to $500.

Grand Valley State College
Joan Boand, Coordinator of Women's
Athletics
College Landing
Allendale, MI 49401
BB, FH, SB, Ten, T&F, VB. Number and
values vary.

Henry Ford Community College
John F. O'Hara, Athletic Director
5101 Evergreen
Dearborn, MI 48128
BB, CC, G, SB, Ten, T&F, VB. 49
scholarships. $270.

Highland Park Community College
Glen R. Donahue, Athletic Director
Third at Glendale
Highland Park, MI 48203
BB, CC, Ten, T&F. 20 scholarships. To
full tuition.

Hillsdale College
Jack McAvoy, Athletic Director
Hillsdale, MI 49242
SB, Ten, VB. 3 tuition scholarships.

Jackson Community College
Chris Kane, Asst. Director
Admissions/Coach
2111 Emmons Rd.
Jackson, MI 49201
BB, SB. 19 scholarships. Values from
$500 to $1000.

Kalamazoo Valley Community College
Dick Shilts, Athletic Director
6767 W. "O" Ave.
Kalamazoo, MI 49009
BB, SB, Ten, VB. 33 scholarships.
Tuition scholarships.

Lake Michigan College
Women's Athletic Director
2755 E. Napier
Benton Harbor, MI 49022
BB, SB, VB. 16 scholarships. Values from
$350 to $500.

Lake Superior State College
Gunile Myers, Women's Athletic Director
Norris P.E. Center
Sault Ste. Marie, MI 49783
BB, Rifl, Ski, SB, Ten, VB. Number and
values vary.

Lansing Community College
Walt Lingo, Athletic Director
419 N. Capitol Ave.
Lansing, MI 48901
BB, G, SB, Swim, Ten, VB. 25
scholarships. Values from $200 to $600.

Macomb County Community College
Ernie Romine, Athletic Director
14500 E. 12 Mile
Warren, MI 48093
BB, CC, SB, S&D, Ten, T&F, VB. 56
scholarships. Partial to full tuition.

Michigan State University
Nell C. Jackson
Jenison Fieldhouse
East Lansing, MI 48824
BB, CC, FH, G, Gym, SB, S&D, Ten,
T&F, VB. 112 scholarships. Values from
partial to full tuition.

Michigan Technological University
Ted Kearly, Athletic Director
Houghton, MI 49931
BB, VB. 8 scholarships. Values from $100
to $1000.

Montcalm Community College
Don Stearns, Athletic Director
Sidney, MI 48885
BB. 10 scholarships. Tuition.

Mott Community College
Athletic Coordinator
1401 E. Court St.
Flint, MI 48503
BB, SB, VB. 29 scholarships. Values
vary—tuition only.

Muskegon Community College
J. Paul King, Athletic Director
221 S. Quarterline
Muskegon, MI 49442
BB, Ten, VB. 22 scholarships. Tuition.

Northern Michigan University
Barbara Patrick, Asst. Athletic Director
Marquette, MI 49855
BB, FH, Gym, S&D, VB. 83 scholarships.
Values to full scholarships.

Oakland University
Corey Van Fleet, Athletic Director
Rochester, MI 48083
BB, G, SB, S&D, Ten, VB. 30
scholarships. Values from $200 to $2600.

Saginaw Valley State College
Marsha Reall, Women's Basketball Coach
2250 Pierce Rd.
University Center, MI 48710
10 BB. Values from $600 to $2900.

Southwestern Michigan College
Dean Ron Gunn, Athletic Director
Dowagiac, MI 49047
BB, CC, Cheerleading, T&F, VB.
Number and values vary.

University of Detroit
Lawrence Geracioti, Director of Athletics
4001 W. McNichols Rd.
Detroit, MI 48221
BB, SB. 20 scholarships. Tuition to full
ride.

University of Michigan
Phyllis Ocker, Associate Director of
Athletics
1100 S. State St.
Ann Arbor, MI 48109
BB, CC, FH, G, Gym, SB, S&D, Sync,
Ten, T&F, VB. 124 scholarships.

Wayne State University
Honor Smith, Coordinator of Women's
Athletics
Detroit, MI 48202
BB, Fenc, G, SB, Ten, T&F, VB. 60 plus
scholarships. Partial to full ride.

Western Michigan University
Carl F. Ulrich
Kalamazoo, MI 49008
BB, CC, FH, Gym, SB, S&D, Ten, T&F,
VB. Tuition.

MINNESOTA

Bemidji State University
Ann Lowdermilk, Women's Athletic
Director
Bemidji, MN 56601
BB, FH, Gym, S&D, Ten, T&F, VB.
Number and values vary.

Golden Valley Lutheran College
Financial Aids Office
6125 Olson Hwy.
Minneapolis, MN 55422
BB, CC, G, SB, Ten, T&F, VB. Number
and values vary.

Mankato State University
Georgene Brock, Women's Athletic
Director
Mankato, MN 56001
BB, CC, G, Gym, SB, S&D, Ten, T&F,
VB.

St. Cloud State University
Gladys Ziemer, Women's Athletic
Director
1st Ave. S.
St. Cloud, MN 56301
BB, Gym, SB, Ten, T&F, VB. Number
and values vary.

Southwest State University
Jeri Madden, Women's Athletic Director
E. College Dr.
Marshall, MN 56258
BB, SB, S&D, Ten, T&F, VB. 68
scholarships. Values from $50 to $2000.

University of Minnesota
Dr. Vivian M. Barfield, Athletic Director
Bierman Field Athletic Bldg., Rm. 238
516 15th Ave. S.E.
Minneapolis, MN 55455

BB, CC, FH, G, Gym, SB, S&D, Ten, T&F, VB. 54 scholarships. Full in-state rides, some full out-of-state rides. Values from $870 to $3000.

University of Minnesota (Duluth)
Linda M. Larson, Athletic Coordinator
2400 Oakland Ave.
Duluth, MN 55812
BB, SB, S&D, Ten, VB. 17 scholarships. Values from $350 to $1000.

Winona State University
Lavonne Fiereck, Women's Athletic Director
Johnson and Sanborn Streets
Winona, MN 55987
BB, G, Gym, SB, S&D, Ten, T&F, VB. Values from $100 to $700.

Worthington Community College
Lynn Barngrover, Women's Coach
College Way
Worthington, MN 56187
BB, T&F, VB. 45 scholarships. Values to $100.

MISSISSIPPI

Hinds Junior College
Rene Warren, Asst. Athletic Director in Charge of Women's Athletics
Box 394 HJC
Raymond, MS 39154
10 BB scholarships. Values vary.

Holmes Junior College
W.A. Miles, Women's Basketball Coach
Box 55
Goodman, MS 39079
BB. 13 scholarships. Values vary.

Jackson State University
Walter Reed, Athletic Director
1325 W. Lynch St.
Jackson, MS 39217
BB, G, Ten, T&F, VB. Number and values vary.

Meridian Junior College
Frankie K. Walsh, Women's Basketball Coach
5500 Hwy. 19 N.
Meridian, MS 39301
BB. 13 scholarships. Values from $500 to $1000.

Millsaps College
Dr. James A. Montgomery, Athletic Director
Jackson, MS 39210
BB, Ten. Number and values vary.

Mississippi State University
Libba Birmingham, Coordinator of Women's Athletics
Drawer 5327
Mississippi State, MS 39762
BB, G, SB, Ten, VB. 27½ scholarships. Values from partial to full.

Mississippi University for Women
Samye Johnson, Athletic Coordinator
W-1400
Columbus, MS 39701
BB, SB, Ten, VB. 38 scholarships. Values to $3088.

Mississippi Valley State University
Davis Weathersby, Athletic Director
Itta Bena, MI 38941
BB, CC, T&F. 32 scholarships.

Northeast Mississippi Junior College
William B. Ward, Athletic Director
Booneville, MS 38829
BB scholarships. Values vary.

Rust College
Ishmell Edwards, Athletic Director
Rust Ave.
Holly Springs, MS 38635
BB, CC, Ten, T&F, VB. Partial to full ride.

Southwest Mississippi Junior College
Linda F. Harper, Athletic Director
Summit, MS 39666
BB. 10 scholarships. Values from $120 to $1460.

University of Mississippi
Warner Alford, Athletic Director
University, MS 38677
BB, Ten, VB. 30 scholarships. Values to
$4823.

MISSOURI

Central Missouri State University
Dr. Roger Denker, Athletic Director
Warrensburg, MO 64093
BB, FH, Gym, SB, S&D, Ten, T&F, VB.
75 scholarships. Values from $315 to
$1910.

Crowder College
Bud Powell, Coach
Neosho, MO 64850
BB, SB. 12 scholarships. Values vary.

Culver-Stockton College
Gene Hall, Athletic Director
Canton, MO 63435
BB, SB, VB. Number varies. Values from
$200 to $800.

Evangel College
Sandra Sorbo, Women's Athletic Director
Springfield, MO 65802
BB, Ten, VB. Number and values vary.

Lincoln University
Yvonne W. Hoard, Director of Women's
Athletics
Jefferson City, MO 65101
BB, SB, Ten, T&F, VB. 32 scholarships.
Values vary.

Mineral Area College
JoAnn Owen, Instructor
Flat River, MO 63601
Ten, VB. 14 scholarships. Values from
$500 to $900.

Missouri Western State College
Rhesa Sumrell, Coordinator of Women's
Athletics
St. Joseph, MO 64507
BB, G, SB, Ten, VB. 20 scholarships.
Values from $100 to $1400.

Northwest Missouri State University
Sherri Reeves, Asst. Athletic Director
Maryville, MO 64468
BB, SB, Ten, T&F, VB. 29 scholarships.
Values from $200 to full ride.

Park College
Don Vandewalle, Athletic Director
Parkville, MO 64152
BB, CC, T&F, VB. 25 scholarships.
Partial to full ride.

School of the Ozarks
Dora Meikle, Associate Professor
Point Lookout, MO 65726
BB, CC, S&D, T&F, VB. Number and
values vary.

Southwest Baptist College
Rex Brown, Athletic Director
Bolivar, MO 65613
BB, SB, Ten, VB. Number and values
vary.

Southwest Missouri State University
Mary Jo Wynn, Athletic Director for
Women
Springfield, MO 65802
BB, CC, FH, G, SB, Ten, T&F, VB.
Number and values vary.

**St. Louis Community College at
Florissant Valley**
Bill Miller, Athletic Director
3400 Pershall Rd.
St. Louis, MO 63135
BB, CC, SB, S&D, Ten, T&F, VB. Half
tuition scholarships.

St. Louis University
David Axelson, Women's Athletic
Director
3672 W. Ine
St. Louis, MO 63108
BB, FH, SB, S&D, Ten, VB. Number and
values vary.

Stephens College
Dorothy L. Jones, Athletic Director
Columbia, MO 65215
G, Swim, Ten, VB. 12 scholarships.
Values from $500 to $3500.

Tarkio College
Chris Ragsdale, Director of Athletics
Tarkio, MO 64491
BB, SB, VB. Number varies. Values from
$100 to $1000.

University of Missouri (Columbia)
G. Jean Cerra, Associate Director of
Athletics
P.O. Box 677
Columbia, MO 65205
BB, G, Gym, SB, S&D, Ten, T&F, VB. 90
scholarships. Values from $630 to $3945.

University of Missouri (Kansas City)
Ken Webster, Athletic Director
5100 Rockhill Rd.
Kansas City, MO 64110
VB. 8 scholarships. $700 each.

University of Missouri (Rolla)
Annette Caruso, Women's Coach
Rolla, MO 65401
BB, SB, VB. 12 scholarships. Values from
$100 to full ride.

University of Missouri (St. Louis)
Judith W. Berres, Women's Athletic
Coordinator
8001 Natural Bridge
St. Louis, MO 63121
BB, FH, SB, VB. Number and values
vary.

William Woods College
Roy Love, Athletic Director
Fulton, MO 65251
BB, SB, S&D, Ten, T&F, VB. 30
scholarships from $500.

MONTANA

Carroll College
Tom Kelly, Athletic Director
Helena, MT 59601
BB, VB. 24 scholarships. Partial to full
tuition.

College of Great Falls
Steve Aggers, Athletic Director
1301 20th St. S.

Great Falls, MT 59405
BB. 6 scholarships. Tuition.

Dawson Community College
Dee Anderson, Women's P.E. Director
Box 421
Glendive, MT 59330
BB, Rodeo. 18 scholarships. Values vary.

Eastern Montana College
Woody Hahn, Athletic Director
Billings, MT 59101
BB, Gym, T&F, VB. 40 scholarships.
Values from $111 to $423.

Flathead Valley Community College
Dr. Gary Parker
Box 1174
Kalispell, MT 59901
BB, T&F, VB. 30 scholarships. Tuition.

**Montana College of Mineral Science and
Technology**
Forrest Wilson, Athletic Director
W. Park St.
Butte, MT 59701
BB, VB. 19 scholarships. Tuition.

Montana State University
Ginny Hunt, Athletic Director
Fieldhouse
Bozeman, MT 59717
BB, CC, Gym, Ski, Ten, T&F, VB. 68
scholarships. Tuition to full ride.

Northern Montana College
Linda Schoenstedt, Coach
Havre, MT 59501
BB, VB. 20 scholarships. Values from
$333 to $1500.

Rocky Mountain College
Frank E. Mathew
1511 Poly Dr.
Billings, MT 59102
BB, T&F. Values to $1000.

University of Montana
Barbara Hollman, Director of Women's
Athletics
Missoula, MT 59801
BB, Gym, S&D, Ten, T&F, VB. 56
scholarships. Values from $333 to $1296.

Western Montana College
Dona Wallace, Coordinator of Women's
Athletics
Dillon, MT 59725
BB, T&F, VB. 36 scholarships. Values
from $111 per quarter.

NEBRASKA

Central Technical Community College
Herbert Kahookele, Athletic Director
Box 1024
Hastings, NE 68901
BB, Ten, VB. 26 scholarships. Values
from $360 to $480.

College of Saint Mary
Kathy Barclay, Athletic Director
1901 S. 72nd St.
Omaha, NE 68124
BB, SB, VB. Number varies. Values from
$200 to $4500.

Concordia College
John W. Knight, Athletic Director
Seward, NE 68434
BB, CC, T&F, VB. Values to $500.

Creighton University
Mary Higgins, Coach
2500 California
Omaha, NE 68178
BB, SB, VB. Number varies. Partial to
full ride.

Hastings College
Dr. Lynn Farrell, Athletic Director
7th and Turner
Hastings, NE 68901
BB, G, Ten, T&F, VB. Values from $100
to $800.

Kearny State College
Allen H. Zikmund, Athletic Director
Kearny, NE 68847
BB, CC, SB, S&D, T&F, VB. 35 tuition-
waiver scholarships.

Mid-Plains Community College
Teri Caswell, Women's Coach
RR #4, Box 1
North Platte, NE 69101

BB, VB. 30 scholarships. Values from
$300 to $500.

Midland College
Don C. Watchorn, Athletic Director
720 E. 9th
Fremont, NE 68025
BB, CC, T&F, VB. 42 scholarships.

Northeast Technical Community College
Will Medow, Athletic Director
801 E. Benjamin Ave.
Norfolk, NE 68701
BB, VB. 17 scholarships. Values from
$245 to $491.

Peru State College
Jerry Joy, Women's Athletic Director
Peru, NE 68421
BB, SB, T&F, VB. Tuition scholarships.

Platte Technical Community College
Marge Burkett, Women's Athletic
Director
Rt. 1
Columbus, NE 68601
BB, VB. 14 scholarships. Values vary.

University of Nebraska
Dr. June Davis, Athletic Director
102 S. Stadium
Lincoln, NE 68588
BB, CC, G, Gym, SB, S&D, Ten, T&F,
VB. Number varies. Partial to full ride.

University of Nebraska (Omaha)
Connie Claussen, Coordinator of
Women's Athletics
Box 688
Omaha, NE 68101
BB, SB, T&F, VB. Number varies. Values
from $260 to full ride.

Wayne State College
John W. Merriman, Athletic Director
Wayne, NE 68787
BB, SB, T&F, VB. 20 scholarships.
Partial to full tuition.

York College
David Simpson, Athletic Director
York, NE 68467
VB. Number varies. Values to $400.

NEVADA

University of Nevada (Las Vegas)
Roger Barnson, Athletic Director
4505 Maryland Parkway
Las Vegas, NV 89154
Number and values vary.

University of Nevada (Reno)
John Legarza, Coordinator of Women's
Athletics
Intercollegiate Athletics
Reno, NV 89557
BB, CC, G, Gym, SB, Swim, Ten, VB. 35
scholarships. Values from $238 to $1738.

NEW HAMPSHIRE

Franklin Pierce College
Beverly A. Holtsberg, Athletic Director
Rindge, NH 03461
BB, SB, VB. Number varies. Values from
$200 to $2000.

Keene State College
Kay Booth, Women's Athletic Director
Spaulding Gymnasium, Apian Way
Keene, NH 03431
BB, FH, Gym, Ski, SB, S&D, Ten, VB.
Partial tuition.

New Hampshire College
Susan M. Murray, Athletic Director
2500 N. River Rd.
Manchester, NH 03104
BB, FH (both AIAW DIV II). Number
varies. Values from $700 to $3000.

University of New Hampshire
Gail Bigglestone, Director of Women's
Athletics
Field House
Durham, NH 03824
BB, CC, FH, Gym, IH, Lax, Ski, SB,
S&D, Ten, T&F, VB. Number varies.
Partial to full ride.

NEW JERSEY

Fairleigh Dickinson University
Ellen J. McEwen, Women's Athletic
Director
1000 River Rd.
Teaneck, NJ 07666

BB, Fenc, VB. Full ride scholarships.

Monmouth College
Joan Martin, Asst. Coordinator
West Long Branch, NJ 07764
BB, S&D. 5 scholarships. Values to $3000.

Princeton University
Mrs. Merrily Dean Baker, Women's
Athletic Director
Box 71
Princeton, NJ 08540
Based on need.

Rider College
John B. Carpenter, Athletic Director
Box 6400
Lawrenceville, NJ 08648
BB, SB, VB. Based on need.

**Rutgers, The State University of New
Jersey**
Athletic Center
P.O. Box 1149
Piscataway, NJ 08854
BB, Crew, CC, FH, G, Gym, Lax, SB,
S&D, Ten, T&F, VB. Number varies.
Partial to full.

Seton Hall University
Sue Dilley, Women's Athletic Director
S. Orange Ave.
South Orange, NJ 07079
BB, SB, Swim, Ten, VB. 20 scholarships.
Values from $1000 to full ride.

St. Peters College
John B. Wilson, Director of Athletics
2641 Kennedy Blvd.
Jersey City, NJ 07306
BB. 12 scholarships.

Upsala College
John Hooper, Athletic Director
Prospect St.
East Orange, NJ 07019
Based on need.

NEW MEXICO

College of Santa Fe
Carol Wellenbrock, Women's Athletic
Director
St. Michael's Dr.
Santa Fe, NM 87501

BB, VB. 24 scholarships. Values from $50 to $1000.

New Mexico Highlands University
Mary Topping, Director of Women's Athletics
Las Vegas, NM 87701
BB, VB. 24 scholarships. Values from $116 to $1056.

New Mexico Junior College
Dale Caton, Athletic Director
Lovington Hwy.
Hobbs, NM 88240
Rodeo, Ten. 15 scholarships. Values from $500 to $1780.

New Mexico State University
Karen Fey, Women's Athletic Coordinator
Box 3145
Las Cruces, NM 88003
BB, SB, S&D, Ten, VB. 62 scholarships. Tuition to full ride.

University of New Mexico
Linda Estes, Director of Women's Athletics
Albuquerque, NM 87131
BB, G, Gym, Ski, SB, S&D, Ten, T&F, VB. 92 scholarships. Tuition to full ride.

NEW YORK

Adelphi University
Lawrence C. Keating, Athletic Director
Garden City, NY 11530
BB, FH, SB, Ten, T&F. Tuition. Values vary.

C. W. Post College
Patricia Lamb, Women's Athletic Director
Greenvale, NY 11548
BB, FH, SB, Ten, VB. Number and values vary.

Canisius College
Dr. Daniel Starr
2001 Main St.
Buffalo, NY 14208

BB, Gym, SB, Ten, VB. Number varies. Values from $250 to full tuition.

Colgate University
Ruth Goehring, Athletic Director
Box 338
Hamilton, NY 13346
BB, FH, Lax, SB, S&D, Ten, VB. Number varies. Values from $500 to $6500.

Fordham University
David Rice, Athletic Director
Bronx, NY 10458
BB, Swim, T&F, Ten. 28 tuition scholarships.

Genesee Community College
Anthony P. Cory, Athletic Director
College Rd.
Batavia, NY 14020
BB, B, FH, SB, VB.

Hofstra University
Eve Atkinson, Director of Women's Athletics
Hempstead, NY 11550
BB, Fenc, FH, Gym, Lax, SB, VB. Number varies. Partial tuition to full ride.

Iona College
Rick Mazzuto, Athletic Director
715 North Ave.
New Rochelle, NY 10801
BB. Tuition.

Ithaca College
Iris M. Carnell, Assistant Athletic Director
School of HPER
Ithaca, NY 14850
BB, FH, Gym, Lax, SB, S&D, Ten, T&F, VB. Values from $500 to $1500. Based on financial need.

The King's College
Howard C. Miller, Athletic Director
Lodge Rd.
Briarcliff, NY 10510
Partial.

Long Island University
Roslyn Beck, Asst. Director of Women's
Athletics
University Plaza
Brooklyn, NY 11201
BB, CC, Gym, T&F, Ten. 31
scholarships. Partial to full ride.

Marist College
Susan Deer, Women's Basketball Coach
Poughkeepsie, NY 12601
BB. 3 scholarships. Values from tuition
to full ride.

Mercy College
Neil Judge, Director of Athletics
555 Boardway
Dobbs Ferry, NY 10522
BB, SB, Ten, VB. 6 scholarships. Values
from $500 to $1700.

Nazareth College
Elaine Brigman, Director of Athletics
4245 East Ave.
Rochester, NY 14610
BB, S&D, Ten, VB. Number varies.
Values from $200.

New York Institute of Technology
Gail Wasmus, Women's Athletic Director
P.O. Box 170
Old Westbury, NY 11568
BB, SB, Ten, VB. 25 scholarships. Values
from $1000 to $2560.

Niagara University
Mary A. Riccio, Athletic Office
Niagara University, NY
BB, S&D, VB. Tuition assistance.

Pratt Institute
Wayne Sunderland, Athletic Director
200 Willoughby Ave.
Brooklyn, NY 11205
BB, CC, Fenc, Ten, T&F, VB. Based on
need.

Roberts Wesleyan College
John A. Fraser, Athletic Director
2301 Westside Dr.
Rochester, NY 14624
BB, SB, VB. Based on need.

Siena College
Joyce Bergman, Women's Athletic
Coordinator
Rt. 9
Loudonville, NY 12211
BB. 11 scholarships. Tuition & fees.

St. Francis College
Mary Convy, Coordinator of Women's
Athletics
180 Remsen St.
Brooklyn, NY 11201
BB, S&D, VB. Values to $5000.

St. John Fisher College
Phillip Kahler, Athletic Director
3690 East Ave.
Rochester, NY 14618
BB, Soccer, VB. 25 scholarships. Values
vary.

St. John's University
Kathleen Meehan, Athletic Director
Jamaica, NY 11439
BB, CC, Fenc, SB, S&D, Ten, T&F.
Values from half tuition to full ride.

St. Thomas Aquinas College
David Possinger
Rt. 340
Sparkill, NY 10976
BB. 2 scholarships. Values from $100 to
$4000.

Syracuse University
Doris Soladay, Director of Women's
Athletics
820 Comstock Ave.
Syracuse, NY 13210
BB, Crew, FH, S&D, Ten, VB. Number
of grants vary. Value $4950 to $8030.

Union College
Richard Sakala, Athletic Director
Schenectady, NY 12308
Based on need.

Utica College of Syracuse University
Joan Kowalewski, Director of Women's
Athletics
Utica, NY 13502
BB, S&D. Number varies. Values from
$100 to $3000.

Villa Maria College
Michael A. Papili, Athletic Director
240 Pine Ridge Rd.
Buffalo, NY 14225
SB, VB. 20 scholarships. Values from $75
to $150.

Wagner College
Peter J. Carlesimo, Athletic Department
631 Howard Ave.
Staten Island, NY 10301
BB, SB, Ten, T&F. Values from $100 to
$6000.

NORTH CAROLINA

Appalachian State University
Judith Clarke, Asst. Athletic Director
Boone, NC 28607
BB, FH, G, SB, S&D, Ten, T&F, VB.
Number and values vary.

Brevard College
Corky Maynor, Athletic Director
Brevard, NC 28712
BB. 6 scholarships. $100 to $500.

Campbell University
Wendell Carr, Athletic Director
Box 1137
Bruies Creek, NC 27506
BB, SB, Ten, VB. Values from $400 to
full ride.

Duke University
Tom Butters, Director of Athletics
Durham, NC 27706
BB, FH, G, Gym, Ten. Number and
values vary.

Durham College
Ralph E. Hawkins, Athletic Director
Durham, NC 27707
BB, Ten, T&F. 23 scholarships. Values
from $200 to $1200.

East Carolina University
Laurie Arrants, Coordinator of Women's
Athletics
Minges Coliseum
Greenville, NC 27834

BB, FH, Gym, SB, S&D, Ten, T&F, VB.
Number varies. $250 to full scholarship.

Elon College
Mary Jackson, Head Basketball/Softball
Coach
Elon College, NC 27244
BB, SB, Ten, VB. Partial scholarships.

Guilford College
Gayle Currie, Women's Coordinator
Friendly Ave.
Greensboro, NC 27410
BB, SB, Ten, VB. Partial tuition.

Highpoint College
Jerry Steele, Athletic Director
933 Montlieu Ave.
Highpoint, NC 27262
BB, FH, Ten, VB. 10 scholarships. Values
from $100 to $4000.

Lenoir Rhyne College
Pat L. Smith, Coordinator of Women's
Athletics
Box 356, College Station
Hickory, NC 28601
BB, SB, Ten, VB. 6 scholarships. Partial
to full ride.

Livingstone College
Dr. Joe R. Robinson, Athletic Director
701 W. Monroe St.
Salisbury, NC 28144
BB, G, SB, Ten, T&F. 40 scholarships.
Tuition.

Mars Hill College
Dr. Barbara Holingsworth, Athletic
Director
Mars Hill, NC 28754
BB, Ten, VB. Number varies. Values
from $500 to $2000.

Montreat-Anderson College
Linn Stranak, Athletic Director
Montreat, NC 28757
BB, Ten, VB. Number and values vary.

Mount Olive College
Bradford Mitchell, Athletic Director
Henderson Dr.
Mount Olive, NC 28365

BB, SB. 11 scholarships. Values from $200 to $2000.

North Carolina A&T State University
Dr. Bert C. Piggott, Athletic Director
312 N. Dudley St.
Greensboro, NC 27411
BB, SB, Ten, T&F, VB. 65 scholarships.
Partial scholarships.

North Carolina State University
Nora Lynn Finch, Coordinator of
Women's Athletics
Hillsborough St.
Raleigh, NC 27607
BB, CC, Fenc, Gym, SB, S&D, Ten, T&F,
VB. Number and values vary.

Peace College
Beth Gorman, Director of Athletics
Peace St.
Raleigh, NC 27604
BB, Ten, VB. Number and values vary.

Pfeiffer College
Tom Childress
Misenheimer, NC 28109
BB, FH, SB, Swim, Ten. 27 scholarships.
Values vary.

Shaw University
Dr. William Spann, Athletic Director
118 South St.
Raleigh, NC 27611
BB, SB, VB. 14 scholarships. Values to
$1500. Based on need.

University of North Carolina (Asheville)
Barbara A. Quinn
Asheville, NC 28804
BB, Ten, VB. Values from $300 to $1300.

University of North Carolina (Chapel Hill)
Coach (of specified sport)
P.O. Box 2126
Chapel Hill, NC 27514
BB, CC, Fenc, FH, Gym, SB, S&D,
Soccer, Ten, T&F, VB. Number varies.
Values from $250 to full ride.

University of North Carolina (Charlotte)
Judy Wilkins, Athletic Dept.
Charlotte, NC 28223

BB, Ten, VB. 14 scholarships. Partial to
full ride.

University of North Carolina (Wilmington)
William J. Brooks
S. College Rd.
Wilmington, NC 28401
BB, SB, S&D, VB. 25 scholarships.
Tuition to full ride.

Wake Forest University
Dorothy Casey, Women's Athletic
Director
Reynolda Station
Winston-Salem, NC 27109
BB, CC, G, Ten, VB. Values partial to
full $5200.

Winston-Salem State University
Marcelene Scales, Athletic Director
Winston-Salem, NC 27102
BB, SB, T&F, VB. 18 scholarships. Values
from $500 to $1000.

NORTH DAKOTA

Bismarck Junior College
Ed Kringstad, Director of Athletics
Schaefer Hts.
Bismarck, ND 58501
BB, T&F, VB. 24 scholarships. Values
from $500 to $800.

Dickinson State College
Jo Lindquist, Women's Athletic Director
Dickinson, ND 58601
BB, CC, T&F, VB. 52 scholarships.
Values from $100 to $700.

Mary College
Al Bortke, Athletic Director
Apple Creek Rd.
Bismarck, ND 58501
BB. 12 scholarships. Values from $4000
to $4500.

Mayville State College
Dr. Martin W. Johnson, Athletic Director
Mayville, ND 58257
BB, Gym, T&F, VB. Number varies.
Partial to full tuition and fees.

Minot State College
Kathy McCann, Women's Athletic
Director
9th Ave.
Minot, ND 58701
BB, T&F. 27 scholarships. Values vary.

North Dakota State School of Science
Edward E. Werre, Athletic Director
Wahpeton, ND 58075
BB, T&F, VB. 15 scholarships. Tuition &
fees.

North Dakota State University
(Bottineau)
Don Thompson, Athletic Director
1st and Simrall
Bottineau, ND 58318
BB, VB. Number and values vary.

North Dakota University (Fargo)
Lynn Dorn, Women's Athletic Director
Fargo, ND 58102
BB, CC, Gym, SB, Ten, T&F, VB.
Number varies. Values from $622 to
$1937.

University of North Dakota
Dr. Helen Smiley, Coordinator of
Women's Athletics
Grand Forks, ND 58202
BB, VB, FH, T&F. 48 scholarships.
Tuition and fees.

OHIO

Ashland College
Gay Whieldon, Athletic Director
College Ave.
Ashland, OH 44805
BB, FH, SB, S&D, Ten, VB. 32
scholarships. Values from $500 to $1000.

Bowling Green State University
Carole J. Huston, Associate Athletic
Director
Bowling Green, OH 43403
BB, CC, FH, G, Gym, SB, S&D, Ten,
T&F, VB. Full grants-in-aid available.

Cleveland State University
Robert Busbey, Athletic Director

E. 24th St. and Euclid Ave.
Cleveland, OH 44115
BB, S&D, VB. 24 scholarships. Values
vary.

The College of Steubenville
Henry J. Kuzma, Athletic Director
Franciscan Way
Steubenville, OH 43952
BB. 6 scholarships. Values vary.

Cuyahoga Community College
Rex Smith, Director of Athletics
1100 Pleasant Valley Rd.
Panta, OH 44130
BB, B, S&D, Ten, T&F. 10 scholarships.
Values $135 each.

Kent State University
Judy Devine, Associate Athletic Director
Kent, OH 44242
BB, CC, FH, Gym, SB, S&D, Ten, T&F,
VB. Number and values vary.

Malone College
Patricia Long, Athletic Director
515 25th St. N.W.
Canton, OH 44709
BB, Ten, T&F, VB. Values from $100 to
$2000.

Miami University
Karen Womack, Women's Athletic
Director
38 Millett Hall
Oxford, OH 45056
BB, FH, SB, S&D, Ten, T&F, VB. 21
scholarships. Tuition to full ride.

Mount St. Joseph College
Jean Dowell, Athletic Director
Mount St. Joseph, OH 45051
BB, VB. Partial scholarships.

Ohio State University
Phyllis J. Bailey, Director of Athletics
410 W. Woodruff Ave.
Columbus, OH 43210
BB, CC, Fenc, FH, G, Gym, SB, S&D,
Sync S, Ten, T&F, VB. 82 scholarships.
Values from $576 to $3500.

Ohio University
Peggy Pruitt, Coordinator of Women's
Athletics
Convocation Center
Athens, OH 45701
BB, CC, FH, Lax, SB, S&D, Ten, T&F,
VB. Number and values vary.

Rio Grande College
Diane Lewis, Athletic Director
Rio Grande, OH 45674
BB, T&F, VB. 36 scholarships. Values
from $200 to $1500.

Shawnee State Community College
Harry Weinbrecht, Athletic Director
940 Second St.
Portsmouth, OH 45662
BB. 10 scholarships. Partial to full
tuition.

Sinclair Community College
Norma Dycus, Athletic Director
444 W. Third St.
Dayton, OH 45402
BB, SB, Ten, VB. Number varies. Values
from $50 to $300.

University of Akron
Gordon Larson, Athletic Director
302 Buchtel Ave.
Akron, OH 44325
BB, SB, VB. Number and values vary.

University of Cincinnati
Jean Tureck, Women's Athletic Director
Clifton Ave., Laurence Hall
Cincinnati, OH 45221
BB, G, S&D, Ten, VB. Number and
values vary.

University of Dayton
Elaine Dreidame, Associate Director of
Athletics
College Park Dr.
Dayton, OH 45469
BB, VB. 18 scholarships. Values from
$500 to $4900.

University of Toledo
Marnie Swift, Coordinator of Women's
Athletics
2801 W. Bancroft St.
Toledo, OH 43606

BB, FH, Ten, VB. 20 full scholarships.

Urbana College
Robert Cawley, Athletic Director
College Way
Urbana, OH 43078
BB, VB. 4 scholarships. Values from $500
to $540.

Wright State University
Peggy L. Wynkoop, Asst. Athletic
Director
Dayton, OH 45435
BB, S&D, VB. 2–4 scholarships per sport.
Tuition to full ride.

Xavier University
Laurie Massa, Coach
Victory Pkwy.
Cincinnati, OH 45207
BB, Ten, VB. Partial to full tuition.

Youngstown State University
Pauline Noe, Asst. Director of Athletics
410 Wick Ave.
Youngstown, OH 44555
BB, FH, Gym, SB, S&D, VB. 30
scholarships. Values from partial to full
ride.

OKLAHOMA

Bethany Nazarene College
Dr. Wanda Rhodes, P.E. Director
Bethany, OK 73008
BB, Ten, VB. 18 scholarships. Values
from $500 to $1000.

Cameron University
Bill G. Shahan, Women's Athletic
Director
2800 Gore Blvd.
Lawton, OK 73505
BB, SB, Ten, VB. Values from $100 to
$1705.

Central State University
Dr. Virginia Peters, Coordinator of
Women's Intercollegiate Sports
100 N. University Dr.
Edmond, OK 73034
BB, Gym, SB, Ten, T&F, VB. 40
scholarships. Values vary.

Eastern Oklahoma State College
Joe Thomas, Athletic Director
Wilburton, OK 74578
BB, Ten, T&F. 18 scholarships. Tuition
to full ride.

El Reno Junior College
Jim Whitworth, Athletic Director
El Reno, OK 73036
BB. 12 scholarships. Values from $250 to
$400.

Northeastern Oklahoma A & M College
Dr. Boyd Converse, Athletic Director
2nd and I
Miami, OK 74354
BB, SB, Ten. 20 scholarships. Values
from $325 to $2300.

Northeastern Oklahoma State College
Dr. Willa Faye Mason, Women's Athletic
Director
Tahlequah, OK 74464
BB, SB, VB. 25 scholarships. Tuition.

Oklahoma Baptist University
David L. Sallee, Athletic Director
500 W. University
Shawnee, OK 74801
BB, SB, VB. Values from $200 to full
ride.

Oklahoma Christian College
Laura Jobe, Women's Coach
Route 1, Box 141
Oklahoma City, OK 73111
BB, VB. 12 scholarships. Values vary.

Oklahoma State University
Susan S. Hall, Women's Intercollegiate
Athletics
Gallagher Hall Field House
Stillwater, OK 74074
BB, G, Gym, SB, Ten, T&F, VB. Full
scholarships.

Oral Roberts University
Bob Brooks, Athletic Director
7777 S. Lewis
Tulsa, OK 74171
BB, Gym, Ten, VB. Values to $5300.

Oscar Rose Junior College
Joe Johnson, VP of Student Affairs
6420 Southeast 15th
Midwest City, OK 73110
BB, Ten. 15 scholarships. Tuition and
books.

Phillips University
Bob Wilson, Athletic Director
Enid, OK 73701
BB. 8 full ride scholarships.

Southeastern Oklahoma State University
Dr. Don Parham, Athletic Director
Durant, OK 74701
BB. 6 scholarships. Tuition.

Southwestern Oklahoma State University
Laura Switzer, Women's Athletic Director
Weatherford, OK 73096
6 BB scholarships. Values from $240 to
$600.

St. Gregory's College
Rev. Paul Zahler, Assistant Women's
Basketball Coach
1900 W. MacArthur
Shawnee, OK 74801
BB. 10 scholarships. Values from $1000
to $3000.

University of Oklahoma
Don Jimerson, Assistant Athletic
Director
151 W. Brooks
Norman, OK 73019
BB, CC, G, Gym, SB, S&D, Ten, T&F,
BV. Number and values vary.

University of Tulsa
Emery Turner, Athletic Director
600 College Ave.
Tulsa, OK 74104
BB, CC, G, Swim, Ten, T&F, VB. Values
from $1000 to $3300.

OREGON

Central Oregon Community College
Doug Muck, Athletic Director
College Way
Bend, OR 97701

BB, CC, G, Ten, T&F, VB. 28
scholarships. Partial tuition.

Clackamas Community College
Chuck Hudson, Athletic Director
19600 S. Molalla
Oregon City, OR 97045
BB, CC, Ten, T&F, VB. Tuition.

George Fox College
Dr. Marjorie Weesner, Coordinator of
Women's Athletics
Meridian St., Newberg, OR 97132
BB, SB, T&F, VB. 40 scholarships. Values
from $100 to $500.

Linfield College
Dr. Jane S. McIlroy, Coach
McMinnville, OR 97128
BB, CC, FH, SB, S&D, Ten, T&F, VB. 29
scholarships. Values $400 to $1000.

Oregon State University
Nancy Gerou, Women's Athletic Director
Gill Coliseum 103
Corvallis, OR 97331
BB, CC, Gym, SB, S&D, T&F, VB. 35
scholarships. Values from $786 to $4069.

Portland State University
Roy Love, Athletic Director
P.O. Box 751, Portland, OR 97207
BB, Fenc, Gym, SB, S&D, Ten, VB.
Values from $121 to $3000.

Southern Oregon State College
Sally Rushing, Women's Athletic
Director
1250 Siskiyou Blvd.
Ashland, OR 97520
Sports, number, values vary.

Umpqua Community College
Cy Perkins, Athletic Director
P.O. Box 967
Roseburg, OR 97470
BB, CC, Ten, T&F, VB. $170 per term.

University of Oregon
Dr. Julie Carson
McArthur Court
Eugene, OR 97403
BB, CC, FH, Gym, SB, S&D, Ten, T&F,
VB. Values from partial tuition.

PENNSYLVANIA

Bucknell University
Margaret L. Bryan, Women's Athletic
Director
Lewisburg, PA 17837
BB, CC, FH, Lax, SB, S&D, Ten, T&F,
VB. Values to $6500. Based on need.

Clarion State College
Frances M. Shope, Women's Athletic
Director
Clarion, PA 16214
BB, Gym, S&D, VB. Number and values
vary.

Drexel University
Mary F. Semanik, Women's Athletic
Director
32nd & Chestnut Sts.
Philadelphia, PA 19104
Arch, Bad, BB, FH, Lax, SB, S&D, Ten,
VB. Values vary based on need.

Duquesne University
Eileen B. Surdoval, Women's Athletic
Director
Locust St.
Pittsburgh, PA 15219
BB, Ten, VB. 32 scholarships. Partial to
full scholarships.

Eastern College
Jean A. Shiffer, Women's Athletic
Director
Fairview Dr.
St. Davids, PA 19087
BB, FH, SB, Ten, VB. Values from $100
to $1000.

Gannon College
Karen Morris, Women's Athletic Director
109 W. 6th St.
Erie, PA 16541
BB, SB, Ten, VB. 15 scholarships. From
$300 to full tuition.

Lafayette College
Sharon Mitchel, Athletic Director for
Women
Easton, PA 18042
BB, FH, Lax, SB, S&D, Ten, VB. Aid
based on need.

LaSalle College
Kathleen M. Wear, Women's Athletic
Director
20th & Olney Ave.
Philadelphia, PA 19141
BB, FH, SB, S&D, T&F, VB. Number
and values vary.

Lehigh University
Judith H. Turner, Assistant Director of
Women's Athletics
Taylor Gymnasium #38
Bethlehem, PA 18015
BB, FH, Lax, SB, S&D, Ten, VB.
Number and values vary.

Lincoln University
Jean White, Women's Volleyball Coach
Lincoln University, PA 19352
BB, VB. Number and values vary.

Lycoming College
Clarence Burch, Athletic Director
Williamsport, PA 17701
Scholarships based on need.

Pennsylvania State University
Della Durant, Assistant Athletic Director
113 White Bldg.
University Park, PA 16802
BB, B, CC, Fenc, FH, Gym, Lax, Rifl,
S&D, Ten, T&F, VB. Number and values
vary.

**Pennsylvania State University—Ogontz
Campus**
Wesley A. Olsen, Athletic Director
1601 Cloverly Lane
Abington, PA 19001
Scholarships based on need.

Point Park College
Jerry Conboy, Athletic Director
201 Wood St.
Pittsburgh, PA 15222
BB. 12 scholarships. Tuition.

Robert Morris College
Albert Applin, Athletic Director
Narrows Run Rd.
Coraopolis, PA 15108
BB, SB, Ten, VB. Values to full
scholarships.

Shippensburg State College
Gwendolyn Baker, Women's Athletic
Director
Shippensburg, PA 15257
BB, CC, FH, Lax, SB, S&D, Ten, T&F,
VB. 102 scholarships. Values to $500.

St. Joseph's College
Ellen Ryan, Women's Athletic Director
54th & City Line Ave.
Philadelphia, PA 19131
BB, FH, SB, Ten, VB. Tuition.

Temple University
Dr. E. Kaye Hart, Women's Athletic
Director
Pearson Hall 201
Philadelphia, PA 19121
Bad, BB, B, Fenc, Gym, Lax, SB, S&D,
Ten, T&F, VB. Athletic Trainers. 80
scholarships. Partial tuition to full ride.

University of Pittsburgh
Sandy Bullman, Women's Athletic
Director
P.O. Box 7436, Athletic Dept.
Pittsburgh, PA 15213
BB, CC, FH, Gym, S&D, Ten, T&F, VB.
83 scholarships. From half tuition to full
ride.

University of Scranton
Gary Wodder, Athletic Director
John Long Center
Scranton, PA 18510
BB, FH, SB, Ten, VB. 8 scholarships.
Based on need.

Ursinus College
Robert R. Davidson, Athletic Director
Main Street
Collegeville, PA 19426
Bad, BB, CC, FH, Gym, Lax, SB, S&D,
Ten, VB. Number varies. Values from
$200 to $3600. Based on need.

Villanova University
Mary Anne Steenrod, Women's Athletic
Director
Villanova, PA 19085
BB, CC, FH, SB, S&D, T&F, Ten, VB.
Values from $1800 to $5950.

Waynesburg College
Hayden Buckley, Athletic Director
Waynesburg, PA 15370
VB. 2 scholarships. $3000 each.

Wilkes College
Doris Sarcino, Women's Athletic Director
Wilkes-Barre, PA 18766
BB, CC, FH, G, SB, S&D, Ten, VB.
Based on need.

York College of Pennsylvania
Jack C. Jaquet, Athletic Director
Country Club Rd.
York, PA 17405
BB, CC, FH, SB, S&D, Ten, VB. Values
to $1000.

PUERTO RICO

University of Puerto Rico
Dr. Jose M. Portela, Athletic Director
Box M, College Station
Rio Piedras, PR 00931
BB, CC, SB, S&D, Ten, T&F, VB.
Tuition.

University of Puerto Rico—Mayaguez Campus
Edmundo Carrero, Athletic Director
Mayaguez, PR 00708
BB, CC, SB, S&D, Ten, T&F, VB. 70
scholarships. $250.

RHODE ISLAND

Providence College
Helen Bert, Women's Athletic Director
River Avenue
Providence, RI 02919
BB, FH, IH, SB, VB. Number and values
vary.

Rhode Island College
Gail H. Davis, Associate Athletic
Director
Providence, RI 02908
BB, CC, Fenc, Gym, SB, Ten, T&F, VB.
Scholarships based on need.

University of Rhode Island
Eleanor Lemaire, Associate Director of
Athletics
Kingston, RI 02881

BB, CC, Gym, FH, SB, Ten, T&F, VB.
Partial to full scholarships. Numbers
vary.

SOUTH CAROLINA

Anderson College
John Edwards, Athletic Director
Boulevard St.
Anderson, SC 29621
BB, Ten. 7 scholarships. Values from
$300 to $3500.

Baptist College
Thad Talley, Women's Athletic Director
P.O. Box 10087
Charleston, SC 39411
BB, Ten, T&F, VB. Values to full ride.

Claflin College
P. Palmer Worthy, Athletic Director
College Ave., NE
Orangeburg, SC 29115
BB, SB, Ten, T&F. 24 scholarships.

Clemson University
Annie Tribble, Coordinator of Women's
Athletics
Clemson, SC 29631
BB, CC, FH, S&D, Ten, VB. Number and
values vary.

College of Charleston
Joan Cronan, Women's Athletic Dept.
Charleston, SC 29401
BB, S&D, Ten, VB. Number and values
vary.

Columbia College
Linda Warren, Athletic Coordinator
Columbia, SC 29203
BB, Ten, VB. Number and values vary.

Francis Marion College
Gerald Griffin, Athletic Director
P.O. Box 7500
Florence, SC 29501
BB, SB, Ten, VB. Values to tuition.

Furman University
Howard Wheeler, Women's Athletic
Director
Greenville, SC 29613

BB, FH, G, Gym, SB, S&D, Ten, VB.
Number varies. Values from $200 to
$5000.

Limestone College
Jay Rhodes, Athletic Director
Gaffney, SC 29340
SB. 13 scholarships. Values to $4300.

Newberry College
Red Burnette, Athletic Director
College St.
Newberry, SC 29108
BB, SB, Ten, VB. 55 scholarships. Values
to $2625.

North Greenville College
Judy Stroud, Women's BB/VB Coach
Tigerville, SC 29688
5 BB, 1½ VB scholarships. Values vary.

Presbyterian College
Cally Gault, Athletic Director
Clinton, SC 29325
BB, Ten, VB. 6½ scholarships. Values to
$4950.

South Carolina State College
Dr. Willis Ham, Athletic Director
Orangeburg, SC 29117
BB, Ten, T&F, VB. Partial to full grants.

Spartanburg Methodist College
Terry Stephenson, Athletic Director
Powell Mill Road
Spartanburg, SC 29301
BB, SB, VB. 5 scholarships. Values to
$3000.

University of South Carolina
Pam Parsons, Director of Women's
Athletics
Columbia, SC 29208
BB, Gym, SB, S&D, Ten, VB. 76
scholarships. Tuition to full ride.

Voorhees College
Kenneth F. Sandiford, Athletic Director
Voorhees Road
Denmark, SC 29042
BB, SB, T&F. 24 scholarships.

SOUTH DAKOTA

Augustana College
Eileen Friest, Coordinator of Women's
Athletics
Sioux Falls, SD 57102
BB, CC, SB, Ten, T&F, VB. Number
varies. From $200 to full ride.

Dakota Wesleyan University
Jan Jirsak, Coordinator of Women's
Athletics
Mitchell, SD 57301
BB, SB, T&F, VB. Number varies. Values
from $100 to $500.

South Dakota State University
Stan Marshall, Director of
HPER/Athletics
Brookings, SD 57006
BB, CC, FH, G, Gym, SB, S&D, Ten,
T&F, VB. Number varies.

University of South Dakota
Mary Zimmerman, Coordinator of
Women's Athletics
Dakota Dome
Vermillion, SD 57069
BB, T&F. 22 scholarships. Values from
$200 to full ride.

TENNESSEE

Austin Peay State University
Athletic Director
Clarksville, TN 37040
BB, Ten, T&F, VB. 44 scholarships.
Partial to full.

Belmont College
Betty Wiseman, Women's Director of
Sports
Athletic Dept.
Belmont Blvd.
Nashville, TN 37203
BB, Ten. Partial tuition.

Chattanooga State Community College
Don Green, Athletic Director
4501 Amnicola Hwy.
Chattanooga, TN 37406

BB, Ten. 8 scholarships. Full ride.

Cleveland State Community College
Jim Cigliano, Dean of Students
P.O. Box 1205
Cleveland, TN 37311
BB, G, Ten. Numbers vary. Values from
$75 to $488.

Columbia State Community College
Elner M. Hamner, Assistant Professor
Columbia, TN 38401
BB. 3 scholarships. Values from $100 to
$300.

Covenant College
Dr. Walter Bowman, Athletic Director
Lookout Mountain, TN 37350
BB, VB. 8 scholarships. Values to $3020.

East Tennessee State University
Janice C. Shelton, Women's Athletic
Director
Box 21340A
Johnson City, TN 37601
BB, Gym, Rifl, Ten, T&F, VB. 50
scholarships. Values from $1900 to $3057.

Lambuth College
Roscoe C. Williams, Athletic Director
Lambuth Blvd., Jackson, TN 38301
BB, Ten, VB. 32 scholarships. Values to
$1000.

Memphis State University
Elma Roane, Women's Athletic Director
Fieldhouse 367
Memphis, TN 38152
BB, G, Gym, Ten, T&F, VB. 66
scholarships. Values from $500 to $4000.

Middle Tennessee State University
Dr. Patricia Jones, Women's Athletic
Director
Memorial Blvd.
Murfreesboro, TN 37132
BB, Ten, T&F, VB. 25 scholarships.
Values to $1654.

Roane State Community College
Phil Allen, Athletic Director
Harriman, TN 37748
BB, Ten. Values from $50 to $1500.

Tennessee State University
Samuel R. Whitmon, Athletic Director
3500 Centennial Blvd.
Nashville, TN 37203
BB, T&F. 17 scholarships. Tuition.

Tennessee Technological University
Marynell Meadors, Assistant Athletic
Director
Box 5057
Cookeville, TN 38501
BB, Ten, VB. 22 scholarships. Values
from $1700 to $2600.

Tennessee Wesleyan College
Dwair Farmer, Athletic Director
Box 40, College St.
Athens, TN 37303
BB, Ten. 16 scholarships. $400.

Trevecca Nazarene College
Carolyn Smith, Women's Coordinator
333 Murfreesboro Rd.
Nashville, TN 37217
Ten, VB. 7 scholarships. Tuition.

Union University
Dr. David Blackstock
Hwy. 45—Bypass North
Jackson, TN 38301
BB. 8 scholarships. Partial to full.

University of Tennessee (Chattanooga)
Sharon Fanning, Women's Athletic
Coordinator
615 McCallie Ave., Athletic Dept.
Chattanooga, TN 37402
BB, G, Ten, VB. 38 scholarships.
Tuition.

University of Tennessee (Knoxville)
Gloria Ray, Women's Athletic Director
115 Stokley Athletic Center
Knoxville, TN 37916
BB, CC, S&D, Ten, T&F, VB. 67
scholarships. Values from $500 to $3300.

University of Tennessee (Martin)
Bettye Giles, Women's Athletic Director
Women's Intercollegiate Athletics
Martin, TN 38238

BB, Ten, VB. 28 scholarships. Tuition to full ride.

Vanderbilt University
Emily H. Harsh, Assistant Athletic Director
Box 120158
Nashville, TN 37240
BB, CC, S&D, Ten, T&F, VB. Partial to full ride.

Volunteer State Community College
Dr. L. G. Reagan, Woman's Coach
Gallatin, TN 37066
BB. 6–8 scholarships. Values from $90 to $270.

TEXAS

Amarillo College
Jim Calvin, Athletic Director
2201 S. Washington, Box 447
Amarillo, TX 79178
BB, Ten. Number and values vary.

Angelina College
Guy Davis, Athletic Director
P.O. Box 1768
Lufkin, TX 75901
BB, Ten. 16 scholarships. Full ride.

Angelo State University
Jane Davis, Women's Athletic Director
2601 W. Avenue N
San Angelo, TX 76901
BB, CC, SB, Ten, T&F, VB. 52 scholarships. Values from $400 to $1800.

Baylor University
Jack Patterson, Athletic Director
Box 6427
Waco, TX 76706
BB, SB, T&F, VB. Number and values vary.

Bishop College
Myrtle Robinson, Athletic Director
3837 Simpson-Stuart Rd.
Dallas, TX 75232
BB, CC, SB, Ten, T&F, VB. 34 scholarships. Partial to full ride based on need.

Brazosport College
Joycelynn Gingson, Associate Professor
500 College Dr.
Lake Jackson, TX 77566
BB, Ten, VB. 24 scholarships. Values from $50 to $900 per semester.

Concordia College
John Faszholz, Athletic Director
3400 N. IH 35
Austin, TX 78705
Ten, VB. 14 scholarships. Values from $650 to $1300.

Cooke County College
Jim Voight, Athletic Director·
Box 815
Gainesville, TX 76240
BB, Ten. 18 full ride scholarships.

East Texas State University
Margo Waters, Director of P.E. & Athletics for Women
Commerce, TX 75248
BB, Ten, T&F, VB. 44 scholarships. Values to full scholarship.

Frank Phillips College
Audie Apple, Athletic Director
Box 5118
Borger, TX 79007
BB, Ten. 15 scholarships. Values from $250 to $1445.

Hardin-Simmons University
Peggy Williams, Women's Athletic Coordinator
Box 884 H-SU
Abilene, TX 79601
BB, Ten, V.B. 21 scholarships. Values from $600 to $2700.

Henderson County Junior College
Leon Spencer, Athletic Director
Athens, TX 75751
BB. 15 scholarships. Values from $1600 to $2000.

Hill Junior College
John Thornton, Athletic Director
P.O. Box 619
Hillsboro, TX 76645

BB, G, Ten. 16 scholarships. Partial to full ride.

Howard College
Don Stevens, Women's BB Coach
Big Spring, TX 79720
BB. 10 scholarships. Values from $300 to $1850.

Howard Payne University
Harold Mayo, Athletic Director
HPU Station, Box 175
Brownwood, TX 76801
BB, VB. Values from $400 to full tuition.

Lamar University
Belle Mead Holm, Women's Athletic Director
10039 University Station
Beaumont, TX 77710
BB, Dance, G, S&D, Ten, T&F, VB. 78 scholarships. Values vary.

Lee College
Gertrude Lyon, P.E. Instructor
Box 818
Baytown, TX 77520
S&D, Ten, VB. 19 scholarships. Values vary.

Midland College
Del Poss, Director of Athletics
3600 N. Garfield
Midland, TX 79701
G, S&D, Ten. 18 scholarships. Values from $450 to $2328.

Midwestern State University
Gerald Stockton, Athletic Director
3400 Taft
Wichita Falls, TX 77308
BB, Ten, VB. 20 scholarships. Values from tuition to full ride.

North Harris County College
Dr. Robert S. Williams
2700 W. Thorne Dr.
Houston, TX 77073
BB, Ten. 18 scholarships. Books, fees, tuition.

North Texas State University
Vicky Guy, Administration Assistant
P.O. Box 13917, NT Station
Denton, TX 76203
BB, CC, G, Ten, T&F, VB. Number and values vary.

Odessa College
Virginia Brown, Assistant Professor
3743 Fern Circle
Odessa, TX 79762
Ten. 12 scholarships. Values from 2000 to $4000.

Pan American University
Kelly Bass, Women's Coordinator, Athletic Dept.
Edinburg, TX 78539
BB, Gym, SB, VB.

Ranger Junior College
Ron Butler, Athletic Director
Ranger, TX 76470
BB, T&F. 18 scholarships. Half to full.

Rice University
Martha Hawthorne, Women's Athletic Director
P.O. Box 1892
Houston, TX 77001
BB, CC, S&D, Ten, T&F, VB. Number and values vary.

San Jacinto College North
Gene Moore, Athletic Director
5800 Uvalde
Houston, TX 77049
BB, G. 17 scholarships. Books, tuition, fees, plus $75 per month.

San Jacinto College Central
Dorothy Brown, Women's P.E.
Spencer Hwy.
Pasadena, TX 77505
Ten, T&F, VB. 33 scholarships. Full ride.

South Plains Junior College
Gayle Nicholas, Women's Basketball Coach
Levelland, TX 79336
BB, Ten. 16 scholarships. Values from $175 to $1400.

Southern Methodist University
Barbara Camp, Assistant Athletic
Director
Moody Coliseum, Box 216
Dallas, TX 75275
BB, G, S&D, Ten. 6 scholarships. Partial
to full.

Southwest Texas State
Dana Craft, Athletic Director
Towers Center
San Marcos, TX 78666
BB, Gym, S&D, Ten, VB. Number varies.
Values from $150 to $1900.

Southwestern Christian Junior College
P.O. Box 10
Terrell, TX 75160
BB, CC, T&F. 12 scholarships. $2083.

Southwestern University
Glada Munt, Athletic Director
Box 272, S.U. Station
Georgetown, TX 78626
BB, VB. 8 scholarships. Values from $500
to $3000.

Stephen F. Austin State University
Sue Gunter, Athletic Director
Box 3016, SFA Sta.
Nacogdoches, TX 75962
BB, SB, Ten, T&F, VB. 21 scholarships.
Values from $1000 to $1800.

Texarkana Community College
Athletic Director
2500 N. Robison Rd.
Texarkana, TX 75501
G, Ten. 16 scholarships. Values vary.

Texas A & I University
Nita Fisher, Athletic Director
Campus Box 202
Kingsville, TX 78363
BB, Ten, T&F, VB. 52 scholarships.
Values from $100 to $875 per semester.

Texas A&M University
Kay Don, Assistant Athletic Director for
Women
College Station, TX 77843
BB, CC, G, SB, S&D, Ten, T&F, VB. 24
scholarships. Values from $500 to full.

Texas Christian University
Carolyn Dixon, Associate Athletic
Director
Forth Worth, TX 76129
BB, G, Gym, S&D, Ten. 25 scholarships.
Values from $1200 to $5000.

Texas Lutheran College
Kathryn M. Yandell, Women's Athletic
Coordinator
Sequin, TX 78155
BB, Ten, T&F, VB. 12 scholarships.
Values vary.

Texas Tech University
Jeannine McHaney
P.O. Box 4079
Lubbock, TX 79409
BB, CC, G, SB, S&D, Ten, T&F, VB. 86
scholarships. Partial to full ride.

Texas Wesleyan College
Miriam Satern, Athletic Coordinator
Fort Worth, TX 76105
BB, SB, Ten, VB. 15–25 scholarships.
Values from $1000 to $2500.

Trinity University
Emille Burrer-Foster
Women's Tennis Coach
715 Stadium Dr.
San Antonio, TX 78284
Ten. 2 scholarships. Value $4134.

Tyler Junior College
Floyd Wagstaff, Athletic Director
East Fifth St.
Tyler, TX 75701
BB, Ten. 16 scholarships. $1500.

University of Houston
Women's Athletic Director
Jeppesen Fieldhouse
Houston, TX 77004
BB, CC, S&D, Ten, T&F, VB. 75
scholarships. Tuition to full ride.

University of Mary Hardin Baylor
Dr. Dan Atha, Athletic Director
College & 10th Sts.
Belton, TX 76513
BB, Ten, VB. 14 scholarships. Partial to
full.

University of Texas (Arlington)
Bill Reeves, Athletic Director
Arlington, TX 76019
BB, SB, T&F, VB. 42 scholarships.
Tuition to full ride.

University of Texas (Austin)
Donna Lopiano, Director of Women's
Athletics
Bellmont Hall 606
Austin, TX 78712
BB, CC, G, Gym, S&D, Ten, T&F, VB.
88 full scholarship equivalents.

University of Texas (El Paso)
Jim Bowden, Athletic Director
El Paso, TX 79968
BB, Gym, T&F, VB. 46 scholarships.
Values from $200 to $1860.

Wayland Baptist College
Bob Clindaniel, Athletic Director
Plainview, TX 79072
BB, Ten. 16 scholarships. Values to
$3150.

Weatherford College
Bob McKinley
308 E. Park
Weatherford, TX 76086
BB, Ten. 11 scholarships. Partial to full.

Western Texas College
Nolan Richardson, Athletic Director
Snyder, TX 79549
BB. 10 scholarships. Values from $300 to
$1900.

Wharton County Junior College
Ann Plumme, Women's Coach
911 Boling Hwy.
Wharton, TX 77488
BB, VB. Number varies. Values from
$180 to $810 per semester.

UTAH

Brigham Young University
Lu Wallace, Women's Intercollegiate
Administrator
295 RB
Provo, UT 84602

BB, CC, G, Gym, S&D, Ten, T&F, VB.
Number and values vary.

College of Eastern Utah
William D. Peterson, Athletic Director
Price, UT 84501
BB, Gym, SB, VB. 11 tuition
scholarships.

Dixie College
Bob Horlacher, Coordinator of Women's
Athletics
225 S. 700 East
St. George, UT 84770
BB, SB, VB. Numbers vary. Partial to
full.

Snow College
Ron Abegglen, Athletic Director
Ephraim, UT 84627
BB, SB, VB. 15 scholarships. Values vary.

Southern Utah State College
Kathryn Berg, Women's Athletic Director
Cedar City, UT 84720
BB, Gym, SB, T&F, VB. 10 scholarships.
Values from $50 to $429.

University of Utah
Fern Gardner, Women's Athletic Director
Special Events Center
Salt Lake City, UT 84112
BB, Gym, Ski, SB, S&D, Ten, T&F, VB.
90 scholarships. Values vary.

Utah State University
Marilyn Weiss, Director Women's
Athletics
UMV 77
Logan, UT 84321
BB, CC, Gym, SB, VB. Number varies.
Value to $3500. Full scholarships.

Utah Technical College Provo/Orem
Sharon M. Benson, Women's Athletic
Director
1395 N. 150 E.
Provo, UT 84601
BB, VB. 10 scholarships. Tuition.

Weber State College
Jane Miner, Women's Athletic Director
3750 Harrison Blvd.
Ogden, UT 84408

BB, CC, G, SB, Ten, T&F, VB. Numbers vary. Partial to full tuition.

VERMONT

St. Michael's College
Sue Duprat, Coordinator of Women's
Athletics
Winooski Park, VT 05404
BB, (FH, SB if also connected with BB),
additional consideration given to 2-sport
athletes. Number varies. Values to $4000.

University of Vermont
Sally Guerette, Assistant Athletic
Director, Coordinator of Women's
Athletics
Patrick Gym—UVM
Burlington, VT 05405
BB, Ski, Ten. Scholarship aid available
in varying number and values.

VIRGINIA

College of William and Mary
Mildred B. West, Director of Women's
Athletics
Williamsburg, VA 23185
Bad, BB, Fenc, FH, G, Gym, Lax, S&D,
Ten, T&F, VB. Numbers vary. Values
from $250 to full tuition.

Emory and Henry College
Eleanor Hutton, Women's Athletic
Director
Emory, VA 24327
BB, Ten, VB. All aid based on need.

George Mason University
Chris Walters, Women's Athletic Director
4400 University Drive
Fairfax, VA 22030
BB, CC, SB, Ten, T&F, VB. 18
scholarships. Partial to full.

James Madison University
Dr. L. Leotus Morrison, Director of
Women's Sports
Harrisonburg, VA 22807
Full grants in BB. Partial grants in FH,
G, Gym, Lax, Swim, Ten, T&F, VB.

Longwood College
Carolyn V. Hodges, Director of Women's
Athletics
Farmville, VA 23901
BB, FH, G, Gym. Number and values
vary.

Old Dominion University
Mikki Flowers, Assistant Athletic
Director
Hampton Blvd.
Norfolk, VA 23508
BB, FH, Lax, S&D, Ten. Number and
values vary.

Randolph-Macon College
Hugh F. Stephens, Athletic Director
Ashland, VA 23005
BB, FH, Ten. 8 scholarships. Values from
$250 to $450

University of Richmond
Carol Reese, Women's Athletic Director
Richmond, VA 23173
CC, FH, Lax, S&D, Sync, Ten, T&F.
Number and values vary.

University of Virginia
Barbara A. Kelly, Associate Director of
Athletic Programs
P.O. Box 3785
Charlottesville, VA 22903
BB, CC, FH, Lax, SB, S&D, Ten, T&F,
VB. Number and values vary.

Virginia Commonwealth University
Elizabeth S. Royster, Women's Athletic
Director
901 W. Franklin St.
Richmond, VA 23284
BB, FH, S&D, Ten, BV. 13 scholarships.
Values from $393 to $1462.

Virginia Polytechnic Institute and State University
Jo K. Kafer, Women's Athletic Director
Washington Street
Blacksburg, VA 24060
BB, FH, S&D, Ten, VB. 40 scholarships.
Partial to full tuition.

Virginia State College
Dr. Claude Flythe, Athletic Director
Box 58, Athletic Department
Petersburg, VA 23803
BB, T&F. Partial.

WASHINGTON

Big Bend Community College
Jim Grant, Athletic Director
24th B Chanute
Moses Lake, WA 98837
BB, T&F, VB. 26 scholarships. Tuition
plus $1000 work-study.

Centralia Community College
Carl Bergstrom, Athletic Director
P.O. Box 639
Centralia, WA 98531
BB, Ten, VB. 11 scholarships. Values
from $100 to $1300 (includes work-study).

Eastern Washington University
C. Peggy Gazette
HPERA
Cheney, WA 99004
BB, Gym, Ten, T&F, VB. 28
scholarships. $618 per year.

Edmonds Community College
Fred Shull, Athletic Director
20000 68th Ave. W.
Lynnwood, WA 98036
BB, SB, VB. 45 scholarships. Tuition,
room and work assistance.

Everett Community College
Wiley Davis, Athletic Director
801 Wetmore Ave.
Everett, WA 98201
BB, CC, Ten, T&F, VB. 23 scholarships.
Values from $102 to $1200. Available
only to WA, OR, ID & BC students.

Fort Steilacoom Community College
Jack Scott, Athletic Director
9401 Farwest Dr. S.W.
Tacoma, WA 98498
BB, SB, Ten, VB. 28 scholarships. Partial
to full tuition.

Grays Harbor College
Diane Smith, Women's Athletic Director
College Heights
Aberdeen, WA 98520
BB, SB, VB. 25 scholarships. Values from
$315 to $1315.

Highline Community College
Don McConnaughey, Athletic Director
Midway, WA 98031
BB, CC, S&D, Ten, T&F, VB. Number
and values vary.

Pacific Lutheran University
Women's Athletic Director
Tacoma, WA 98447
BB, CC, Crew, FH, SB, Ski, Swim, Ten,
T&F, VB. Based on need.

Seattle Pacific University
Keith Phillips, Athletic Director
3307 Third Ave. W.
Seattle, WA 98119
T&F. 7 scholarships. Values from $500 to
$3800.

Seattle University
Cathy Benedetto, Women's Athletic
Director
Seattle, WA 98122
BB, Gym, Ten. Number varies. Values to
full ride.

University of Puget Sound
Dawn Bowman, Women's Athletic
Director
1500 Warner St.
Tacoma, WA 98415
BB, CC, SB, S&D, Ten, VB. 38
scholarships. Values from $200 to $4000.

University of Washington
Catherine Green, Associate Director of
Intercollegiate Athletics
Seattle, WA 98105
BB, CC, G, Gym, S&D, Ten, T&F, VB.
Number and values vary.

Walla Walla Community College
Mary Lynn Worl
500 Tausek Way
Walla Walla, WA 99362
BB, Ten, VB. Number and values vary.

Washington State University
Joanne Washburn, Athletic Director
Pullman, WA 99164
BB, CC, FH, Gym, Ski, S&D, Ten, T&F,
VB. Number and values vary.

WEST VIRGINIA

Concord College
Georgia Kelly, Women's Coordinator
Athens, WV 24712
BB, SB, Ten, T&F, VB. Values from $220
to $1160.

Davis & Elkins College
Edward McFarlane, Athletic Director
Elkins, WV 26241
BB, FH, Ten. 27 scholarships. Values
from $500 to $4000.

Marshall University
Dr. Lynn Snyder
P.O. Box 1360
Huntington, WV 25715
BB, G, SB, Ten, T&F, VB. 28
scholarships. Values from $3432.70.

Salem College
Loyal Park, Athletic Director
Main St.
Salem, WV 26426
BB, SB, VB. 25 scholarships. Values from
$400 to $1000.

University of Charleston
Robert A. Francis, Assistant Athletic
Director
MacCorkle Ave.
Charleston, WV 25304
BB, SB, Ten, VB. Number varies. Values
from $100 to $1000.

University of West Virginia
Dr. Jan Stocker, Assistant Athletic
Director
Morgantown, WV 26505
BB, CC, Gym, SB, Swim, Ten, T&F, VB.
Values vary.

West Liberty State College
Janet Pannett, Director of Women's
Athletics
West Liberty, WV.26074
BB, SB, Ten, VB. 12 scholarships. Values
from $200 to $1100.

West Virginia Institute of Technology
Neal Baisi, Athletic Director
Montgomery, WV 25136
BB. 6 scholarships. Values from $110 to
$550.

West Virginia State College
Robert Maxwell, Athletic Director
Institute, WV 25112
BB. 6 scholarships. $210 in-state. $1160
out-of-state.

WISCONSIN

Carthage College
Dianne M. Mizerka, Athletic Director
2001 Alford Drive
Kenosha, WI 53141
Bad, BB, SB, S&D, Ten, T&F, VB.
Number varies. Values from $100 to $800.

Marquette University
Tat Shiely, Coordinator of Women's
Athletics
1532 W. Clybourn
Milwaukee, WI 53233
BB, CC, Ten, T&F, VB. 44 scholarships.
Values from $1000 to $3620.

University of Wisconsin (Madison)
Kit Saunders, Director of Women's
Athletics
1440 Monroe St.
Madison, WI 53706
Bad, BB, CC, Fenc, FH, G, Gym, S&D,
Ten, T&F, VB. 100 scholarships. Values
from $919 to $5388.

University of Wisconsin (Parkside)
Coach (of specific sport)
Kenosha, WI 53140

BB, Fenc, SB, S&D, Ten, T&F, VB.
Number and values vary.

WYOMING

Casper College
Jean Wheatley, Women's Athletic
Director
125 College Dr.
Casper, WY 82601
BB, Gym, Ten, VB. 20 scholarships.
Values vary.

Central Wyoming College
Tony Masters, Athletic Director
Riverton, WY 82501
BB, G, Ten, VB. Values from $100 to
$1700.

Eastern Wyoming College
Verl E. Petsch, Women's Athletic Director
Torrington, WY 82240
BB, T&F, VB. 21 scholarships. Values
from $300 to full ride.

Northwestern Community College
Tom Case, Athletic Director
Powell, WY 82435

BB, Ten, T&F, VB. 25 scholarships.
Values from $300 to $2000.

Sheridan College
Teddy Peterson, Women's Athletic
Director
Sheridan, WY 82801
BB, VB. 20 scholarships. Values from
$300 to $2000.

University of Wyoming
Bob Hitch, Athletic Director
P.O. Box 3414
University Station
Laramie, WY 82071
BB, CC, Ski, SB, S&D, T&F, VB. 72
scholarships. Values to full ride.

Western Wyoming College
Susan Kuehl, Women's P.E. Director
Box 428
Rock Springs, WY 82901
BB, VB. 18 scholarships. Values from
$350 to $1500.

APPENDIX 2:
WOMEN'S SPORTS FOUNDATION SPORTS CAMP GUIDE

ARCHERY

The World Archery Center
Director: Mrs. Myrtle K. Miller
67 Old Stone Church Rd.
Upper Saddle River, NJ 07458
Phone: (201) 327-2170; July and August
(717) 421-3180
Skill Level: From neophyte to top
Age Range: Coed; all ages

BASEBALL

Michigan State University Summer Sports School (See general listing.)

BASKETBALL

Bowling Green State University (See general listing.)

Carolina Girls' Basketball Camp
Director: Pam Parsons
University of South Carolina
Women's Athletic Department
Round House
Columbia, SC 29206
Phone: (803) 777-3829
Skill Level: Beginning, intermediate, advanced, separated by age and ability
Age Range: Girls 8–18

Center for Professional Development and Public Service at Florida State University
Director: Janice Dykehouse
Women's Athletics
Florida State University
Tallahassee, FL 32306
Phone: (904) 644-1007
Skill Level: All
Age Range: Girls 12–18

Connecticut Girls Sports Camps, Inc.
(See general listing.)

Sam Jones Girls Basketball School
Director: Sam Jones
Center Court, Ltd.
P.O. Box 6324

Silver Springs, MD 20906
Phone: (301) 598-5887
Skill Level: Beginning to advanced
Age Range: Girls 11–18

Pat Kennedy Girls Basketball Camp
Directors: Pat Kennedy, Robert Kennedy
P.D. 4 Box 95
Stroudsburg, PA 18360
Phone: (717) 595-2886 (winter); (717) 595-6343 (summer)
Skill Level: All separated by ability
Age Range: Girls 9 and up

Pat Kennedy Invitational Basketball Camp
Director: Pat Kennedy
P.O. Box 228
Mountainhome, PA 18342
Phone: (717) 595-7686
Skill Level: All separated by ability
Age Range: Girls to 17

Madison Basketball School
Director: Betty Jaynes
James Madison University
Godwin 27
Harrisonburg, VA 22807
Phone: (703) 433-6153
Skill Level: All
Age Range: Girls 14–18

Medalist Sports Camps (See general listing.)

Milwaukee Bucks Basketball Camps
Director: Ron Blomberg
10206 North Port Washington Rd.
Mequon, WI 53092
Phone: (414) 241-8680
Skill Level: All
Age Range: Coed 8–18

Billie Moore Girls Basketball Camp
Director: Billie Moore
UCLA Head Coach
8245 Ronson Rd.
Suite D
San Diego, CA 92111
Phone: (714) 279-7800; toll-free in California (800) 542-6005

Skill Level: All levels, separated by age and ability
Age Range: Girls 12–21

Ellen Mosher Basketball Camp
Director: Ellen Mosher
3087 Evelyn St.
Roseville, MN 55113
Phone: (612) 631-2336
Skill Level: All
Age Range: Girls 10–20

Rutgers University Sports Camps (See general listing.)

Syracuse University Girls Basketball Camp
Director: Barbara Jacobs
820 Comstock Ave.
Syracuse, NY 13210
Phone: (315) 423-2508
Skill Level: All
Age Range: Girls 11–18

Texas A & M Girls Basketball Camp
Director: Cherri Rapp
Athletic Dept.
Texas A & M University
College Station, TX 77843
Phone: (713) 845-1051
Skill Level: All, separated by ability
Age Range: Girls 10–18

Wes Unseld Basketball Fundamentals Camp
Directors: Wes Unseld, Chuck Laur
7912 Marfield Pl.
Baltimore, MD 21236
Phone: (301) 661-7060
Skill Level: All
Age Range: Coed 8–17

USD Girls Basketball Camp
Director: Kathleen Marpe
University of San Diego
Alcala Park
San Diego, CA 92110
Phone: (714) 291-6480, ext. 4272
Skill Level: All, separated
Age Range: Girls 11–19

John Wooden Girls Basketball Camp
Director: John Wooden
Former UCLA Head Coach
8245 Ronson Rd.
Suite D
San Diego, CA 92111
Phone: (714) 279-7800; toll-free in California (800) 542-6005
Skill Level: All levels, separated by age and ability
Age Range: Girls 10–21

BOWLING

Professional Bowling Camps, Inc.
Director: Dorman Spencer
361 N.E. Gilman Blvd.
Issaquah, WA 98027
Phone: (206) 392-0300
Skill Level: All
Age Range: Coed juniors 11–21 and adults

CHEERLEADING

Connecticut Girls Sports Camps, Inc.
(See general listing.)

CROSS-COUNTRY

Bowling Green State University (See general listing.)

Michigan State University Summer Sports School (See general listing.)

Rutgers University Sports Camps (See general listing.)

Sauk Valley Farm (See general listing.)

Shippensburg State College Camps (See general listing.)

Tobybanna Sports Camp, Inc. (See general listing.)

Walton's Grizzly Lodge Summer Camp for Boys and Girls (See multi-sport listing.)

DIVING

Bowling Green State University (See general listing.)

Michigan State University Summer Sports School (See general listing.)

Shippensburg State College Camps (See general listing.)

FIELD HOCKEY

Camp Maple Lake
Director: Carol Houk
605 Country Club Dr.
Bloomsburg, PA 17815
Phone: (717) 784-6431
Skill Level: Beginning, intermediate, advanced
Age Range: Girls 13–20

Connecticut Girls Sports Camps, Inc. (See general listing.)

Eastern Field Hockey Camp, Inc.
Director: Judith Wolstenholme
9 E. Rhodes Ave.
West Chester, PA 19380
Phone: (215) 696-4523
Skill Level: All
Age Range: Girls 14–18

Harris Field Hockey Day Camp
Director: Mary Ann Harris
581 Groffs Mill Rd.
Harleysville, PA 19438
Phone: (215) 256-9467
Skill Level: All
Age Range: Girls, grades 9–12

Madison Field Hockey School
Director: Dee McDonough
James Madison University, Godwin 27
Harrisonburg, VA 22807
Phone: (703) 433-6463
Skill Level: All
Age Range: Girls 14–18

Mercersburg Field Hockey Camp
Director: Carol R. Anderson
21 Woodbridge St.
South Hadley, MA 01075
Phone: (413) 533-2161
Skill Level: Beginning to advanced
Age Range: Girls 12–22

Merestead Hockey and Lacrosse Camps
Director: Caroline Haussermann
20 E. Sunset Ave.
Philadelphia, PA 19118
Phone: (215) 248-3771
Skill Level: All
Age Range: 15–60

Mount Pocono Hockey and Lacrosse Conferences
Directors: Mrs. Francis Regan, Mrs. Robert Miller
Camp Tegawitha
Tobyhanna, PA 18466
Phone: (717) 894-8694
Skill Level: Beginning, intermediate, advanced
Age Range: Girls, high school and college

R & R Sports Academies (See general listing.)

Rutgers University Sports Camps (See general listing.)

Sauk Valley Farm (See general listing.)

Tobybanna Sports Camp, Inc. (See general listing.)

USFHA Olympic Development Camps
Director: Cindy Munro
4415 Buffalo Rd.
North Chili, NY 14514
Phone: (716) 594-4300
Skill Level: Beginning, intermediate, advanced
Age Range: Girls 19–20

GOLF

Bowling Green State University (See general listing.)

Billy Casper California Golf Camp
Director: Billy Casper
8245 Ronson Rd.
Suite D
San Diego, CA 92111
Phone: (714) 279-7800; toll-free in
California (800) 542-6005
Age Range: Girls 10–18

GYMNASTICS

**American Gymnastic Camp/Olympic
Lake Sports Camp**
Director: Dr. Frederic M. Pierce
416 Prentice Rd.
Vestal, NY 13850
Phone: (607) 797-9418 (winter); (717) 623-
2606
Skill Level: All, separated by ability
Age Range: Girls 8–18

Bowling Green State University (See
general listing.)

**Eastern Washington University
Gymnastics Camp**
Director: Jo McDonald
Continuing Education Center, EWU
Cheney, WA 99004
Skill Level: All
Age Range: Girls 8–18

Elon College Gymnastics Camp
Director: Barbara Yarborough
P.O. Box 2195
Elon College, NC 27244
Phone: (919) 584-1161 or 584-9711, ext.
226
Skill Level: All
Age Range: Girls, grade 6–college

M.A.G.I.C. Gymnastics Camp
Directors: Paula Kilpatrick, Barbara
Yarborough
737 E. Davis Street
Burlington, NC 27215
Phone: (919) 584-1161
Skill Level: All, separated by ability
Age Range: Girls 6–18

Medalist Sports Camps (See general
listing.)

Rutgers University Sports Camps (See
general listing.)

**SCI Modern Rhythmic Gymnastics
Camp**
Director: James C. Peterson
734 Alger SE
Grand Rapids, MI 49507
Phone: (616) 247-1575
Skill Level: All
Age Range: Girls 10 and up

U.S. Gymnastics Training Centers
Directors: Michael Jacobson, Robert
Pataky
Box 1090
Cotuit, MA 02635
Phone: (617) 428-6371
Skill Level: All, separated by ability and
size
Age Range: Coed, 8–16

**Walton's Grizzly Lodge Summer Camp
for Boys and Girls** (See multi-sport
listing.)

**YWCA Blue Mountain Gymnastics
Camp**
Director: Wendy Helm
YWCA, 8th and Washington
Reading, PA 19601
Phone: (215) 376-7317
Skill Level: Beginning to advanced
Age Range: Girls 7–16

LACROSSE

R & R Sports Academies (See general
listing.)

Rutgers University Sports Camps (See
general listing.)

MULTI-SPORT CAMPS

University of San Diego All-Sports Camp
(Aquatics, Basketball, Racquetball,
Soccer, Softball, Tumbling, Volleyball)
Director: John Martin
Alcala Park
San Diego, CA 92110

Phone: (714) 291-6480, ext. 4272
Skill Level: All, separated
Age Range: Girls 9-14

**Walton's Grizzly Lodge Summer Camp
for Boys and Girls** (Cross-Country
Running, Gymnastics, Soccer)
Director: Joseph M. Stein
P.O. Box 965
Campbell, CA 95009
Phone: (408) 243-1867
Skill Level: Beginning
Age Range: Coed 7-17

RUNNING

**Bonne Bell Women's Running Camp—
Colorado**
Director: Ben Barron
18519 Detroit Rd.
Lakewood, OH 44107
Phone: (800) 321-9985
Skill Level: All
Age Range: Girls 17 and over

SKIING

Neige Sans Fromtiere
Director: Alain Lazard
P.O. Box 2283
Olympic Valley, CA 95730
Phone: (916) 583-2768
Skill Level: Advanced A and B, separated
by ability
Age Range: Coed 12-30

SOCCER

Bowling Green State University (See
general listing.)

George Logan California Soccer Camp
Director: George Logan
San Diego State Head Coach
8245 Ronson Rd., Suite D
San Diego, CA 92111

Phone: (714) 279-7800; toll-free in
California (800) 542-6005
Skill Level: All levels, separated by age
and ability
Age Range: Girls 7-14

Medalist Sports Camps (See general
listing.)

**Michigan State University Summer
Sports Camps** (See general listing.)

R & R Sports Academy (See general
listing.)

Rutgers University Sports Camp (See
general listing.)

Sauk Valley Farm (See general listing.)

SCI/USA Soccer Development Camp
Director: James C. Peterson
734 Alger SE
Grand Rapids, MI 49507
Phone: (616) 247-1575
Skill Level: All
Age Range: Coed 9 and up

The Soccer Farm
Director: Jim Kuhlmann
265 Alma Dr.
Fairfield, CT 06430
Phone: (203) 255-3617
Skill Level: All, separated by ability
Age Range: Coed 8-18

Tobybanna Sports Camp, Inc. (See
general listing.)

University of San Diego Soccer Camp
Director: Seamus McFadden
University of San Diego
Alcala Park
San Diego, CA 92110
Phone: (714) 291-6480, ext. 4272
Skill Level: All, separated
Age Range: Coed 6-18

Walton's Grizzly Lodge Summer Camp
(See multi-sport listing.)

SOFTBALL

Connecticut Girls Sports Camps, Inc.
(See general listing.)

Sharron Backus California Girls Softball Camp
Director: Sharron Backus, UCLA Head Softball Coach
8245 Ronson Rd., Suite D
San Diego, CA 92111
Phone: (714) 279-7800; toll-free in California (800) 542-6005
Skill Level: All, separated by age and ability
Age Range: Girls 12–21

Center for Professional Development and Public Service at Florida State University
Director: Jo Ann Graf
Women's Athletics
Florida State University
Tallahassee, FL 32306
Phone: (904) 664-1581
Skill Level: All
Age Range: Girls 10–18

Michigan State University Summer Sports Camp (See general listing.)

Joan Joyce Softball Camps
Directors: Fran D'Angelo, John Salerno
Winner's Choice
P.O. Box 408
Southington, CT 06489
Skill Level: All
Age Range: Coed 10 and over

Mott-Leeney Sports Camp
Directors: Jack Mott, Fred Leeney
19 Grove St.
Madison, NJ 07940
Phone: (201) 377-7142
Skill Level: All, separated by ability
Age Range: Girls 7–17

Sauk Valley Farm (See general listing.)

Shippensburg State College Sports Camps (See general listing.)

Tobybanna Sports Camp, Inc. (See general listing.)

SOFTBALL—FAST PITCH

R & R Sports Academy (See general listing.)

St. Mary's College Youth Women's Softball Camp
Director: Fred Williams
St. Mary's College Athletic Camp
Moraga, CA 94575
Phone: (415) 376-0545
Skill Level: Intermediate, advanced
Age Range: Girls 13–17

Tobybanna Sports Camp, Inc. (See general listing.)

SWIMMING

Michigan State University Summer Sports School (See general listing.)

Shippensburg State College Sports Camps (See general listing.)

USD Competitive Swim Camp
Director: Gary Becker
University of San Diego
Alcala Park
San Diego, CA 92110
Phone: (714) 291-6480, ext. 4272
Skill Level: Advanced
Age Range: 12–18

SYNCHRONIZED SWIMMING

R & R Sports Academy (See general listing.)

TENNIS

Bowling Green State University (See general listing.)

Medalist Sports Camps (See general listing.)

Michigan State University Summer Sports School (See general listing.)

Rutgers University Sports Camps (See general listing.)

Shippensburg State College Sports Camps (See general listing.)

Four Star Tennis Academy
Director: Mike Eikenberry
P.O. Box 790
McLean, VA 22101
Skill Level: All
Age Range: Coed 9–18

University of San Diego Tennis School
Director: Ed Collins
University of San Diego
Alcala Park
San Diego, CA 92110
Phone: (714) 291-6480, ext. 4272
Skill Level: All, separated by ability
Age Range: Coed 10–18

TRACK & FIELD

Jim Bush Track and Field Camp
Director: Jim Bush, UCLA Head Coach
8245 Ronson Rd., Suite D
San Diego, CA 92111
Phone: (714) 279-7800; toll-free in
California (800) 542-6005
Skill Level: All levels, separated by age
and ability
Age Range: Girls, grades 5–11

Connecticut Girls Sports Camps, Inc.
(See general listing.)

Michigan State Summer Sports School
(See general listing.)

Rutgers University Sports Camps (See
general listing.)

VOLLEYBALL

Biola Volleyball Camp
Director: Connie A. Taroneberry
Biola College
13800 Biola Ave.
La Mirada, CA 90639
Phone: (213) 944-0351, ext. 3428
Skill Level: All levels; camp divided into
two divisions
Age Range: Girls, grades 7–12

Bowling Green State University (See
general listing.)

Cardinal Volleyball Camp
Director: Scott Luster
Women's Athletics, Belknap Gym
University of Louisville
Louisville, KY 40208
Phone: (502) 588-5577, 459-8907, 588-5577
Skill Level: Beginning, intermediate,
advanced, separated by ability

Connecticut Girls Sports Camps, Inc.
(See general listing.)

**Center for Professional Development and
Public Service at Florida State University**
Director: Cecile Reynaud
Women's Athletics
Florida State University
Tallahassee, FL 32306
Phone: (904) 644-1216
Skill Level: All
Age Range: Girls 10–21

**Mary Dunphy Volleyball Fundamentals
Camp**
Director: Mary Dunphy, Pepperdine
University Head Volleyball Coach
8245 Ronson Rd., Suite D
San Diego, CA 92111
Phone: (714) 279-7800; toll-free in
California (800) 542-6005
Skill Level: All levels, separated by age
and ability
Age Range: Girls 13–18

**Michigan State University Summer
Sports School** (See general listing.)

R & R Sports Academies (See general
listing.)

Sauk Valley Farm (See general listing.)

**Shippensburg State College Sports
Camps** (See general listing.)

Sports Camps International
Director: James C. Peterson
734 Alger SE
Grand Rapids, MI 49507
Skill Level: All
Age Range: Coed 14 and up

USD Girls Volleyball Camp
Director: John Martin

University of San Diego
Alcala Park
San Diego, CA 92110
Phone: (714) 291-6480, ext. 4272
Skill Level: All
Age Range: 14–18

University of Wisconsin—Oshkosh Volleyball Camp
Director: Wendy Saintsing
110 Albee Hall
University of Wisconsin—Oshkosh
Oshkosh, WI 54901
Phone: (414) 424-1392
Skill Level: Beginning, intermediate, advanced, separated by ability
Age Range: Girls, grade 10–college

WRESTLING

Michigan State University Summer Sports School (See general listing.)

GENERAL LISTING

Bowling Green State University
(Basketball, Cross-Country, Diving, Golf, Gymnastics, Soccer, Tennis, Volleyball)
Director: Gary Palmisano
Athletic Dept.
Bowling Green State University
Bowling Green, OH 43402
Phone: (419) 372-2401
Skill Level: All
BASKETBALL CAMP:
Age Range: Girls 10–17
CROSS-COUNTRY CAMP:
Age Range: Coed 8–12
DIVING CAMP:
Age Range: Coed 10–17
GOLF CAMP
GYMNASTICS CAMP
SOCCER CAMP:
Age Range: Coed 10–17
TENNIS CAMP:
Age Range: Coed 12–17
VOLLEYBALL CAMP:
Age Range: Girls 27–31

Connecticut Girls Sports Camps, Inc.
(Basketball, Cheerleading, Field Hockey, Gymnastics, Soccer, Softball, Track and Field, Twirling, Volleyball)
Director: Betty Ann Krayeske
P.O. Box 87
Eatertwon, CT 06795
Phone: (203) 274-3102, 0843
Skill Level: All, separated by age and ability
Age Range: Girls 8–18

Medalist Sports Camps (Basketball, Tennis, Soccer)
Director: Ron Blomberg
10206 No. Port Washington Rd.,
Mequon, WI 53902
Phone: (414) 421-8580
Skill Level: Separated by ability
Age Range: Coed 8–18

Michigan State University Summer Sports School (Baseball, Cheerleading, Cross-Country, Diving, Field Hockey, Football, Golf, Ice Hockey, Soccer, Softball, Speed Swimming, Tennis, Track, Volleyball, Wrestling)
Director: Gene Kenney
Athletic Department
Jenison Fieldhouse
Michigan State University
East Lansing, MI 48824
Phone: (517) 355-5264
Skill Level: All
Age Range: Coed 9–17

R & R Sports Academy for Girls and Women (Field Hockey, Lacrosse, Soccer, Fast-Pitch Softball, Synchronized Swimming, Volleyball)
Directors: Mary Ravsa, Mary Jo Ruggieri
Box 21150
Columbus, OH 43221
Phone: (614) 299-9438
Skill Level: All levels, separated by age and ability
Age Range: Girls 8 and up
FIELD HOCKEY CAMP
LACROSSE CAMP
SOCCER CAMP
FAST-PITCH SOFTBALL CAMP

SYNCHRONIZED SWIMMING CAMP
VOLLEYBALL CAMP

Rutgers University Camps (Basketball, Cross-Country, Field Hockey, Gymnastics, Lacrosse, Soccer, Softball, Tennis, Track and Field)
Rutgers University
P.O. Box 1149
Piscataway, NJ 08854
Phone: (201) 932-4251
Skill Level: All, separated by ability
BASKETBALL CAMP:
Director: Theresa Shank Grentz
Age Range: Girls 8 and up
CROSS-COUNTRY CAMP:
Director: Frank Gagliano
Age Range: Girls 8–17
FIELD HOCKEY CAMP:
Director: Ann Petracco
Age Range: Girls 10 and up
GYMNASTICS CAMP:
Director: Sandra Buys Salvas
Age Range: Girls 8–18
LACROSSE CAMP:
Directors: Ann Petracco, Heidi Faith
Age Range: Girls 10 and up
SOCCER CAMP:
Director: Geza Kiss
Age Range: Girls 8–17
SOFTBALL CAMP:
Director: Pat Willis
Age Range: Girls 10–18
TENNIS CAMP: '
Director: R. Richard Johnson
Age Range: Girls 8–17
TRACK AND FIELD CAMP:
Director: Frank Gagliano
Age Range: Girls 9–18

Sauk Valley Farm (Cross-Country, Field Hockey, Soccer, Softball, Volleyball)
Directors: Mr. and Mrs. Richard C. Schaefer
Irish Hills
Brooklyn, MI 49230
Phone: (517) 467-2061

Skill Level: All, separated by ability
Age Range: Girls, junior high through college
CROSS-COUNTRY CAMP
FIELD HOCKEY CAMP
SOCCER CAMP
SOFTBALL CAMP
VOLLEYBALL CAMP

Shippensburg State College Camps (Basketball, Cross-Country, Diving, Softball, Swimming, Tennis)
Director: Kenneth C. Washinger
P.O. Box 442
Shippensburg State College
Shippensburg, PA 17257
Phone: (717) 532-1256
Skill Level: All levels, separated by ability
CROSS-COUNTRY CAMP:
Age Range: Girls 12–17
DIVING CAMP:
Age Range: Girls 8–18
SOFTBALL CAMP:
Age Range: Girls 9–18
SWIMMING CAMP:
Age Range: Girls 9–17
TENNIS CAMP:
Age Range: Girls 10–17
VOLLEYBALL CAMP:
Age Range: 12–18

Tobybanna Sports Camp, Inc. (Basketball, Cross-Country, Field Hockey, Soccer, Softball)
Director: James Quick
Box 192
Mountainhome, PA 18352
Phone: (717) 595-7970
Skill Level: All levels
Age Range: Girls 8–18
BASKETBALL CAMP
CROSS-COUNTRY CAMP
FIELD HOCKEY CAMP
SOCCER CAMP
SOFTBALL CAMP

FOOTNOTES

Chapter 2

1. John H. Douglas and Julie Ann Miller, "Record Breaking Women," *Science News* (Vol. 112, September 10, 1977), p. 173.
2. "The Weaker Sex? Hah!," *Time* (June 26, 1978), p. 60.
3. Ibid.
4. "Sporting Life," *Ms.* (August 1978), pp. 28–29.
5. Douglas and Miller, "Record Breaking Women," p. 173.
6. Ibid.
7. Jesse Owens, "The Times They Are A-Changing," *Women's Sports* (March 1980), pp. 7–8.
8. Barbara McDowell, Hana Umlauf, et al., "Women in Sports," *The Good Housekeeping Almanac* (New York: Newspaper Enterprise Assoc. Inc., 1977), p. 410.
9. Norris McWhirter, et al., *Guinness Book of Women's Sports Records* (New York: Sterling Publishing Co., 1979), p. 107.
10. Peter Swerdloff, *Men and Women* (New York: Time-Life Books, 1975), p. 11
11. Douglas and Miller, "Record Breaking Women," p. 172.

12. The next few pages summarize information in John A. Lucas and Ronald A. Smith, "From Corsets to Bloomers—Women in Sport," *Saga of American Sport* (Philadelphia: Lea and Febiger, 1978), p. 250–266.
13. Peggy J. Woodeson and Denise Watts, *Schoolgirl Athletics* (London: Stanley Paul and Co., Ltd., 1966), p. I.
14. Lucas and Smith, *Saga of American Sport*, p. 360.
15. Billie Jean King with Kim Chapin, *Billie Jean* (New York: Harper and Row Publishers, 1974), p. 143.
16. Lucas and Smith, *Saga of American Sport*, p. 360.
17. Ibid.
18. Ibid., p. 361.
19. Sam Smith, "She Won 1st Gold for U.S. Women," *Chicago Tribune* (January 27, 1980), Sec. 3, pp. 1, 6.
20. Bill Jauss, "Janie's Back! . . . and She May Hustle into Action Saturday," *Chicago Tribune* (December 20, 1979), Sec. 4, p. 2.
21. Sally Helgesen, "On the Loose: See Jane Run, See Dick Run Faster," *Inside Sports* (April 30, 1980), p. 118.
22. King, *Billie Jean*, pp. 100–101.

Chapter 3

1. American Civil Liberties Union, "Sex Discrimination in Athletics and Physical Education," Women's Rights Project (January 1975) as reprinted in Bonnie L. Parkhouse and Jackie Lapin, *Women Who Win: Exercising Your Rights in Sports* (Englewood Cliffs, N.J.: Prentice-Hall, Inc., a Spectrum Book, 1980), pp. 86–87.
2. Katherine Ley, "Women in Sports: Where Do We Go From Here, Boys?" *Phi Delta Kappan* (October 1974), p. 129.
3. Parkhouse and Lapin, *Women Who Win*, pp. 95–96.

Chapter 4

1. "New Grades for America's College," reprinted from *The Chronicle of Higher Education* (1979) in the *Chicago Tribune* (October 14, 1979), Sec. 2, pp. 1–2.
2. John Underwood, "The Writing on the Wall," *Sports Illustrated* (May 19, 1980), pp. 36–48.
3. Julia E. Johnsen, *The Reference Shelf* (New York: H. W. Wilson Co., Vol. VI, No. 2, March 1929), p. 16.

Chapter 5

1. Bob Gaillard, "Recruiting and How to Handle It," *Handbook for the Young Athlete* (Palo Alto, Calif.: Bull Publishing Co., 1978), p. 183.
2. Ibid., p. 184.
3. Hassan O. Rosell, "He Offered Me a Car to Help My Mother Out," *Young Chicago* (Vol. I, Spring 1979), p. 15.

Chapter 7

1. "Here and There," *Athletic Journal* (November 1976), p. 8.
2. Gary Reinmuth, "High School Sports Injuries: It's Time to Face the Facts," *Chicago Suburban Tribune* (April 17, 1980), pp. 15–16.
3. David Marcotte as quoted in Sally Helgesen, "On the Loose: The Quick Fix Is Slow Torture," *Inside Sports* (June 30, 1980), p. 30.

Chapter 8

1. Janice Kaplan, *Women and Sports* (New York: The Viking Press, 1979), p. 87.
2. Ibid.
3. Lloyd Percival as excerpted in Bryant J. Cratty, *Psychology in Contemporary Sport: Guidelines for Coaches and Athletes* (Englewood Cliffs, N.J.: Prentice-Hall, Inc., 1973), p. 240.
4. Ibid., p. 241.

BIBLIOGRAPHY

Ackermann-Blount, Joan. "Up in Arms About My Arm," *Sports Illustrated,* July 16, 1979, pp. 40+.

American Civil Liberties Union. "Sex Discrimination in Athletics and Physical Education," Women's Rights Project, January 1975. Parts reprinted in Parkhouse, Bonnie, *Women Who Win.*

Athletic Journal. "A Review of Athletics in the High Schools," June 1930, pp. 43+.

———. most issues, 1976–80, Evanston, Ill.

Bell, Taylor. "Cross Going in Circles–tentatively: Purdue Coach Left Holding Bag." *Chicago Sun-Times,* June 3, 1980, p. 88.

Campbell, Gail. *Marathon: The World of the Long-Distance Athlete.* New York: Sterling Publishing Co., Inc., 1979.

Chronicle of Higher Education, as excerpted in "Ranking the Top Colleges," *Chicago Tribune,* October 14, 1979, Sec. 2, pp. 1–2.

Cowley, Susan Cheever. "Women on the Run," *Newsweek,* November 14, 1977, p. 100.

Crase, Darrell. "The Continuing Crises in Athletics," *Phi Delta Kappan,* October 1974, pp. 99–101.

235

Cratty, Bryant J. *Psychology in Contemporary Sport: Guidelines for Coaches and Athletes.* Englewood Cliffs, N.J.: Prentice-Hall, Inc., 1973.

Douglas, John H., and Miller, Julie Ann. "Record Breaking Women," *Science News,* Vol. 112, September 10, 1977, pp. 172–174.

Forbes. "Saruday's Hard-Pressed Heroes," November 15, 1976, pp. 77–80.

Gaillard, Bob, et al. *Handbook for the Young Athlete.* Palo Alto, Calif.: Bull Publishing Co., 1978.

Gipe, George. *The Great American Sports Book.* Garden City, N.Y.: Doubleday and Co., Inc. 1978.

Helgesen, Sally. "On the Loose: See Jane Run, See Dick Run Faster," *Inside Sports,* April 30, 1980, pp. 118–119.

——. "On the Loose: The Quick Fix Is Slow Torture," *Inside Sports,* June 30, 1980, pp. 98–99.

Human Behavior, "Female Jocks: Why Women Are Making It in Sports," June 1978, p. 51.

Jauss, Bill. "Janie's Back! . . .and She May Hustle into Action Saturday" *Chicago Tribune,* December 20, 1979, Sec. 4, p. 2.

Jeansonne, John. "Body and Soul: After the Sprain. . .Where to Treat an Injured Foot," *Inside Sports,* June 30, 1980, pp. 104–105+.

Johnsen, Julia E. *The Reference Shelf,* Vol. VI, No. 2, March 1929, New York: H. W. Wilson Co.

Kaplan, Janice *Women and Sports.* New York: The Viking Press, 1979.

——. "Are Girls Catching Up to Boys in Sports," *Seventeen,* December 1976, pp. 112–113+.

——. "What Price Victory?" *Nutshell,* 1978/79, reprinted in *Social Issues Resources Series,* Vol 1, Article #60.

——. "Locker-Room Philosopher," *Seventeen,* May 1977, pp. 104, 108.

Kelly, Jill, et al. "Who Says Athletes Can't Be Pregnant?" *Ms.,* July 1978, pp. 47–48.

King, Billie Jean, with Chapin, Kim. *Billie Jean.* New York: Harper and Row Publishers, 1974.

Klafs, Carl E., and Lyon, M. Joan. *The Female Athlete: Conditioning, Competition, and Culture.* St. Louis: The C.V. Mosby Co., 1973.

Kleiman, Carol. "Women Are No Longer Stuck with Half a Court," *Chicago Tribune*, Sec. 3, pp. 1, 3.

Klein, Frederick C. "Is Your Youngster a Badminton Whiz? It Could Pay His Bills," *Wall Street Journal*, April 24, 1980, p. 1.

Lamb, Julia. "Not Yet Ready to Burn Their Bridges," *Sports Illustrated*, June 6, 1977, pp. 55–56+.

Larned-Romano, Deborah, and Leavy, Jane. "Athletics and Fertility: A New Medical Controversy That Raises Old Questions," *Ms.*, October 1979, pp. 38–39.

Ley, Katherine. "Women in Sports: Where Do We Go From Here, Boys?" *Phi Delta Kappan*, October 1974.

Leavy, Jane. "Evonne Goolagong—Playing Winning Tennis Again," *Ms.*, July 1978, pp. 49–51.

Lucas, John A., and Smith, Ronald A. *Saga of American Sport.* Philadelphia: Lea and Febiger, 1978.

Maddox, Elliot. "Blending Athletics and Academics," *The New York Times*, June 15, 1980, Sec. S, p. 2.

Maslow, Jonathan Evan. "At Tackle, Ms. Tammy Lee Mercer," *Saturday Review*, November 26, 1977, pp. 49–50.

McDowell, Barbara, and Umlauf, Hana. "Women in Sports" in *The Good Housekeeping Almanac.* New York: Newspaper Enterprise Association, Inc., 1977.

McWhirter, Norris, et al. *Guinness Book of Women's Sports Records.* New York: Sterling Publishing Co., 1977.

Mitchell, Fred. "Cross Changes His Mind, Signs to Attend Purdue," *Chicago Tribune*, June 13, 1980, Sec. 4, p. 1.

Ms. "Sporting Life," August 1978, pp. 28–29.

Neal, Patsy. *Sport and Identity.* Philadelphia: Dorrance and Co., 1972.

Newsweek. "Equal Play, Equal Pay," September 5, 1977, p. 83.

Owens, Jesse. "The Times They Are A-Changing," *Women's Sports*, March 1980, pp. 7–8.

Parkhouse, Bonnie L., and Lapin, Jackie. *Women Who Win: Exercising Your Rights in Sports.* Englewood Cliffs, N.J.: Prentice-Hall, Inc., 1980.

Peterson, Lex and McDonald, Jean. "The Trouble with Women's Sports," *Champaign-Urbana News-Gazette*, February 22, 1980, Sec. T, pp. 9–12.

Pogge, Mariann. "From Cheerleader to Competitor," *Update on Law-Related Education*, in Social Issues Resources Series, Vol. 1, Article 57.

Reinmuth, Gary. "High School Sports Injuries: It's Time to Face the Facts," *Chicago Suburban Trib*, April 17, 1980, pp. 15–16.

Rodeo News, "Barrel Racing Champ Started Early," May 1980, pp. 17+.

Rohrbaugh, Joanna Bunker. "Femininity on the Line," *Psychology Today*, August 1979, pp. 30–42.

Rosell, Hassan O. "He Offered Me a Car," *Young Chicago*, Vol. I, Spring 1979, pp. 15–16.

Sabock, Ralph J. *The Coach*. Philadelphia: W. B. Saunders Co., July 1973.

Smith, Sam. "She Won 1st Gold for U.S. Women," *Chicago Tribune*, January 27, 1980, Sec. 3, pp. 1, 6.

Sports Illustrated, many issues, 1979–1980.

Swerdloff, Peter. *Men and Women*. New York: Time-Life Books, 1975.

Time. "Comes the Revolution: Joining the Game at Last, Women Are Transforming American Athletics," June 26, 1978, pp. 54–59.

———. "The Weaker Sex? Hah!" June 26, 1978, p. 60.

Tutko, Thomas and Bruns, William. *Winning Is Everything and Other American Myths*. New York: Macmillan Publishing Co., Inc., 1976.

Underwood, John. "The Writing on the Wall," *Sports Illustrated*, May 19, 1980, pp. 36–48+.

U.S. News and World Report, "School Sports: Victims of Their Own Success," October 22, 1979, pp. 89–90.

Women's Sports, all issues, 1979–80.

Wood P. S. "Sex Differences in Sports," *The New York Times Magazine*, May 18, 1980, pp. 30–33+.

Woodeson, Peggy J., and Watts, Denise. *Schoolgirl Athletics*. London: Stanley Paul and Co., Ld., 1966.

Wright, James E. *Anabolic Steroids and Sports*, U.S. Army Research Institute of Environmental Medicine, Natick, Mass.: Sports Science Consultants, 1978.

INDEX

239